Henry John Heinz: The Founder, age 74, 1918.

IN GOOD COMPANY

125 Years at the Heinz Table

(1869–1994)

Illustrated with Photographs

ELEANOR FOA DIENSTAG

Edwin C. Lehew, photo editor

WARNER BOOKS

A Time Warner Company

Warner Books, Inc., 1271 Avenue of the Americas, New York, NY 10020

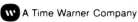 A Time Warner Company

Printed in the United States of America
First Printing: September 1994
10 9 8 7 6 5 4 3 2 1

Library of Congress Cataloging-in-Publication Data
Dienstag, Eleanor Foa.
In good company : 125 years at the Heinz table, 1869–1994 /
Eleanor Foa Dienstag.
p.   cm.
Includes bibliographical references and index.
ISBN 0-446-51797-6
1. H. J. Heinz Company History. 2. Heinz, H. J. (Henry John),
1844–1919. 3. Food industry and trade—United States—History.
4. Businessmen—Pennsylvania—Pittsburgh—Biography. 5. Heinz
family.   I. Title.
HD9321.9.H4D54   1994
338.7′664028′092—dc20

[B]   94-497
                                                                  CIP

Book design by Giorgetta Bell McRee

Contents

PREVIOUS BOOKS BY ELEANOR FOA DIENSTAG

WHITHER THOU GOEST:
The Story of an Uprooted Wife

Foreword

The histories of America's great companies are more than mere chronicles of personal or corporate achievement. They are also revealing portraits of the nation's evolution. Inspired by the American ethos, stimulated by new technology and sustained by a diverse, expanding infrastructure, legendary entrepreneurs helped define the United States and shape its destiny in the late nineteenth and early twentieth centuries. Some of the enterprises they created have had a lasting presence, achieving international stature and influence as the new century approaches.

H. J. Heinz Company is one of these American paradigms. It began shortly after the Civil War in a family garden near Pittsburgh, Pennsylvania. Its founder, Henry John Heinz, was a pioneer in food processing and product marketing. Son of German immigrants, he found himself at the center of an emerging urban, industrial society. He recognized the opportunities of this new world, seized them, and in the course of doing so, devised principles and practices that set the standard for an entire industry.

Succeeding generations sustained the company and maintained its public following throughout a period of enormous social, political, and economic upheaval. The constancy of Heinz proved a great comfort in times of depression and world war. At the same time, the radically changing world opened new avenues for growth. In this respect, history has revealed the true genius of Heinz, the man and the enterprise: the ability to anticipate and respond to change.

The past two decades have generated some of the most significant changes ever experienced by American business. A global economy is emerging, uneven but inexorable. A technological revolution is erupting, equal in impact to the one that gave rise to America's classic nineteenth-century enterprises. A new scale of competition is unfolding, placing consumers, workers, and managers in cosmopolitan contention for labor, capital, materials, and services. In this context, the Heinz story is especially instructive and stimulating. The company's response to a vastly changing environment, under the leadership of Tony O'Reilly, is an excellent case study in alert, progressive management.

This is not to say that *In Good Company* is a business textbook. It is, like American history itself, a lively, dramatic account of people and ideas, of fortunes won and lost, of heroic triumph and human fallibility. It also is a tale of many cities   from Pittsburgh to London, from Toronto to Sydney, from Milan to Athens, from Tokyo to Auckland, from Harare to Guangzhou—where people from distant cultures have come to share a common bond as Heinz employees and consumers. They are the new inheritors of the noble Heinz tradition.

In the course of 125 years, Heinz has grown from an American dream to a global brand. That achievement is testament to the universal appeal of the Heinz ideal of pure food and healthful, affordable nutrition. It is also a tribute to the tenacity, inventiveness, and dedication of generations of Heinz employees around the world. Their story, contained in this volume, is one that reflects a much broader account of human aspiration and accomplishment. It also is the prelude to a volume yet to be written by many hands in many countries. As a new generation of consumers enters a widening world marketplace, the appeal of the Heinz ideal remains unceasingly durable and filled with promise.

—HENRY KISSINGER

Acknowledgments

~ ~

Given the scope of this undertaking, I owe a debt of thanks to hundreds of people who helped me along the way.

To begin with, though I spent much time in the archives, this book is mainly based on two years of interviews with present and retired Heinz employees around the world. Many spent hours helping me to see, feel, and smell the past. A great deal of that material is included, directly and indirectly. However, in the end, not every story and affiliate history could be included. In truth, I gathered enough material for a book many times this size, and, if I have any regret, it is that I could not do full justice to every story.

Nevertheless, whether quoted by name or not, I wish to emphasize that each and every person to whom I talked helped me write this book. I gained insights from every conversation, and deeply appreciated the time so many took, often far beyond the call of duty, to acquaint me with their country and city, to locate retirees, plan itineraries, dig up old photographs and albums, share meals, memories, and moments. For me it has been a wonderful adventure and rare privilege to enter so many lives, and I thank each and every one of you for sharing your personal histories, which were so entwined with the history of the company.

There are some people to whom I owe a special debt of gratitude. First, within the company, chairman, president, and CEO Tony O'Reilly, who understood the value of such a project, supported its birth, and, by opening his door, helped open all others. Also, Ted Smyth and Debbie Foster, who guided the undertaking from beginning to end. Their contribution was invaluable. Finally, a cadre of fact checkers tried to prevent obvious errors. I thank them for their efforts.

I am also indebted to Frank J. Kurtik, Heinz family archivist, for sharing with me his immense knowledge of the Heinz family, and for making available to me a wealth of documents that filled out many missing pieces in the family story. Also, WQED of Pittsburgh, for sharing some of the material it collected while assembling its television documentary of the Heinz family.

Finally, I am grateful to friends and colleagues who sustained me on this long journey, in ways big and small. They include Robert S. Davis, Anne Eisenberg, Leon Balter, Dorothy Beach, and the American Society for Journalists and Authors (ASJA), through which this project first arrived.

I am acutely aware that no single interpretation can do justice to the simultaneous experiences of thousands of people who labored around the world for the H. J. Heinz Company. I hope, however, that what follows rings true for those who remember, and brings to life for every reader the complex and colorful mosiac of the past.

Introduction

⌁

Nineteen ninety four is a significant year in the life of the H. J. Heinz Company. It marks the 125th anniversary of the company. It also marks Heinz in the mid-1990s, vigorous and "full of beans," both executing today's strategies and forging those that will become the foundation of Heinz in the 21st century, the Heinz of tomorrow.

This book is a portrait of both Heinz today—history in the making—and Heinz past and future. It is about a vibrant, successful company that, in ways small and large, still reflects and is a direct descendant of the historic Heinz and its leaders.

So direct a descendant that even H. J. "Jack" Heinz II remarked in 1985, at the company's Annual Meeting, on the uncanny similarity between his grandfather, Henry John Heinz, the Founder, and today's chairman, president, and CEO, A. J. F. "Tony" O'Reilly. "I can think of nothing more complimentary to say of him than to compare his energy, vitality, and genius for worldwide salesmanship and statesmanship most favorably with the man who founded the company."

The H. J. Heinz Company is constantly looking backwards into the future and forward into the past. As Tony O'Reilly once noted to a gathering of New York security analysts, "Heinz started its future long ago."

One hundred and twenty-five years ago, to be exact, when America was emerging from a calamitous civil war, and Pittsburgh—brimming with energy and an abundance of resources—was on the verge of becoming one of the great boom towns of the industrial revolution.

Henry John Heinz, in novelist Edith Wharton's phrase, was one of the "Lords of Pittsburgh," a man both ahead of his time and rooted in his time. And what a time it was for Pittsburgh! Its mills and army of laborers forging iron, steel and glass; its three-river port overflowing with commerce; its citizens devoted to business; its sooty skies a testament to prosperity; the entire city bent to the creation of profit and wealth. In fact, as the short story writer O'Henry observed, "Everybody worked in Pittsburgh, and it wasn't for lack of money."[1]

Out of the post–Civil War soil of Pittsburgh rose five titans of industry—Carnegie, Mellon, Westinghouse, Frick, and Heinz. Their names still resonate in our ears. So do three of their five businesses. This is indeed a remarkable record since by 1947 only 30 of the 825 firms in operation in 1873 still were independent operations, most of them iron and steel. Of the 63 firms making food in 1873, only one survives: Heinz.

By U.S. standards, the Heinz Company—at 125—is an old company, hoary with age and tradition. It is also one of a dwindling number of surviving companies, fewer and fewer since the take-over days of the 1980s, to still bear the name of its founder. But by any standards, it is a remarkably distinguished and successful company, genuinely beloved by the citizens of its hometown, as well as by loyal employees and customers around the globe.

Its brand name has increased in stature and value over the years, as has its reputation for world-class employees, management, and products. That would not have surprised the Founder, since so much of what the H. J. Heinz Company is today, he envisioned. His prescience continues to astonish.

Henry John Heinz was a remarkable man. An energetic, entre-

---

1. Stephen Potter, *The Magic Number: The Story of "57."* London: Max Rheinhardt, 1959, p. 24.

preneurial boy from a pastoral village near Pittsburgh ("Oh, we country boys work"), who was not only a business genius, but a man of high moral principle and personal rectitude.

In 1869, when he founded the company, those qualities rarely coexisted in business. It was an age when horses were often better treated than workers, when the unchecked exploitation of men, women, and children was as common as influenza.

Henry John Heinz was different. He behaved as though his factory was still his mother's spotless kitchen. Others might cook and package their food in filthy warehouses under unsanitary conditions. In his factories, floors were hosed and swept regularly. Others might bribe and break laws to gain new markets. He paid grocers to remove aging Heinz products from their shelves. Others might hide cheap fillers in tinted glass to increase profits. He insisted on the best ingredients and clear jars to display the purity of Heinz products.

Henry John Heinz also treated his employees as though they were members of his family. He believed that if you treat people fairly and decently, they will be happier and more productive in their labor. In 19th-century America, that was a radical approach to employer–employee relations, especially with regard to women on an assembly line.

Imagine—not only did Henry John Heinz provide his assembly-line workers with clean clothes and indoor facilities for washing (when most had no indoor plumbing), but he insisted on providing a weekly manicure to those who worked with food. A weekly manicure!

Later, too, as business boomed, he built two roof gardens (one for men and one for women), where employees could relax, stroll, and get a bit of fresh air. He also built a gymnasium, swimming pool, library, auditorium for free lectures and concerts, and male and female dining rooms (replete with a piano to be played by a talented fellow worker), and made available to employees a Heinz carriage and team of horses, so they could be driven, like men and women of leisure, through the city's parks.

Known as the "Prince of Paternalism," his philosophy may have had its limitations—no dialogues about workers' rights were ever recorded—but it's clear that the deeply religious, teetotaling Henry Heinz, a stalwart of the Sunday School movement, was a man who rewarded hard work, and prized fairness, honesty, integrity, and quality.

He did not simply mouth these principles, he lived them. To the astonishment of many of his employees, he never abided sharp or deceptive practices, yet he still managed to turn quite a profit. Indeed, the peripatetic Henry John Heinz, rarely at his desk, always on the go—across the country, around the world—turned a small, local business into an international food business and one of the country's great family fortunes.

His vision was practical and immediate, as well as far-reaching. He saw the forest *and* the trees.

Above all, Henry John Heinz understood and loved people. He knew what America's homemaker wanted and empathized with her. He knew what America's grocer and farmer wanted, and put himself in their place. He understood that he was in a business that sustained and nourished people. Consciously or unconsciously, he founded and expanded a company that did more than employ and pay workers. It also sustained and nourished individuals. It made them feel part of a special family. Generations of workers in Pittsburgh and at other company locations considered themselves fortunate to be hired. They still do.

Long after the Founder's death in 1919, the Heinz Company continued to be known as "a good place to work." It was neither the best-paying company in town nor the most profitable. But still, people wanted to work there. They still do.

Why? Because to be a member of the Heinz Company was to be "in good company," part of a warm, extended family, a lively family proud of its products and the values that produced them.

This book is a tribute to that extended family—past, present, and future—and its unique character.

A company's character—its heart, soul, and culture—is its fate, which explains both the past and the range of its future dreams and possibilities.

While the company has changed, its character has not. Initially created in the image of Henry John Heinz, carried forward by his son Howard and grandson Jack, then by two nonfamily leaders, Burt Gookin and Tony O'Reilly, it has remained amazingly true to the values and beliefs of the Founder.

Of course, like any family, Heinz has had its ups and downs, its successful and less-successful ventures, inspired ideas, lucky accidents, missed opportunities, fiascos, and funny stories. However, its devotion to quality products and people has never wavered. Or as O'Reilly has said, "Brands and brains made the company in the past."

To brands and brains, one has to add the harder-to-pin-down qualities—call them herbs and spices—of charm, warmth, and humor that, at any party, around any table, make the difference between failure and success.

This book is not about false nostalgia for "the good old days." In truth, as colorful as the past may have been, the good old days are today. And to be part of the Heinz family today—whether at the oldest or newest Heinz facility—is to be "in good company," among smart, funny, welcoming people.

The Founder had a dry—in every sense of the word—humor. When asked how he felt on the morning of his 71st birthday, instead of giving a verbal reply, he jumped over a chair.

Today's chairman is a born storyteller and wit who is fond of "defying gravity with a touch of Irish levity."

What a pleasure it was, and is, to be in their company.

Indeed, being "in good company" may be the essence of the company's character; the secret ingredient in every Heinz product. Next to the Founder's magic number, "57," it may explain, as nothing else can, the company's remarkable longevity.

Join us at the Heinz table and see for yourself.

Section I

TODAY'S HEINZ

For the H. J. Heinz Company, 1991 turned out to be a uniquely difficult year. Bad news abounded: plummeting prices in the pet-food market; intense competition in tuna; unprecedented competitive assaults in the diet food and meeting programs markets; a soup war in the United Kingdom; negative foreign currency movements; tomato and potato gluts that increased the price spread between Heinz and private-label products, thus adversely affecting gross profit.

All of these factors, combined with the longest recession since World War II—moving like a tidal wave around the globe—created an environment more challenging than anything chairman, president, and chief executive officer (CEO), Anthony J. F. O'Reilly, had seen in 20 years.

It galvanized O'Reilly and the company.

Senior management understood that a profound sea change was taking place. Nineteen ninety-one, though unique in some ways, was not a temporary blip, but the beginning of a new era marked by deflation, unprecedented competition, and structural change.

Strategies that had worked for Heinz in the inflationary environment of the 1980s would work less well in the slow-growth environment of the 1990s. Not only were price-obsessed consumers trading down to private-label and generic brands, but, more significant in the long run, new retail distribution outlets were demanding higher discounts for volume orders from suppliers like Heinz. Margins were being squeezed.

O'Reilly, who loves not only to compete, but to win, took the challenge personally. He embraced the role of inside change agent.

O'Reilly has said, "Leadership is about defining the problem, then making when necessary the rather lonely decision to change." Following his own script, over the next few years he and his management team dramatically grappled with an unprecedented array of economic and competitive challenges, revolutionized strategic thinking, and initiated a series of changes, both short-term and long-term, that resulted in a strengthened and renewed Heinz.

During the spring and summer of 1991, O'Reilly, described by some as a "player-coach" chief executive, went on the offensive with a series of lightning quick moves that immediately improved the company's portfolio of businesses.

In April, he sold Caribbean Restaurants, Inc. In June, he created a new Weight Watchers Food Company, assembling under one roof over 240 Weight Watchers brand products that, for more than a decade, had been manufactured and marketed by two different affiliates, Ore-Ida and Heinz U.S.A. Also in June, he sold The Hubinger Company, a corn wet-milling operation, for a handsome pretax profit of about $221 million. In August, he acquired JLFoods, a major food-service business with annual sales of nearly $500 million. It catered to the away-from-home dining market, ranging from restaurants, cafeterias, and pizzerias to quick-service chains, hotels, diners, and institutions.

In themselves good strategic plays—exiting a slow-growth and commodity business for a fast-growing, value-added business— these moves also financed and jump-started other corporate changes, which, like ripples in a pond, continued to spread.

In September 1991, O'Reilly announced "a quiet restructuring" and a new marketing offensive to shareholders at the annual meeting in Pittsburgh. The goal: to cut costs, regain marketing momentum, and position the company for the 1990s.

Remaining profits from the Hubinger sale would be used in two ways: to increase marketing support for major brands, particularly in tuna, pet food, and weight-loss; and to accelerate cost reductions in the company's "relentless pursuit of low-cost-operator status."

Changes to come would include investments in new technologies, reconfiguration and rationalization of plants, new product development, and organizational realignment.

THE "NEW" HEINZ

In February 1992, at a worldwide Growth Forum attended by the company's top 35 managers, O'Reilly and his senior advisors discussed the inside-and-outside changes taking place and forcefully presented the twofold challenge: to immediately turn the business around and deliver a major improvement in market share and profit and, more basically, to question sacred cows, scrutinize old ways of doing business, and implement radical change.

O'Reilly's vision was clear. He foresaw a "new" Heinz that, while carefully managing its current business, would become more entrepreneurial and aggressive in creating new products and carving out fresh markets. His language was blunt. The 1990s were not the 1980s. Business as usual would not do.

Management would have to be "vigorous, visionary, and determined." World Headquarters would work closely as a partner with each affiliate, sharing the risk and debating the options. Closer and more frequent communication would be essential. It would be a year in which senior managers would "live in each other's pockets," stay close to the action, and run the business as if they owned it. It would be a time of bold action, major growth strategies, and productivity gains. It would require hard work and tough choices.

To help management rigorously examine productivity and cost issues, and better leverage the company's global strengths, O'Reilly established three international, interaffiliate task forces. Led by senior managers, they focused on procurement, overhead costs and restructuring, and European marketing efficiency. Following a long-standing Heinz tradition of doing more with less, each member did double duty, with task-force work piled on top of regular, full-time responsibilities.

Heinz has always prided itself on its decentralized management structure and continues to nurture initiative and accountability. Over the years, O'Reilly has used interaffiliate task forces to meet new corporate challenges. Functioning like in-house consultants, they have proved to be quick, efficient vehicles for cutting through bureaucracy and surfacing new people and ideas. When the hierarchy is flattened, as it is when senior managers, including O'Reilly, work side by side with, say, a tinplate purchasing manager, fresh concepts and tactics emerge.

In fact, a revolutionary idea did emerge from one of the task forces: to replace the company's decentralized purchasing system with a centralized negotiation strategy. In other words, to reduce prices by consolidating purchasing among a few, global low-cost suppliers.

The very day the company was wrestling with the advantages and disadvantages of centralized procurement, O'Reilly found himself addressing Richard Cyert's "Leadership" class at Carnegie Mellon University's business school.

Cyert, former president of Carnegie Mellon, professor of economics and management, and a Heinz board member since 1984, views O'Reilly as "a charismatic leader," one of a handful of CEOs who "really understand the leadership function." He had invited O'Reilly to talk about his ideas and answer questions, a session he videotaped.

It was a vintage O'Reilly off-the-cuff performance, beginning with his late arrival ("Tony is always late," colleagues and friends agree), his quotes from Marx—both Groucho and Karl, his fountain of facts, his gift for mimicry and Irish eloquence.

O'Reilly was refreshingly candid about the changing dynamics within the food business, as well as the procurement debate then being wrestled to the ground at Heinz.

Basically, Heinz contemplated doing to suppliers exactly what the Wal-Marts and warehouse clubs of the world—already about $25 billion of the $340 billion annual retail market for food in the United States[1]—were doing to manufacturers.

---

1. *Fortune*, January 11, 1993.

Though leveraging the company's global strength made eminent financial sense—it would save the company millions over the next decade—the solution would violate Heinz's decentralized structure and culture. Surely it would not be welcomed with open arms. Or, as O'Reilly humorously put it, "One of the three biggest lies in the world is, 'We're from World Headquarters and we're here to help.' "

"Yet in the end," as O'Reilly pointed out, "only one person in the entire organization can ordain such a change. And that happens to be the chief executive officer. You're not asked to do it very often, but when you're asked . . . you'd better step up to bat and do it. Sacred cows will be shot, jobs will be lost, careers will be changed, but making such difficult decisions is essentially what leadership is all about."

Procurement of key materials was centralized.

Another significant step away from decentralization was the creation of a new, Pittsburgh-based Heinz Service Company to consolidate and streamline North American customer order processing, invoicing, credit, and receivables for products from Heinz U.S.A., Heinz Canada, StarKist, Ore-Ida, and Weight Watchers brands. Basically a customer-driven move, it would also lower costs.

In the area of marketing, Heinz began to challenge conventional wisdom about media spending. Taking a more flexible and timely approach to trade, consumer, and point-of-purchase promotions, as well as media buys, affiliates aimed more of their marketing dollar toward consumer promotion and shelf pricing.

Heinz, already enjoying a $2 billion business in the European Community, targeted further growth. Luigi Ribolla, about to become senior vice president for Europe, headed up a task force to, as O'Reilly put it, "lead the charge for volume growth across the entire continent."

During 1992 and 1993, a charged-up O'Reilly and senior management hammered out new (reasonable, but demanding) goals for each affiliate and successfully led the company out of the complacency and "if it ain't broke don't fix it" mentality that inevitably accompanies two decades of unparalleled financial growth and profitability.

In March 1992, O'Reilly addressed the New York Society of

Securities Analysts. The company's strategies were working; market shares were up for major brands, such as ketchup, 9-Lives cat food, Ore-Ida potatoes, and Weight Watchers brand entrées and desserts.

In October 1992, with an eye to the dynamic Asia–Pacific market, Heinz made its largest offshore acquisition, purchasing Wattie's Limited, a mini-Heinz in New Zealand, for $300 million. It impressed, among others, Nomi Ghez, an analyst with Goldman Sachs, who noted that Wattie's "is the largest food company in Australasia with not only leading market shares in New Zealand but $70 million in exports to Japan." An excellent complement to existing Heinz operations in Australia, Japan, and China, the new acquisition "would significantly strengthen its presence in this fast growing region of the world."[2]

In September 1993, to shareholders at the Annual Meeting, O'Reilly amplified the strategies and shared the good news. Heinz management had engineered an impressive turnaround. A "new" Heinz had emerged, poised for substantial growth in the 1990s and beyond. Heinz had been sorely tested, and not found wanting. O'Reilly relished the victories.

Since meeting the challenge of change has always been a key ingredient in the company's ongoing success, today's "new" Heinz will surely not be its last incarnation. In a 125-year history of renewal and growth, continual transformation—through panics, world wars, recessions, depressions, new technologies, new competition, new distribution systems, and shifting consumer tastes—has kept the company healthy, growing, and, as O'Reilly likes to describe it, "ahead of the curve."

----

2. Goldman, Sachs & Co. investment commentary, October 7, 1992.

Heinz Today

The H. J. Heinz Company, with global sales of over $7.1 billion, remains a decentralized federation of companies with a lean 180-member worldwide headquarters staff that operates as overall strategist, banker, auditor, information facilitator, and coordinator. World Headquarters is located on the 59th and 60th floors of the handsome, triangular steel-and-glass USX tower in downtown Pittsburgh.

Reporting to the chairman, president, and chief executive officer are senior vice presidents, who work closely with the heads of a number of business affiliates and who, in a sense, communicate ideas, information, policies, and strategies back and forth between the coach and his players on a weekly and sometimes daily basis.

Senior vice presidents generally do not run an affiliate, but indirectly oversee many. For example, it is their job to champion the cause of—and get corporate headquarter funds for—their affiliates' new products, promotions, capital investments, marketing campaigns, etc. To do so means staying in close touch, constantly discussing marketplace pressure points, as well as people and ideas. Ideally, it's a partnership rather than an arms-length relationship, with a mutual appreciation of the risks and opportunities ahead.

Senior vice presidents are the linchpin in the partnership. Their role—more akin to that of CEO—requires diplomatic and balancing skills somewhat different from those needed for heading a single business. Thus it is generally viewed, as it was for O'Reilly, as a stepping-stone to the top job.

Senior vice presidents, plus the heads of functional staff areas—such as corporate affairs, planning, development, organization, finance, technology, legal—make up the CEO's "college of cardinals," with whom he constantly consults and on whom he depends. Add to this handful of advisors the top officers of major affiliates and you have the key people—fewer than 40 or so individuals—who oversee the geographically vast and immensely profitable H. J. Heinz Company.

They do so with a minimum of paper and a maximum of personal accessibility. Nobody (well, almost nobody) writes memos or position papers, gets points for belonging to a lot of industry organizations or creating a paper trail. Nobody has the staff or the time. As 30-year corporate-veteran George Greer, vice president for organization development and administration, said, "People know what's important, what isn't, and what we can just toss in the wastebasket. 'It-would-be-nice-if's' just don't get done around here. We all do double duty."

By and large, staff heads function with a secretary and, maybe, an assistant. Decisions are made by strolling down the hall to an office, picking up the phone, or calling a meeting. (No one has yet figured out a way to eliminate meetings.)

The company's nonbureaucratic management style—which puts a premium on sharing information, collectively solving problems, and open lines of communication ("If Tony has a specific issue down the line, he'll just pick up the phone and call")—may be one of the true secrets of its success. David Sculley, senior vice president and a member of the board since 1989, calls Heinz "the largest small company in the world."

News travels fast at Heinz, in large part because of this style, and because senior managers—individually and together—travel a lot. The only tools for staying in touch and getting things done seem to be a phone, a fax, and a secretary who knows how to find you 24 hours a day anywhere in the world. (For example, during one crisis, O'Reilly arose from his table at a 75th birthday party for Jack Heinz, attended by, among others, the queen of England, to take an emergency call. Pittsburgh had just received a serious tampering threat regarding baby food. It precipitated a 10-week crisis during which O'Reilly was in continuous communication with the crisis team at all hours and on every continent.)

So desks are often at 40,000 feet, and senior managers are often to be found, sleeves rolled up, down in the trenches where the action is—on the factory floor, at affiliate meetings, walking supermarket aisles, going to "cuttings" (food industry lingo for "tastings"), monitoring focus groups, and generally helping line managers anticipate and solve problems.

This open, informal, peripatetic style may be the only one that works for global companies bent on staying close to the marketplace with entrepreneurial swiftness and efficiency. Few have managed to resist empire building and bureaucracy so well.

Increasingly, too, there are more face-to-face get-togethers between O'Reilly and affiliate presidents. In July 1991, O'Reilly initiated once-a-month "President's Meetings," in addition to the normal cycle of budget and planning presentations and reviews. These meetings have forged closer ties, franker talk, a quicker sharing of new ideas, and a more entrepreneurial style. As one affiliate president put it, "Everyone now realizes the biggest sin is the sin of omission rather than commission."

The meetings are a natural extension of O'Reilly's collegiality philosophy, which he has nurtured since the first day he joined Heinz. O'Reilly has succeeded in creating an extended-family feeling among senior management, even, with rare exception, among those who are no longer with the company. This has been aided and abetted by the fact that management longevity at Heinz is the rule rather than the exception. So by the time a manager reaches the top, that manager has worked with, around, or next to everyone else for years, and often decades.

O'Reilly is naturally sociable and regularly assembles his "college of cardinals" for intense brainstorming sessions. Whether they are gathered around his long table at Castlemartin, his Irish residence, or around multiple tables at a downtown Pittsburgh hotel, whether they are toasting and roasting vice chairman Joe Bogdanovich on his 80th birthday in Bermuda or enjoying a summer picnic in O'Reilly's suburban Fox Chapel backyard, it's clear that the former star rugby player loves being around and heading up a spirited team. It's also clear how much goodwill, in addition to information, is generated.

A Global Player

Heinz today, a global player in the food business, specializes in providing processed food products and nutritional services. Famous for its "57 Varieties," it now actually markets more than 3,000 varieties to consumers in over 200 countries. It is well balanced geographically, with about 43 percent of its sales coming from non-U.S. operations. With business in more than 200 countries and territories, Heinz employs approximately 37,700 people full time, plus thousands of part-time workers during seasonal peaks.

In the food business, brand dominance ensures quality earnings. As O'Reilly explained to Cyert's class, "The food industry's capital investment characteristics are very pleasing if you are brand dominant. For example, Heinz in the United Kingdom, which has 10 major market leaders and where Heinz is the dominant brand presence in the retail trade, can provide for all its capital needs and pay a 75 percent dividend to World Headquarters without increasing its borrowing."

The company's powerful brand names, in addition to Heinz, include Weight Watchers, Ore-Ida, StarKist, 9-Lives, and many others, such as Plasmon in Italy, with number-one brands accounting for a hefty 60 percent of sales.

OUTSTANDING STOCK PERFORMER

For a decade and a half, since O'Reilly became CEO, the company's performance has made it a darling of the marketplace.

In fact, since 1980, the company has more than doubled its sales. During that time, operating income has grown at an average annual rate of 9.8 percent; net income has grown at an average of 10.6 percent. Over the same time period, total return to shareholders (including investing dividends) has been more than 1,500 percent.

Heinz stock has outperformed the Standard and Poor's 500 Index, as well as its 10 U.S. food industry peers, Borden, CPC International, Campbell's, ConAgra, General Mills, Gerber, Kellogg, Quaker, Ralston Purina, and Sara Lee. Over a 10-year period beginning in 1983, the S&P appreciated 229 percent, the average share price of its peer group 439 percent, and Heinz's stock price by 459 percent.

Without increasing its number of shares, the company's market capitalization on the New York Stock Exchange has gone from $908 million in 1979 to nearly $1 billion in 1994.

This has produced a bonanza for Heinz shareholders, nearly all of whom are American. The combination of price appreciation and increasing dividends yield has meant that anyone who reinvested dividends during the 10 years starting in 1983 realized a total return of 551.5 percent, equal to a 20.6 percent compounded annual rate of return. The S&P's annual compounded total return for the same period was 15.6 percent.

Most Heinz salaried employees own stock in the company through a variety of savings plans. O'Reilly has always believed in building stock equity into compensation, or, as he has said, in "creating a reward structure consistent with what the company wants to achieve," which is above-average growth.

Focus on Performance

Another key to the company's success is its single-minded focus on performance. For managers, well-rewarded performance means a combination of relatively low base pay and incentive options. More than most CEOs, O'Reilly has shared with middle and upper management—through using long-term stock options—the rewards of success.

Overall, with stock ownership the universal icon, turf wars have been kept to a minimum, strong bonds of loyalty forged, and fortunes made. If the company as a whole does well, so do employees from Tokyo to Toronto.

Sustaining profitable growth does not get easier, but, in effect, with the ante continually being upped, management continues to bet on itself.

GEOGRAPHIC AND PRODUCT DIVERSITY

Heinz takes great pride in its geographic and product diversity, and is fond of describing itself as "a basket of companies and a basket of currencies."

Each of the company's nearly 50 affiliates is encouraged to hire and promote local talent, to develop and market products that appeal to local needs and tastes—indeed, to develop the local company and its business to full potential. No two affiliates are alike in product mix or brand strengths.

• *Heinz U.S.A.* Across the Allegheny River and slightly to the northeast of World Headquarters—from where its red-brick buildings and smokestacks are distinctly visible—lies the original 21-acre Heinz factory complex on the North Side of Pittsburgh. Today, the complex is headquarters for the largest affiliate in the Heinz family, Heinz U.S.A. It houses scientific and technical personnel plus a state of the-art, highly computerized Pittsburgh factory. There are a dozen other Heinz U.S.A. factories throughout the country.

Still the heart of the business, Heinz U.S.A. produces its flagship Heinz-labeled core products for the retail and food-service market. These include ketchup, baby foods, pickles, vinegar, and sauces. It also manufactures more than 90 percent of private-label soups, and operates Chef Francisco, the number-one producer of premium frozen soups for the food-service industry.

The company's other main domestic affiliates are:

• *Star-Kist Foods, Inc.*, with headquarters in Newport, Kentucky, across the river from Cincinnati, includes two divisions:

Heinz Pet Products (created in 1988), a premium pet-food supplier, whose brands include 9-Lives cat food, touted by media star "Morris the Cat," Jerky Treats, and Skippy premium dog food;

StarKist Seafood (acquired in 1963), with factories in Puerto Rico, Ecuador, Ghana, Samoa, France, and Portugal. StarKist created a national market for tuna and made "Charlie the Tuna" a household name. It remains a leading worldwide supplier of "dolphin-safe" tuna-based products.

Together they employ about 8,000 in 9 locations around the world.

• *Ore-Ida Foods* (acquired in 1965), with headquarters in Boise, Idaho, is the number-one processor of frozen potatoes for the retail market. Serving both the retail and food-service markets, it has acquired other frozen-food businesses, including Gagliardi Brothers, which markets Steak-umm sandwich steaks; Celestial Farms, a top processor of frozen baked-potato products; Bavarian Specialty Foods, which sells frozen baked goods to the food-service trade; Continental Delights, a manufacturer of frozen pocket sandwiches; Moore's, which makes onion rings, breaded cheeses, and other appetizers; Domani, in the frozen-pasta business; and Delicious Foods, maker of coated vegetable and cheese products. Ore-Ida employs about 4,000 people at 12 factories and its Boise headquarters.

• *Weight Watchers International* (acquired in 1978), with headquarters in Jericho, New York, is the world's largest weight-control service system. It operates meetings in 24 countries around the world, with attendance of nearly one million members per week. Through Weight Watchers Publishing Inc., it publishes a national magazine with a readership of about 5 million, as well as cookbooks and video- and audiotapes. Weight Watchers International also manages fitness facilities and a Personal Cuisine line of foods for sale at meeting sites.

• *Weight Watchers Food Company* (established in 1991), has headquarters in Pittsburgh. It offers more than 250 products. The Weight Watchers brand is the number-seven trademark by dollar volume in U.S. supermarkets, and offers retail frozen, refrigerated, and shelf-stable products, as well as products for the food-service market. Its frozen desserts are the number-one brand in the supermarket.

Internationally, the Founder and his son Howard extended the company's core products to countries with American–English tastes and eating habits. The earliest international companies, once known as the ABC affiliates, were Australia (established in

1935), Britain (established in 1905), and Canada (established in 1909). For decades, Heinz U.K. was the jewel in the crown, surpassing U.S. profits and volumes.

Following World War II, led by the Founder's grandson Henry J. "Jack" Heinz II and R. Burt Gookin, a second wave of international expansion took place. Heinz acquired facilities, and has remained, in the Netherlands (1958), Venezuela (1959), Japan (1961), Italy (1963), and Portugal (1965).

O'Reilly, in turn, spearheaded growth in rapidly growing regions of the world, such as Africa, Asia/Pacific, and Eastern Europe. They include affiliates in Zimbabwe (1982), the People's Republic of China (1984), Korea (1986), Thailand (1987), Spain (1987), Botswana (1988), Greece (1990), Egypt (1992), Hungary (1992), and New Zealand (1993).

Continuity of Philosophy

Despite the growth and change of 125 years, there has been a remarkable continuity of philosophy within the company. Many of today's business ideas and buzzwords—global vision; global brands; think global, act local; decentralized management; health and nutrition; respect for the earth; product quality and purity; doing well by doing good—have been an integral part of the company's basic values, goals, and beliefs since its inception.

That is because they flow directly from the Founder, whose "modern" vision inspired and guided every CEO who followed. His philosophy of ethical behavior toward employees, suppliers, and consumers and his enlightened notions of self-interest have been a source of pride to Heinz men and women for generations. It has made them feel part of a special place where people count, quality counts, and humanistic values count. Indeed, the Founder's favorite motto, "To do a common thing uncommonly well brings success," is as inspiring today as it was in 1869.

Section II

Five Chief Executives
at the Heinz Table

There have been only five chief executives at the Heinz table during its 125-year history: three family members and two nonfamily professional managers. The spotlight has shone more brightly on some than on others. Best known is the Founder, Henry John Heinz, whose life has been written about in a full-length biography, The Good Provider, *by Robert C. Alberts. Least known and largely forgotten is his son Howard, whose personality and times did not lend themselves to the publicity enjoyed by his son Jack. And, of course, modern business journalism has closely tracked the careers and accomplishments of Burt Gookin and Tony O'Reilly. Thus the following brief profiles attempt to cast a more even light on our knowledge of these men. Only by placing each man's contribution to the company in fuller perspective can we begin to understand the reasons for its remarkable survival and success.*

Young Henry John Heinz, age 24, 1868.

Henry John Heinz:
The Founder

$\sim\!\sim$

(1844–1919)

First and foremost, as is evident on every page of the 20 volumes of his diaries spanning the years 1875 to 1897, Henry John Heinz (called Harry or Henry by his family) was a country boy and practical man. Each diary entry begins with a notation about the weather, often followed by seasonal observations about crops. The man who helped transform food growing and processing was rooted in the rhythms of an agricultural age.

His mother was the family gardener, and Harry was very much his mother's son. The formidable Anna Margaretha Schmitt, a deeply religious, disciplined woman who managed a household of 10, must have been a clever, thrifty, energetic, immaculate, and humane organizer. Harry certainly thought so. In an early company biography, edited by the Founder, his success was ascribed to "the moral and business qualities inherited from his mother."[1]

In 1843, Harry's parents, Henry and Anna, met, married, and began a family in Birmingham, Pennsylvania, across the Monongahela River from Pittsburgh. Each had left a small village in southern Germany—Kallstadt and Kruspis—for a better life in

---

1. Robert C. Alberts, *The Good Provider*. Boston: Houghton Mifflin Co., 1973, p. 5. Alberts' biography provides a full-scale portrait of the man and his times.

21

America. Harry, the first of eight surviving children (four boys and four girls), was born October 11, 1844. Six years later, Henry Heinz purchased a brickyard and relocated his family to Sharpsburg, a young community (founded in 1841) and canal town on the northern banks of the Allegheny. Eight miles east of Pittsburgh, its good farmland may have reminded John and Anna of the Rhine Valley.

Henry used brick from his own yard to build a house for his family on Main Street. As was the custom, he ran the business and Anna was in charge of the family garden. Her bountiful tract, stretching back in neat rows from the family house to the river, regularly produced a surplus. She launched her son's lifelong career in the food business by entrusting to him the job of selling the garden's surplus. He was a born salesman.

By the age of 12, the family's budding entrepreneur had expanded his personal garden to three and a half acres and invested part of his profit in a horse and cart, to better peddle his wares. At the same time, he walked three miles a day to and from a Lutheran church school in the village of Etna, worked for his father in his brickyard, brought home extra money by picking potatoes for a neighboring farmer and leading horses along the canal towpath. His energy was legendary throughout his long life.

Never a desk man or bookish type (his son Howard suggested that reading gave him a headache), the only action of which he seemed incapable was sitting still.

At 15, Harry joined his father as a practical assistant in the brick business. He also attended Duff's Mercantile College in Pittsburgh and became his father's bookkeeper. He may have been a self-invented business genius, but he was not unschooled or ignorant of basic financial practices. At Duff's, for example, he learned double-entry bookkeeping and other practical accounting skills. An 1866 account book for Heinz & Ray (a partnership in a short-lived ice business) testifies to his thorough grounding in the nuts and bolts of managing a business.

Harry also supervised his brothers and sisters in the garden, and, with the help of his mother, began to sell her prepared horseradish. An eye-watering, knuckle-scraping misery to produce at home, horseradish bottled in vinegar was already popular among housewives, who normally shunned prepared food. In

"The House Where We Began," built in 1854 on Main Street by the Founder's father, John Henry Heinz, a brick manufacturer. The family's first home in Sharpsburg, it was surrounded by four acres of rich farmland where Harry's mother planted her garden. Later the house became the Anchor Brand firm's first office and factory, with bottled horseradish packed by three employees in the basement. As the company grew, it took over the entire house. In 1872, after Heinz, Noble & Company leased a four-story building in downtown Pittsburgh, it remained a warehouse for the firm's 160 acres of farmland along the Allegheny River.

In 1904, the Founder floated "The House Where We Began" five miles down the Allegheny to a hallowed spot nestled within the Heinz Company's North Side plant in Pittsburgh. Finally, in 1954, the Little House was dismantled and rebuilt in Greenfield Village, Michigan, where it now can be visited, along with other historical American homes.

fact, there was a brisk trade in the product, which was generally sold in colored glass so as to obscure cheap fillers like turnip. Harry offered his mother's superior product bottled in clear glass to show its purity, and peddled it to grocers and to managers of hotel kitchens, as well as to housewives. (By 1870, 68 factories in Pittsburgh produced half the nation's glass. The city was also the country's oil-refining center and a producer of two fifths of its iron.)

It was Harry's first business triumph and led to two insights, or what biographer Robert Alberts termed Important Ideas—eight of them altogether—upon which he would later found and guide the H. J. Heinz Company: housewives will pay someone else to do their more difficult cooking chores; and a pure article of superior quality, properly packaged and promoted, will find a ready market on its merit.

By 1868, the 21-year-old Harry, by saving his profits, had accumulated enough money to acquire a half interest in his father's business. No small feat in itself, it was followed by an amazing act of devotion—and one that suggested in its role reversal a shifting of family power from father to son. Upon his father's return from a long visit to Germany, Harry surprised him with a new house. Not only was it larger and grander than their original home, but young Harry had commissioned its design and paid for it by cleverly collecting so-called uncollectible debts from his father's business.

HEINZ & NOBLE FOUNDED

The year 1869 proved to be a seminal one in the life of Henry J. Heinz and the history of the food business. He and his Sharpsburg friend and neighbor, L. Clarence Noble, founded Heinz & Noble, thus laying the foundation for today's global company.

The partners, who had been together in the brick business for a year, turned to what they knew best, producing and selling bottled food products under the Anchor brand, probably chosen because it was a Christian symbol. They hired two women and a boy, and operated out of the original Heinz family home on Main

Heinz, Noble & Company,
Anchor Brand logo,
circa 1869.

Sarah "Sallie" Heinz,
wife of the Founder, 1895.

Street in Sharpsburg. Of course, their first product was the Heinz family's pure and superior grated horseradish in a clear bottle.

Heinz & Noble got off to such a fine start that later that year Harry married Sarah "Sallie" Sloan Young, a daughter of Irish immigrants from County Down, descendants of a respected Northern Irish Presbyterian family. Harry was 25.

Heinz & Noble were fortunate in their timing. The transcontinental railroad and subsequent inventions of the 1870s and beyond—railroad refrigeration, the steam pressure retort (or cooker), inventor Amanda Jones's vacuum method of canning food[2]—created unimagined opportunities for the national expansion of the new processed-food industry. Heinz pioneered its large-scale growth in the factory and in the fields.

In 1872, as the business grew, Clarence's brother, E. J. Noble, joined the partnership, which became Heinz, Noble & Company. Despite the depression of 1873 and a subsequent financial panic, the company appeared well on its way to success. By 1875, it had become a major producer and purveyor of a range of processed condiments, including celery sauce, pickled cucumbers, sauerkraut, and vinegar. It employed 150 people in peak season, and could turn out 300 barrels of sauerkraut, 15,000 barrels of pickles, and 50,000 barrels of vinegar.

Fortunately, a number of Harry's record books from the earliest days of his business have survived. They are a repository of new ideas, recipes, tricks of the food trade, informal market studies, lists of food jobbers, ingredients, notes on seed cultivation, horses, machinery, sales calls, and charitable donations. (In 1870, he began to tithe himself 10 percent of his business profits.)

Ever the farmer, he worked with various government research stations and county agents to experiment with breeding plants for greater yield, early maturity, and other advances. It led to his third Important Idea: to improve the finished product, you must improve it in the ground.

The evidence of these ledgers, together with diaries, scrapbooks, and company records, reveals his boundless curiosity and

---

2. Anne L. MacDonald, *Feminine Ingenuity, Women & Invention in America*. New York: Ballantine Books, 1992.

multiplicity of talents as agronomist, inventor, recipe collector, bricklayer, salesman, manager, buyer, packager, designer, and legendary innovator in the realm of advertising, promotion, and public relations. It never occurred to this entrepreneurial go-getter that he shouldn't have a hand in every aspect of his business.

The records also show that from his very first week in business Heinz was a compulsive traveler. His order books are filled with lists of grocers and restaurants he visited in Titusville, Meadville, Jamestown, Greenville, Warren, Oil City, Akron, and many other towns and cities within a radius of hundreds of miles north, south, east, and west of Pittsburgh. In one 24-hour period, he traveled by railroad from Pittsburgh to Atlantic City, Philadelphia, Washington, D.C., then back to Pittsburgh. (Trains, like the mail, were more frequent than now.)

The three partners oversaw a complex business operating in four locations—Pittsburgh, St. Louis, Chicago, and Woodstock, Illinois—with divided lines of authority. Heinz supervised a four-story factory, office, warehouse, and retail store in downtown Pittsburgh at 167 and 169 Second Avenue (Boulevard of the Allies), plus 160 acres of crops, workers, horses, and wagons in and around Sharpsburg. He also dealt with the banks and covered all Woodstock expenses. E. J. Noble managed the vinegar factory in St. Louis and the jobbing trade in major cities. Clarence, such a beloved friend that Heinz named his first-born son after him, oversaw the warehouse in Chicago, ran the Woodstock operations, and wrote checks to farmers as the crops came in, payable in Pittsburgh.

One of Clarence Noble's responsibilities was to negotiate the preharvest price with farmers. In 1875, to ensure a steady supply of produce, the company agreed to buy the total cucumber and cabbage crop (for 60 cents a bushel and $10 a ton, respectively) from 800 acres of land in Woodstock. It proved to be the fledgling company's undoing.

A CATASTROPHIC YEAR

We have a clear, dramatic, and compulsively readable account of this catastrophic year. Harry's 1875 diary entries are powerful and gripping. They not only add up to a vivid portrait of the man and his times, but gradually turn into an unbearably moving human drama.

The year begins cheerfully enough with reports of "good sleighing" and colorful experiences on the railroad. "Met governor of New Mexico with 10 Indian Chiefs on their way home from Washington." Harry's optimism and enthusiasm are everywhere evident, as are his creative mind and visual flair, visible in the company's early logos, labels, and carriages (see color insert). On May 27, he writes, "Left word to have our wagons painted pea green running gear and plum colored bodies. Never saw or heard of such colors in running gear." The flamboyant and innovative advertiser is already visible.

At the same time, his uneasiness mounts over the company's lack of capital. "Feel depressed and have headache . . . heartsick when Capt. McLean sent for us . . . Sharpsburg check for the first time came back. No funds."

Matters get worse in April. On the 21st, he writes, "This was the hardest day for money and finances I ever had, and entirely alone." On the 24th, "I had the hardest day I ever had, worse than yesterday."

In July, the strain is beginning to take its toll. "I am wearing brain and body out . . . I fear I shall break down if times don't soon change."

Omens of disaster increase. The economic picture is bleak: tight money, hard times, and financial panic.

When the hyperactive Harry, who could always find time to go to church, writes, on July 25, "I didn't feel like attending prayer meeting, nor church, nor Sunday School. Seem exhausted," it's clear he's on the edge of mental and physical collapse.

The whole family is in bad shape. Harry stays home (an event so rare as to be almost without precedent). Sallie, continually sick, loses 10 pounds. Peter, his brother, goes on another drinking spree, then signs the temperance pledge.

In August, he writes, "Seemingly I have lost all ambition. Hope soon to get better."

He does get better, but tragedy is around the corner. It arrives in the unexpected form of phenomenal harvests, "especially in Illinois and especially in cucumbers. By the end of August, cucumbers were coming in from the fields at Woodstock and piling up at the salting stations at the appalling rate of 2,000 bushels a day. Costs of payroll and purchases soared."[3]

In October, he writes, "I have been nearly killed and crazed at times meeting and protecting checks." He is constantly sick and develops boils.

The entries for December, brief, heartrending, read like a Dickens novel. Harry is arrested twice for apparent fraud, and released on bail. He will subsequently be exonerated. But he must admit the shattering truth, first to himself and then to his family, that the business cannot go on. This young man who has never experienced failure must now deal with public humiliation ("Trio in a Pickle," screams a local newspaper headline) and personal defeat.

"Oh, what a thought," writes Heinz on Monday, December 13, after a sorrowful meeting with his family. "To give it all up after working hard for 10 years, besides getting many friends and parents into trouble with us. The pen cannot describe all of our feelings. We did not retire until late. I told them that the pickle business, for some time, has been driving me away from the Cross instead of closer to it, that my mind was so worried and unsettled that I could not worship my God acceptable. Oh, what a thought. What doth it profit us if we gain the whole world and lose our own souls?"

December 17 (Friday) at 5 P.M., Heinz, Noble & Company officially files a "voluntary petition in bankruptcy." Friends and business associates fall away. A coolness even develops—or perhaps inevitably develops—between the Nobles and Heinz.

There is no money for Christmas presents. There is no help from relatives. His parents' house, pledged as collateral, and monies lent to Harry by various members of the family appear to be lost. Only banker-and-neighbor Covode remains "a true friend."

---

3. *The Good Provider*, p. 18.

Excerpt from Harry's diary, December 16–18, 1875, when, after months of struggle, Heinz, Noble & Company finally filed for bankruptcy. "We filed a voluntary petition in bankruptcy on the 17th (Friday) at 5 P.M., as our creditors were forcing us in and our attorney insisted it was better voluntary." Despite the terrible toll it took on the Founder and his family, within a few months, he had regrouped with his brother and cousin, and was back in business.

And yet, on Friday, December 31, in his last entry for the year, Harry's basic optimism and inner strength break through.

"Home and city. Beautiful 60 degrees. For one week past we have had weather like summer or April weather. We were this day and until midnight working at our (bankruptcy) schedule. Came home on midnight train . . . God bless the coming year to us all."

RECOVERY AND RENEWAL

Today we know that this real-life drama had a happy ending. However, before recounting it, let us pause to underscore certain aspects of his personal recovery and the company's renewal.

First, Harry had the courage to plunge back into business within a few months of his bankruptcy. Second, he turned the very instrument of his downfall—the common cucumber pickle—into the company's lucky charm and one of the greatest promotional ideas in America. Third, he vowed to discharge his "moral obligations" to his creditors, and did so over a period of nine years. Fourth, the experience remained so painful that for decades the "official" Heinz history never mentioned the bankruptcy. Instead, in newspaper and company publications, the H. J. Heinz story appeared to be one of unbroken success. From these small but telling details, we can infer the complex character and strength of the man. (His father, on the other hand, was so shattered by the ordeal that he never fully recovered his mental health and spent many years in a Philadelphia sanitarium.)

In 1876—on Valentine's Day—he regrouped with brother John and cousin Frederick, and with $3,000 launched the F & J Heinz Company. Harry, an undischarged bankrupt, unofficially ran the show as their salaried manager. That year they added ketchup (first written "catsup") to their line of pure, quality condiments. From then on, the company prospered, due, in large part, to Harry's business skills, moral force, international vision, eye for talent, and willingness to delegate responsibility so that the organization could grow.

FIRST TRIP ABROAD

By 1886, Harry felt secure enough about the business to leave it for his first extended trip to Europe with the entire family. It included a two-week stay in London, which marked the beginning of a long love affair between the Heinz family and the English.

In 1898, the struggling British business moved to "real premises" at 99–101 Farringdon Road, which contained a warehouse and convention space, as well as offices. Also, as is apparent in this 1903 photograph of the London Branch House, the building served as an immense billboard from which to trumpet Heinz and its 57 Varieties.

The Founder returned to England yearly for three decades. In fact, once he had tasted the pleasures of foreign travel, hardly a year went by that he did not venture to the remotest corners of the earth, acquiring art and artifacts along the way.

Unlike fellow millionaire Frick, whose art (housed in his former New York City mansion) still ranks as one of the country's finest private collections, the Founder was a gilded-age innocent abroad, an enthusiastic amateur whose tastes were inclusive rather than exclusive. With money to spend and boundless curiosity, his private museum housed a hodgepodge of "souvenirs," ranging from stones from the Great Wall of China to "collectibles," some valuable, some not. He wanted people to enjoy what he enjoyed, whether it was an alligator from Florida, carved Japanese ivories, or Parisian timepieces. His collection was sold and dispersed after his death.

Between 1890 and 1914, the Founder traveled to Europe every year but four, and crisscrossed the United States as if it were the next county. For a man who never went to college, travel became a form of higher education and Heinz remained a permanent student.

During his initial visit to London, he made his famous—in

Heinz company lore—unannounced sales call on Fortnum and Mason, purveyors to the royal family. Dressed in silk hat and frock coat, as if he were calling on the queen, he strode through the front door, asked for the head of purchasing, and, no doubt talking all the while, proffered his sample of condiments. To his amazement, the gentleman said, "I think we will take them all."

This event forever enshrined the Founder's awesome talents as a salesman, his vision as a businessman, and the quality of Heinz products. In fact, his first international sale gave rise to his fourth Important Idea, which anticipated the global economy by a century: our field is the world.

Heinz became one of the first U.S. companies to expand internationally, with sales branches and factories established in the United Kingdom in 1905 and in Canada in 1909.

The firm's name was officially changed to the H. J. Heinz Company in 1888 when cousin Frederick and brother John were bought out. Business was so good that on December 24, Harry noted in his diary, "I purchase the most extravagant gift of my life today, a diamond pin (3 stones) . . . for $710, but concluded that a woman so modest and kind was deserving of something while I could pay cash and had no debts." The gift also may have assuaged his guilt for rarely being home.

In total charge at last, the Founder—a decisive, action-oriented man—immediately bought land along the banks of the Allegheny River and launched his ambitious plan to build a "model" factory complex. It was to be based on his fifth Important Idea, also ahead of its time: harmonize the business system of today and you will have the remedy for the present discontent that characterizes the commercial world and fosters a spirit of enmity between capital and labor.

The Founder had observed during his travels the positive effects of paternalism in German factories, and reflected on the negative consequences of poorly treated workers in Pittsburgh, especially the horrors of the 1877 Pittsburgh railroad strike and riots. In remarkable contrast to ruthless captains of industry, such as Carnegie and Frick, who parked their moral precepts at the factory door, the Founder's philosophy of management was enlightened and benevolent. He was a deeply religious man who practiced what he preached. From an early age, his twin passions—morality and business—were interwoven in his character and formed the central tapestry of his life.

The Prince of Paternalism's credo, "Heart power is better than horse power," summed up his eminently practical view of economic and spiritual life. It was a philosophy that, as journalists noted with universal approval, really worked. By 1896, Heinz was already referred to in the press as "a millionaire" and his company, free of management–employee strife, regarded as a workers' utopia.

In 1890, the company began its move from downtown Pittsburgh to the North Side and into the glazed, pressed, hard-brick Romanesque buildings on either side of Progress Street. The factory was built to the Founder's specifications with "the best of everything." Between 1890 and 1898, 17 structures arose around a green, open courtyard. Everything was so well thought out that the Baltimore and Ohio Railroad ran directly into the Vinegar Building.

Heinz, a natural public relations wizard, shrewdly promoted his immaculate model factory complex. On September 29, 1897, he and his managers resolved that "guides showing visitors through the factory make hourly trips from 9 to 11 and from 1 to 3." From then on, any visitor to Pittsburgh took a tour of the "Heinz Pickle Works."

As with so many of his promotional ideas, he originated the concept. By 1900, 20,000 visitors a year were being guided through the model stables (dubbed an "equine palace"), the resplendent Time Office, the printing department, box and can factories, preserving kitchens, packing departments, factory girls' dining room, Baked Bean Building, and Pickle Bottling Department. Not on the tour but equally impressive were the dressing rooms, restrooms, an emergency hospital, roof gardens, indoor swimming pool and gymnasium, meeting hall, and classrooms. Visitors were given food samples, a lecture in the auditorium, and a pickle pin.

Facilities for female employees were exemplary for their day and often far superior to workers' facilities at home. For example, factory women changed from their street clothes into their freshly laundered uniforms, aprons, and caps (which they were expected to sew from material bought at cost from the company) in a spotless, downstairs dressing room lavishly appointed with marble washbasins, hot and cold running water, and bathrooms with showers. They stowed their clothes in private wooden lockers locked with immense keys. At left, two 1906 Pittsburgh factory "girls" in uniform stand in front of their locker room keys. Also available to the "girls" were a free company doctor and dentist, and a weekly manicurist for those handling food.

The Pickle Pin

The pickle pin, another unprecedented piece of merchandising, seems to have been born—like so many good ideas—in a moment of desperation. Thirty years later, in the midst of the Great Depression, the Founder's son Howard delivered a rip-roaring speech to his managers about how, during the 1893 World's Columbian Exposition in Chicago, it all came about.

> The World's Fair came on, and the Founder had to go to the bank to borrow enough money to put up an exhibit at Chicago, the most remarkable exhibit of a food line that had ever been known . . . Borrowed the money! Had the courage in the midst of the panic (of 1892–93) to go through! And then what? Everything looked like defeat and failure. Why? Because they decided to put the food products up 44 steps to the gallery of the Agricultural Building. The people were flocking to the ground floor. Men like Armour and Swift stood still with drooped heads and hands looking failure in the face. But within one week, the Founder devised a simple method of cornering that enemy that will go down in history. He had little boys scatter thousands of pasteboard checks on the ground—they looked like everyone's brass baggage check—and on one side of the check invited people up to the Heinz exhibit for a free individual souvenir: the pickle pin. They brought such a crowd, the police were called because the gallery began to break down.[4]

One million green plaster (gutta-percha) pickle watch charms with a metal loop at the top were given away in Chicago, and delighted fellow-food exhibitors gave the Founder a dinner and an inscribed silver loving cup. The charm turned into a pin sometime later.

---

4. December 7, 1932. Managers' midwinter convention banquet.

Heinz pickle charms designed and distributed by H.J. Heinz as a free souvenir to every visitor—over one million, as it turned out—who climbed the stairs to the H.J. Heinz Company's second-floor exhibit, pictured below, at the 1893 World's Fair, also known as the Columbian Exposition,

in Chicago. Sometime later, the charm became a pin. (The pickle charm with an American flag was reputedly worn by the Founder.)

The pickle pin has become one of the most popular souvenirs in the history of American advertising. More than 100 million have been handed out at expositions, trade fairs and on plant tours. They continue to be sent out to new generations of pickle-pin devotees who request them.

By 1897, the company had officially resolved to use the pickle, bearing the word "Heinz's," as its logo "in all signs, labels, advertisements, etc., wherever practicable and that it be given greater prominence than the trade mark." Later that year, the board resolved to drop the "s" from Heinz and to add an "h" to Pittsburgh. (Between 1891 and 1911, the town's official spelling was without an "h," although local usage was divided. The Point Park Museum notes that Pittsburg without an "h" is the German spelling and Pittsburgh with an "h" is the Welsh spelling.[5])

Over the years, the Heinz pickle, in all its incarnations, would become one of the most famous product symbols in history. Its success illustrated another Important Idea: let the public assist you in advertising your products and promoting your name. In his diary, Heinz wrote, "We keep our shingle out and then let the public blow our horn, and that counts. But we must do something to make them do this."[6]

COMPANY EXPANSION

In 1888, the Founder's sister Elizabeth and his first cousin, Sebastian Mueller, married. Mueller then became general manager of manufacturing and a member of the advisory board. Over the next few years, the company grew by leaps and bounds, and the Founder, constantly on the road, relinquished routine control of the business. The board, now chaired by Mueller, met daily and made most operating decisions. There was much to decide.

By 1901, according to a "Looking Backward" editorial in the employee newsletter *Pickles*, the company was planting "18,000 acres with its own seeds and gathering fruits of many thousands more." In addition to Pittsburgh's 17 large factory and administrative buildings, the company boasted 38 salting stations, nine

---

5. Rich Gigler, *The Pittsburgh Press*, December 23, 1991.

6. Alberts, *op. cit.*, p. 123.

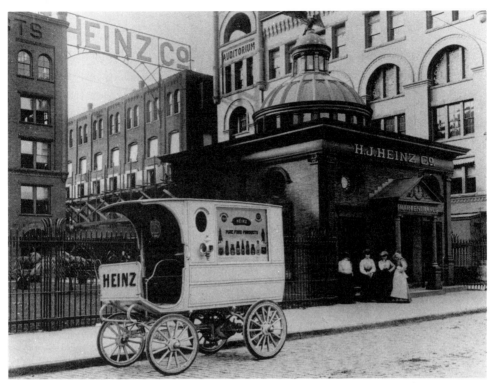

Male and female employees clocked in and out (through separate doors and facilities) of the Time Office, which also served as the company's hiring office. An elegant little building, inside and out, this 1906 photograph shows its central location in the Pittsburgh factory. Parked in front is a Heinz wagon.

branch factories, and 26 branch warehouses and offices (including England), and employed a steady workforce of 2,500. Wheelbarrows had expanded into "huge drays and speedy automobiles and a host of Heinz refrigerator and tank cars running throughout the United States."

The Pickle Army, known as "traveling men," was purveying a range of 200 products nationally and internationally. Expositions in Buffalo and Glasgow depicted "the varieties of goods and styles of packages" furnished by the company. The Founder picked up two gold medals at the 1900 Paris exposition, one for the quality of the products exhibited and one for "the policy of the firm tending to the improvement of its factory conditions . . . for the sociological features of its business as exhibited by means of photographs."

In 1905, Heinz incorporated. Six board members became stockholders of the private corporation. They included, in addition to the Founder (president and general supervisor), his son Howard Covode (assistant to the president), cousin Frederick (head of farms and gardens), brother-in-law Mueller (in charge of manufacturing and branch factories), W. H. Robinson (finance), and R. G. Evans (sales).

May 26, 1909, meeting—the first attended by all members—of the board of directors of the H.J. Heinz Company in the president's office. From left to right: Howard Heinz, W.H. Robinson, Nevin G. Woodside, J.N. Jeffares, Clarence N. Heinz, Henry John Heinz, and Sebastian Mueller.

ADVERTISING AND MARKETING INSPIRATIONS

The Founder now focused on a range of advertising and marketing ideas, an area in which he was unrivaled.

The most durable of his many inspirations came to him in 1896 while he was riding in an elevated train in New York. One of the car cards advertised "21 styles" of shoes, and while he was already manufacturing more than 60 products, his mind kept turning to the number "57" and the phrase "57 Varieties." He was so taken with the magic number that, according to his diary, he "jumped off the train . . . began the work of laying out my advertising plans . . . and within a week the sign of the green pickle with the '57 Varieties' was appearing in newspapers, on billboards, signboards and everywhere else I could find a place to stick it."

Other inspirations followed. They included the Heinz Ocean Pier at Atlantic City, built in 1899 and washed away by the hurricane of 1944, and a six-story Heinz sign, New York's first electric display, which boasted 1,200 incandescent lights. Advertising "good things for the table," as well as the Heinz Pier, it was erected in 1900 at the corner of Fifth Avenue and 23rd Street, and was eventually replaced by the famous Flatiron Building.

Basically, like the gilded-age pickle king that he was, the Founder believed more was more. He plastered the Heinz name across America and Europe, on the sides of delivery carriages, buses, wagons, and trucks; on color cards in streetcars; on three-dimensional signs (the product names change as one moves around the sign); in newspapers and magazines (never on Sunday); on billboards, along railroad tracks, and carved into hillsides; on pickle cards, spoons, showcards, calendars, souvenir books, and in electric lights (the last one remained in Wenceslaus Square, Prague, until the 1968 uprising in Czechoslovakia).

He never lost an opportunity to get the Heinz name before the public. For example, the Founder had a keen eye for horseflesh, which he turned to practical advantage. Housed in his model stables were 200 black Percheron draft horses, which pulled wagons and performed prominently in political and civil parades, as well as other promotional events.

From the beginning, too, the Founder was sensitive to the mar-

One of the earliest "57 Varieties" ads, created circa 1896 for a display on the inside of a horse-drawn street car. Also, a 1901 view of the company design shop.

New York City's first large electric display, built in 1900, with 1,200 incandescent lights. It also displayed the Founder's genius for advertising and promotion. Located at 23rd Street and Fifth Avenue, then bustling with fashionable shopping emporiums, it was eventually replaced by the architecturally renowned Flatiron Building.

keting value of quality packaging and design. The company owned its own glass factory in Sharpsburg, which produced the finest bottles, hand-blown from molds, in a variety of shapes. A stable of designers turned out elegant signs and labels, such as the keystone-shaped (from the keystone state) ketchup label, as well as display and point-of-sales materials. No expense seems to have been spared. According to Ed Lehew, who has worked in the advertising and sales areas of the company for over 40 years, many of the old labels were of such high quality that they could not be reproduced today at any price. Printed on lithographic stones, often with 20 colors, their registration and deep jewel-like tones are a marvel.

An unfortunate example of the Founder's unceasing quest for new promotional opportunities—embedding the number 57 in concrete on hillsides—despoiled the landscape and often enraged local citizens. The Founder always found a way to emerge from the fray looking like a hero. If, for example, negative rumors spread about his buying a scenic hillside for a sign or billboard, he would either protest that he had no such plans or confess and scrap his plans, then turn the hillside over to the city. His only self-imposed advertising restrictions: no billboards in the Pittsburgh area and no advertising in Sunday newspapers.

A 1903 Heinz delivery wagon drawn by a pair of prize-winning draft horses favored by Henry John Heinz, an expert on horseflesh. The company's more than 200 horses, mostly pure black Percherons, and all of which had to conform in weight, size, and type, pulled white wagons with green trimmings. The company was noted for the elegance of its delivery service.

It's also clear that elaborate displays and food tastings at fairs, food shows, expositions, and grocery stores—accompanied by free samples and money-back guarantees—were brilliant marketing devices. They continued through the 1950s.

Of course, the Founder viewed his army of travelers as merchandisers, not just order takers. Informed and inspired twice a year at midwinter and midsummer conventions, they ministered to their customers like priests to their flocks. Under strict orders to deposit and serve samples upon arriving in a store and to "clean up old unsaleable goods" before leaving, they spread the gospel of Heinz quality, purity, and integrity wherever they went. Unlike so many in the food business, the Founder had nothing to hide.

PURE FOOD AND DRUG ACT

Indeed, if anything held back the explosive growth of the industry, it was the general suspicion with which the average consumer viewed most commercially processed food. And rightly so! Without government regulation, manufacturers regularly turned out dreadful and sometimes lethal concoctions. They added dyes and chemicals, such as formaldehyde, to improve flavor and color, stop fermentation and decay, and mask poor quality. Mislabeling and false advertising were routine.

The Founder opposed adding chemicals as preservatives or filler, such as sawdust, to prepared foods. Always at the forefront of change, he actively supported and promoted the passage of a pure food and drug law that would mandate minimum safety standards for the industry. Indeed, his seventh Important Idea was that government regulation would help the food processing industry to grow.

The Founder stood virtually alone within the industry on this issue and related issues of health and sanitation. What he saw as "good business," others viewed as government invasion of personal liberty. It was the age of the robber baron; it was the high tide of monopolies, price-fixing trusts, government nonintervention.

Nevertheless, the Founder worked closely on this issue with Dr.

Harvey Wiley, chief (and first) chemist at the U.S. Department of Agriculture. A magnificent orator, Wiley led—from the mid-1890s on—the crusade for pure food, campaigning against the vested industry interests he viewed as "the hosts of Satan."[7]

The Founder appointed his son Howard and Sebastian Mueller to lead the fight. They forged a coalition of civic and religious groups, newspapers, scientists, politicians, and enlightened citizens. They even went to the White House to convince Teddy Roosevelt of the need for federal legislation. He was skeptical, as were many Americans. Rumors were spread that the company was in favor of prohibition, which led to boycotts of Heinz products by some customers, especially saloons. The fight was vicious.

Gradually, however, the public relations campaign began to work. Also, through the revelations of muckraking journalists, the public became alarmed. Upton Sinclair published his shocking exposé of the Chicago stockyards, *The Jungle*, in early 1906. Congressional hearings were held on adulterations in meat, drink, and drugs. Wiley scientifically demonstrated the deleterious effects of seven chemicals commonly used as preservatives.

According to Wiley, it was only when the good doctor demonstrated to Roosevelt the transformation of cheap whiskey through adulteration into so-called 10-year-old scotch that the president's ire was finally aroused. "If a man can't get a good drink of whiskey when he comes home from work," said Roosevelt, "then there ought to be a law to see that he does."[8]

On June 23, 1906, Congress finally passed the first Pure Food and Drug Act. It was the day the modern food-processing industry was born. Legitimized and sanitized, the industry boomed, and the H. J. Heinz Company with it.

---

7. Alberts, *op. cit.*, p. 170.

8. Alberts, *op. cit.*, p. 177.

A WORLDWIDE CELEBRITY

By now, the Founder was a worldwide celebrity and a one-man band proclaiming the Heinz philosophy and its "57 Varieties." He also pursued a growing range of nonbusiness interests—in the Sunday School movement, local and national politics, and civic and philanthropic organizations, including building the Sarah Heinz Settlement House—and continued to travel. Wherever he went, from Peking to Paris, from Johannesburg to Japan, he carried his samples and proffered his maxims to the press. Colorful and quotable, he was a reporter's dream.

The Founder was a brilliant communicator. In his hands, for example, his mother's character-building aphorisms became inspired instruments of leadership, the equivalent of today's "sound bites." He used them to convey his deepest values and highest ideals, and even embedded them in the stained-glass windows along the staircase in the Administration Building, which opened in 1908.

Many conveyed the essence of the company's culture: "Quality is to a product what character is to a man"; "We are working for success and not for money. The money will take care of itself"; "It is neither capital nor labor that brings success, but management, because management can attract capital and capital can employ labor." Indeed, after 125 years, his most famous maxim—"To do a common thing uncommonly well brings success"—still says it best.

In 1913, a newspaper profile of the Founder described his career as "a business romance" and noted that "he now employs between 5,000 and 6,000 persons . . . has 12 immense factories in the United States, one in Canada, one in England, and one in Spain . . . and his three sons are in business with him."

Toward the end of his life, the Founder became as well known for his zealous commitment to the World's Sunday School Association—also a world peace movement—as for his business success. Heinz, active in Sunday School work from the age of 12, rose from pupil, teacher, superintendent, director of the county association, and president of the Pennsylvania Sabbath School Association (succeeding John Wanamaker in 1906) to member of the executive

H.J. Heinz visited China in May 1913 on a 6,000-mile, six-month world tour with 13 other business and professional men and women, delegates to the seventh convention in Zurich of the World Sunday School Association. Other countries visited included Japan, Korea, Russia, Poland, and Germany. Heinz took a number of cases of Heinz products, as well as one son, Clarence. As this photograph of a 1918 food tasting in China demonstrates, the Founder was pioneering yet another market for Heinz products.

committee of the International and World's Sunday School Associations. Of over 28 million World Association members, 17 million lived in the United States, two million of them in Pennsylvania. In 1913, at the age of 65, with 13 other business and professional men and women, he made a six-month, 6,000-mile tour around the world—Japan, Korea, China, Russia, Poland, Germany, Switzerland—to attend the Seventh Convention of the World Association in Zurich.

A racially and culturally integrated organization, the Sunday School Association brought him, in the spring of 1905 at the

vigorous age of 70, to a huge rally in California. A reporter for the *Stockton California Evening Record* vividly described the torchlight parade of thousands and the Founder's remarks on "The Business Man of Tomorrow." First, the Founder welcomed Afro-American Captain Potter, "the oldest man in the hall, who is 104 years young," and then advised the gathered throng to "make chums of your boys, but if you do, be prepared to get the truth, just like I do." It's worth noting, however, that the Founder was exceedingly competitive with his boys. For example, after being the fifth person to ride in Glenn H. Curtiss's hydroaeroplane, as a local newspaper noted, "He boasted that he had surpassed his sons who, up to this time, had done nothing more exciting than ride an automobile."

Nevertheless, how contemporary his remarks sound. And how astute. The reporter found him "original, entertaining, a great kidder." Then he added, "Heinz can be summed up in one word. He's a corker. Heinz would be the first to use the expression himself."

Truer words were never written. The man was astounding. Indeed, he had become a man of mythic proportions—a man who revolutionized food processing, marketing, and the public's eating habits; an industrialist who was personally likable and treated his workers according to the Golden Rule; a model Victorian who collected "art objects" and venerated mass-produced consumer goods; a success whose Horatio Alger life story embodied the opportunities offered by democratic, abundant America.

However, Harry Heinz was far from perfect. As is often the case with larger-than-life people, his strengths were also his weaknesses. It's clear, for example, that he was a hard taskmaster to those family members, especially brothers and sons, who did not follow his puritanical (some might call them priggish) ways or embrace his workaholic notions of the good life. It's equally clear that any emotional instability in family members may have been exacerbated by Harry's inability to tolerate frailty and imperfection.

Reading between the lines of his diary, one detects a formidable temper. It suggests he may have been a bit of a bully. Harry whipped his youngest brother, Jacob, for not attending school regularly; and he was constantly angry with brother John for his poor work habits. It's fairly clear that family members who could not live up to Harry's expectations left town. Brother John wound up in Indiana, and Harry's invalid son, Clarence, was cared for by Harry's brother Peter and his wife, Pauline, in Lake Geneva, Wisconsin, instead of at Greenlawn, his father's 30-room Pittsburgh mansion. His diary also suggests he was as hard on himself as on others. In short, despite efforts by his private secretary, E. D. McCafferty, to transform him into a saint—in a biography written four years after the Founder's death—and despite subsequent efforts by Howard and the company to deify him, he was a complex individual with his fair share of imperfections. That, in the face of his all-too-human frailties, he became an enlightened and visionary American industrial giant makes his accomplishment more, not less, impressive.

The Founder lived to be 75. Energetic and optimistic to the end, he was a hard act for his sons to follow.

Howard Heinz, age 28, at Bad Kissingen, Germany, in 1905.

Howard Covode Heinz:
The Spirit of the House

~~~

(1877–1941)

Howard Covode Heinz, second son and third child of Henry John and Sarah, presided over the House of Heinz for 22 critical years, from 1919 to 1941. Despite his impressive accomplishments, he has remained something of a mystery, a man about whom there has been much speculation and few facts. There are a number of reasons why.

First, unlike his father, who sought, enjoyed, and was a master at personal publicity, Howard avoided the spotlight. He was a private man who ran a privately held company close to the vest, leaving a meager public record and paper trail. The year he died, *Fortune* dubbed the H. J. Heinz Company "one of the big American corporate mysteries."[1]

Second, Howard revered his father and constantly attributed his every thought and action to the Founder's ideas, philosophy, and wisdom. The press generally believed this simplistic view. *Fortune* went on to note, "Mr. (Howard) Heinz goes his way serenely, at all times and everywhere attributing the major part of his and his company's success to the practices and principles laid down by his father. . . . Under him, as a matter of fact . . . nearly

---

1. "The House of Heinz," *Fortune* magazine, February 1941, p. 76.

all the company's virtues (and its weaknesses, too) can be traced back to the Founder." It was difficult to judge the son apart from the long shadow his father cast.

Finally, the aloof, aristocratic Howard, though widely admired, was not as likable or as colorful as his father. "He revolts," said *Fortune*, "at such crude appellations as 'ketchup king' or 'pickle king.' "[2]

After Howard's death, the young and more personable Jack Heinz quickly moved stage center. He was better copy. He was clever enough to hire Ed Parrack, head of Ketchum, the advertising and public relations agency headquartered in Pittsburgh, to deal more openly with the press. And once he took the company public in 1946, the old, secretive Heinz became a thing of the past.

By 1949, Howard was already the man in the middle, overshadowed by both his father and son. Today, few remember the man or know why he might be worth remembering.

It turns out that Howard is well worth remembering. Indeed, without him, there might not be an H. J. Heinz Company to remember. As a *Saturday Evening Post* article suggested eight years after his death, Howard was "quite possibly a better businessman (than his father) . . . the savior of the Heinz business during the depression."[3]

That is no exaggeration. Throughout the roller-coaster ride of the 1930s (with two depressions in 10 years), while other food companies collapsed left and right, Howard not only saved the company, but expanded it, adding new products, new people, new plants, new territories and branch houses around the world.

As a businessman, Howard inherited most of his father's strengths: self-confidence, optimism, courage, fiscal prudence, and marketing boldness. Luckily for Heinz, these were precisely the right qualities for such a perilous time.

Today, through family scrapbooks and speeches, we have more information about his leadership.

---

2. "The House of Heinz," *Fortune* magazine, February 1941.

3. Arthur Baum, "In Grandpa's Shoes," *The Saturday Evening Post*, June 23, 1949.

The Young Howard

Howard and his older brother, Clarence, learned the business in overalls from the bottom up. On occasion, eight-year-old Howard put in six-hour days at the office and factory, while also attending public school in Sharpsburg. His apprenticeship continued during summer vacations, working in Heinz factories and salting stations around the country.

Howard was more his father's child than either of his brothers, and he fit into the family business as if into a hand-tailored suit. Clarence and Clifford, the youngest son, seem to have lacked Howard's emotional toughness. Clarence, with an artistic flair, worked briefly as advertising manager for the company, retired in 1914 due to poor health, and died in Lake Geneva, Wisconsin, in 1920. (He was cared for by a physician privately in his home.) Clifford died in Palm Springs in 1935.

Howard attended Shadyside Academy and Yale, graduating and taking up full-time duties at the firm in 1900—the dawn of the 20th century. Letters between son and father reveal Howard's loving concern for his father (on August 20, 1894, "Don't work too hard and let the western trip do you some good"), his dedication to the business, and how hard he worked to live up to the old man's expectations and talents.

They also demonstrate how seriously he took his religious and moral duties, especially to young people. He started a Boys' Club in New Haven, and launched a similar club near the Heinz plant on the North Side. His father emulated and honored his son's work by creating, in 1913, the vastly more ambitious Sarah Heinz House. Howard supervised its construction and activities.

In 1906, Howard married Elizabeth Granger Rust. In 1908, she gave birth to their first son, named for his illustrious grandfather, Henry John "Jack" Heinz II. In 1913, their second son, Rust, was born.

Sons Howard, Clarence, and Clifford with their father in 1904. Howard spent summers in different parts of the family business, including company salting houses where fresh pickles were received and cured.

In 1900, the year he graduated from Yale and began full-time work at Heinz, the 20-year-old bachelor, Howard, appeared to have it all. Tall, handsome, heir to an industrial fortune, he zipped between factory and his father's mansion, Greenlawn, in his beloved French Flyer, or Red Devil. A two-cylinder, six-horsepower Panhard-Levassor with a Daimler Phoenix engine, purchased in Paris while father and son attended the exposition, it reached an astounding speed of 40 miles an hour and manufactured its own acetylene for the headlights. No one in Pittsburgh had ever seen anything like it.

Sarah Heinz House, dedicated to "Youth, Recreation, Character and Service," and nationally recognized for its community work, was built by the Founder as an expression of approval of his son Howard's efforts and as a memorial to his wife.

A home away from home to generations of North Side children and their parents, over 80,000 members have benefited from its summer camp and year-round sports, social, and educational programs. The building, whose interior resembles an elegant turn-of-the-century home with wooden beams and stained-glass windows, still stands within the shadow of the original factory complex, now Heinz U.S.A., and is funded by the Howard Heinz Endowment.

In 1901, Howard started a modest boys' club, called Covode House. In 1903, it was expanded to include girls. The Founder loved children, as did his wife, known for her charitable work, particularly with the Children's Aid Society. In dedicating the building in 1915, the Founder wrote, "No sectarian bias will influence the work of this institution. . . . It is our desire to surround the boys and girls of the neighborhood with such good influences that they will never want to depart from the right paths."

An elegant pair, Howard and his wife, Elizabeth, strolling on the boardwalk in Atlantic City in the 1930s. Also, a 1914 portrait of Howard and his son, Henry John "Jack" Heinz II, age six. Named for his illustrious grandfather, Jack Heinz was destined from an early age to run the company.

The Beginning of Quality Control

Howard majored in chemistry, studied nutrition, and fought his father's general distrust of college men, scientists, and chemists. In 1912, he hired Herbert N. Riley, one of the company's first bacteriologists, who rose to become executive vice president under Howard. Riley, and those who followed, began to apply scientific methods to the processing, preservation, and production of food, eventually replacing the secretive gods who presided over their fiefdoms as if they alone could read the entrails. In 1918, they also began to apply scientific controls to quality in the laboratory and on the factory line. According to Riley, Heinz may have been the first U.S. company to coin the term "quality control department."

"In those days," said Riley, "Every operation was secret and the man who possessed the secret guarded it jealously. Everything was in code, and was locked in the safe."[4]

Riley found himself an unwanted man and realized he'd have to take on the factory's awesome pickle salter.

"Our pickle salter was a fellow named 'Shady' Graves, and he was one hell of an important person. He had a little hard top hat on and a cutaway coat and a professional business air about him. He wouldn't let anyone come into the place while he was at work. His great thing was to put a finger into the pickle tanks, take it out with a great sweep, shove it into his mouth, suck it and say, 'Ah—yes—two bushels of salt in *there* . . . three bushes of salt in *here*.'

"But the biggest prima donna of the lot was the Italian operatic tenor in charge of spaghetti, specially brought over from Italy. It is a very simple job, really. The point is that if spaghetti dries unevenly, you get a broken strand. This colorful gentleman was always yelling around the place and being 'the big boss.' I had to get a pass to see him, too. They knew when I came around there would be trouble coming. I used to watch him. He would flicker his hands around as if he was fingering lace cuffs. He would stick

---

4. Alberts, *ibid.*, p. 215.

his hand out of the window to 'feel' the air, rubbing the tips of his fingers together, to determine just how to adjust his drying process."[5]

Riley replaced them with a $400 hygrometer and high school students using a salimeter.

In 1917, after the United States entered World War I, Howard distinguished himself in food relief work. He performed so outstandingly in Pennsylvania that, after the war, Herbert Hoover cabled from Paris to ask him to become director general of American Relief for southeast Europe and Asia Minor. It was an immense and heart-rending job cut short by his father's unexpected death, at the age of 75, of double pneumonia.

HOWARD AND THE TWENTIES

Howard, 42, rushed home. A seasoned executive who had worked in every area of the company, no man was better prepared to assume the presidency of the H. J. Heinz Company.

The 1920s were years of prosperity for the company and the country. Howard embraced and personified the laissez-faire capitalism of the roaring twenties, and reveled in the role of businessman-statesman with easy access to his powerful Republican friends, such as Treasury Secretary Andrew Mellon and Presidents Harding, Coolidge, and Hoover. A captain of industry, he was the youngest man ever elected to the board of the Pennsylvania Railroad.

In 1920, Howard launched a new company tradition, Founder's Day, which every October honored not only his father's birth, but the ongoing bond between employer and employee. By 1924, it had become an extravaganza and technological miracle.

Ten thousand employees listened to identical speeches and dined together at 62 identical banquets in cities throughout the United States, Canada, England, and Scotland, linked by a new

---

5. Alberts, *ibid.*, pp. 215, 216.

Chemist in the H.J. Heinz Company laboratory in 1901, five years before the passage of the Pure Food and Drug Act, which regulated and, to consumers, legitimized the commercial food industry. Howard, a chemist by training, vigorously promoted a scientific approach to quality testing and measurement in food processing. The Heinz Company pioneered quality-assurance standards and procedures.

Three generations of H.J. Heinz Company leaders: the Founder, with son Howard and grandson Jack, December 15, 1917, attending a reception and dinner for the 30th Annual Convention of branch house managers and assistants in the Founder's Pittsburgh mansion, Greenlawn.

invention, shortwave radio. President Coolidge addressed Heinz employees from the White House by radio. Even Coolidge was in awe of the radio hookup, which ran from the White House over a special wire to station KDKA in East Pittsburgh, and was then relayed over the air by the Westinghouse Electric & Manufacturing Company. The event, with its pioneering use of technology, was widely covered by the press. Howard obviously had inherited his father's flair for drama and public relations.

In 1924, the company was exceedingly self-sufficient. It oversaw 150,000 acres of crops, and boasted 150,000 crop harvesters, 25 branch factories, 116 pickle-salting stations, 170 raw-product receiving stations, 755 owned or operated railroad cars, 69 branch offices and warehouses, 1,337 travelers (including 160 in England and their colonies), plus it owned and operated bottle, box, and can factories, as well as seed farms and plant-propagating greenhouses.

How did Howard run this vast empire? By maintaining, like his father, a dizzying pace of travel. Also, by granting a high degree of autonomy to a small circle of exceptionally talented, hardworking, dedicated senior managers in Spain, Canada, Britain, and throughout the United States. They were proud to be extended members of the Heinz Company family and its burgeoning line of quality products.

Few enjoyed the exalted reputation of the remarkable Charles Hellen, originally the company's Boston branch manager. In 1905, the Founder picked Hellen, his best manager, to run the English branch. He retained the post until evacuated to New York on the eve of World War II.

Hellen, a brilliant strategic thinker, tempered by Howard's practical hand, created an immensely successful organization with a decentralized sales and warehouse system. Through 1926, England imported from the United States and Canada baked beans, spaghetti, ketchup, chutney, and three varieties of soup.

In fact, during the teens and twenties, operations and products north of the U.S. border developed a distinctly Canadian personality and taste. Headquartered in Leamington, Ontario, the factory (which processed cucumbers, beans, cabbage, cauliflower, and tomatoes from nearby farms) further expanded: launched its own educational service department, working with local growers to

On October 11, 1924, Founder's Day was simultaneously celebrated by 10,000 Heinz employees and officers who dined together at 62 identical banquets served in cities throughout the United States, Canada, England, and Scotland. They listened to the same addresses by the same speakers, including U.S. President Calvin Coolidge, linked by a new invention, shortwave radio. The Pittsburgh banquet, here pictured, gathered 3,000 employees in one vast room of the Shipping Building in the Pittsburgh factory. Other statistics of the event were impressive: 3,500 feet of dining room table, 25 kitchens, 30,000 pieces of china and glass, 5,000 chickens consumed, and 200 chefs. Howard Heinz also unveiled a full-length statue of the Founder, which still presides over Heinz U.S.A.'s reception area.

In 1926, the 57th anniversary of the company became the occasion for another radio linkup between employees in the United States, Canada, and Great Britain, where those at the Bristol branch, pictured above, celebrated with a banquet as they listened to Howard Heinz and marveled at the technology.

increase yields and develop tomatoes more suitable for processing; and boasted nine coast-to-coast sales branches covering 10 provinces.

In the United States, Howard Heinz, according to his private secretary, A. L. Schiel, was much more of a desk-and-paper man than was his father. He ran a hierarchical organization over which he kept close watch, maintaining daily contact—by phone or in person—with senior Pittsburgh executives in purchasing, manufacturing, sales, and finance. Twice a week, he met and lunched with his board (the same senior men), grilling them on details of the business.

Basically, Howard made most of the key decisions—on pricing, new products, research, and advertising. And in the area of finance, he trusted no one. He alone, it turned out, knew the world wide profit-and-loss picture. Rumor has it that once a year he scribbled and added up numbers reported to him on the back of an envelope.

Howard played a prominent role at summer (August) and winter (January) "conventions," which kicked off the main selling seasons, and at monthly one-day sales conventions held at branch and regional offices in the United States, Canada, and Britain.

At the H. J. Heinz Company, salesmen (still called travelers) were gods. The branch manager system—indeed, the entire organization—revolved around supporting and enhancing their sales and merchandising efforts. One of the first companies to adopt the sales convention idea, under Howard the week-long Pittsburgh gatherings of salesmen and branch managers became increasingly elaborate and expensive events. Part tent revival, part Elks Club bonhomie, part personal politics and perquisite, banners and banquets, songs and sermons were all part of the atmosphere—one in which Howard was a star performer. "Each day," according to Schiel, "his major address would require at least an hour's time and frequently an hour and a half."[6]

Howard was a thrilling orator, and his inspirational speeches were legendary. In fact, on the podium, the stern, aloof, and reserved Howard transformed himself into a warm and caring

---

6. A 1943 affidavit to the Commonwealth of Pennsylvania, County of Allegheny.

With Western Europe again on the verge of war, and the United States still gripped by depression, Howard Heinz commemorated the 70th anniversary of the "firm's founding" with a ringing speech in support of "free enterprise," "rugged individualism," and "free trade." On December 28, 1939, he spoke from the company's Pittsburgh auditorium while diners in 70 banquet halls throughout the United States and Canada listened to the address. Jack Heinz was toastmaster and other speakers included senior managers from New York City; Berkeley, California; and Toronto, Canada.

corporate father, a passionate drummer boy for the house of Heinz—its products, philosophy, and what he called, "The Spirit of the House."

Here, for example, is Howard in 1915.

> The new men ought to understand something about the Spirit of the House. . . . You know ordinarily the idea in the East is that a corporation is a stone-hearted thing that knows nothing but dollars and cents. If I thought this was the kind of organization the H. J. Heinz Company was I would quit my job today . . . neither do I expect you to work

for such an organization. . . . Classed a corporation . . . it is nothing more or less than a partnership in which there are some members of the family, in addition to about 30 men grown up in this business. We have presented them with stock. There isn't a man who cannot get stock if he has the ability and character . . . I mean to say that it is a business that belongs to the employees . . . it is just as much your business as it is my Heinz.

In Howard's hands, the Founder's philosophy of "kindly care and right treatment" became a Horatio Alger version of the American Dream. If his father reigned as the Prince of Paternalism, Howard deserved to be crowned its King.

HOWARD AND THE DEPRESSION

Howard's speeches, like his father's diaries, also provide us with a blow-by-blow account of the 1929 and 1939 depressions and how he overcame them. They are a window into his and the company's heart and soul.

At first, there is nothing but good news.

Early in 1929, for example, addressing a Branch Factory Managers Convention on January 30, Howard asked: "Who would like to be the first to volunteer to go to Australia?" Demand for "57 Varieties" had sent Howard on a trip in 1928 to Australia, New Zealand, the Fiji Islands, and Honolulu. He'd already been searching for a suitable manufacturing site.

Later that year, on September 12, to his Detroit salesmen he boasted, "There are over 11 thousand men in our business. It takes three years to visit the branch houses, factories and receiving stations. . . . There are now 300 salesmen in England."

Howard continued to expand in Pittsburgh as well as abroad. On July 9, *The 57 News* announced that the company would build in Pittsburgh "a theater and service building for the use of employ-

Howard Heinz carried out another grand gesture of paternalism before the curtain of the depression descended. Surrounded by employees who filled the streets and windows of nearby buildings, the cornerstone was laid for the new Auditorium and Service Building at Progress and Heinz Streets at noon on Tuesday, January 8, 1930. After it was placed in position by Howard Heinz, Sebastian Mueller sealed a cornerstone box beneath it. The building was to be used solely for employee activities and comfort. It was built because, said Howard, "people have a right to enjoy such facilities," and because, "in this great partnership of employer and employee, it is the company's duty to make this contribution to the welfare of the other partner." The sealed box contained a history of the company, photos, coins, and other memorabilia.

Lillian Weizmann (right), a child from Pittsburgh's Troy Hill section, joined the company in 1902 at the age of 14 as a pickle bottler. Following in the footsteps of Agnes Dunn, she rose to become a general forewoman and, after World War I, as this 1921 photo documents, head of the first employment department for women. She never married, reigned as dean of Heinz women until her 1953 retirement after 51 years of service, and ultimately became one of two managers of Eden Hall Farm.

ees and visitors at the Main Plant." Indeed, 1929 was "the best year in the history of the company and 1930 will be still better."[7]

On December 19, in an address to a Branch Factory Managers Conference, Howard mentioned the October 27 stock market crash for the first time. It's clear he had no inkling of its implications. "The Wall Street flurry doesn't bother us . . . Wall Street has nothing to do with Main Street. . . . We will enter perhaps not more than a period of a couple of months until the readjustment takes place."

On May 1, 1930, he remained unworried. "I am an optimist, and my father was an optimist before me," he told the annual banquet of the Men's 57 Club. However, by 1931, as Howard later admitted to *Forbes*, "It was evident that world depression had developed."[8]

Howard, it turned out, was in an excellent position to survive. Haunted by his father's bankruptcy, as well as subsequent panics and depressions, from his first day as president he had resolved "to play it safe . . . to get the company so well-heeled financially,"[9] it could survive anything.

That is why, unlike almost every other business leader, he had spent the 1920s getting the company out of debt instead of into debt. Resisting the lure of easy money, through either bank borrowing or the speculative frenzy taking place around him, he'd sacrificed dividends and invested profits in government bonds. His financial prudence saved the company. When banks began to crumble, the debt-free Heinz had no fear of crumbling with them. But Howard did far more than just ride out the 1930s. He went on the offensive.

His strategy was clear. First, cut costs but resist cutting wages so as not to "ruin the spirit, the esprit de corps, the enthusiasm for the House of Heinz and its methods."[10] Second, add a new line of ready-to-serve "quality" soups and a new line of baby or "strained" foods. Third, increase year-round product advertising and pro-

---

7. *The '57' News*, January 14, 1930, p. 1.

8. B.C. Forbes, "Howard Heinz: Sales Booster," March 1, 1939.

9. Speech to Pittsburgh Sales Convention, September 5, 1933.

10. Howard Heinz, speech to managers, August 13, 1931.

motion. As he later explained to *Forbes*, "I decided that we must have more staples, more new products, more salesmen, more advertising, that instead of pulling in our horns, we must push out our horns farther and more vigorously."[11]

It was a gutsy move, and no one was more enthusiastic about it than Howard Heinz. "I ask you whether you ever had a merchandising plan to equal what you have now . . . Never! Look at that line of soups . . . just look at it! . . . If you'd have told a Heinz salesman 10 years ago that you'd have a 10-cent line of cream-of-pea soup and celery soup—if you'd ever told him you had a 15 cent price or a 2 for 25 cents back in 1918, he would have thought you were crazy!"

That was on December 30, 1931. A year later, the tide had not yet turned for the company, but Howard was not discouraged. His speeches were filled with martial metaphors. "Fellow fighters, we are met on the field of battle, and we will win the fight!. . . We are here to make new plans for our campaign . . . We are here to size up the enemy . . . THE HEINZ MARCH IS ON."[12]

By the midsummer convention of 1933, the strategy had paid off. Sales were increasing, and Howard confessed to his salesmen in an August 14 speech: "When I think what we have gone through in this country and where we stand by comparison with other institutions . . . well I just get down on my knees at night and thank the good God."

The company was emerging from the depression "with more varieties and the discovery of the biggest variety we have in the business. Soup!" It had shot to the top of the Heinz hit parade, ahead of ketchup, pickles, beans, and spaghetti.

Christmas 1933 was a joyous occasion. "We have today . . . 60 percent more people on our payroll than we had a year ago . . . more people than at any time in the history of the Company," he proclaimed at holiday festivities on December 23.

England was also growing—there were now 1,500 employees and an addition had been built to the Harlesden plant. In 1934,

---

11. *Forbes*, March 1, 1939.

12. December 7, 1932, Banquet, Managers Midwinter Convention.

Canada built a new plant in Leamington for the processing of tomatoes, and began the production and sales of baby food.

On September 6, 1934, a surprise party in honor of Howard's 57th birthday—"I am 57 years young"—brought forth an outpouring of gratitude by employees. Surprise parties all over the world also celebrated "65 years of happy business family life," with an international telephone hookup.

In 1934, Jack headed to Australia to put up a new factory. At the same time, Hellen, head of Heinz U.K., was building a small factory in Ireland, and the company's baby-food business was growing. Heinz was "making some money" but not anywhere equal to "the days of 1920 to 1929."

By 1936, the company's employment was at a record high of 15,400, and "the consuming trade"—hotels and restaurants—was coming to life. Howard predicted that it would one day "far exceed the chain-store business . . . and threaten the total amount of sales in the retail grocery stores."[13] Also, "the strained-food business" was the second largest product in the line.

HOWARD AND THE UNIONS

The only cloud on the horizon was the issue of labor costs and labor relations. Howard's paternalistic philosophy was on the verge of becoming hopelessly outdated. The coming of the unions would absorb, obsess, and distress him for the rest of his life.

The company had never paid the highest wages in town (the employee word was, "You'll never make a lot of money working at Heinz, but you'll always have a job"), but working conditions were good, no salaried worker had been laid off during the depression, and a person could rise on merit. What more, Howard wondered, could anyone want?

In 1937, a wave of unionism and strikes washed over Pittsburgh. Howard was shocked to discover that some Heinz employees

---

13. Howard Heinz remarks at stockholders' luncheon, December 8, 1936.

wanted a union. During April and May, a hastily formed company-sponsored union fought Local 325 of the Canning and Pickle Workers (an AFL union) for recognition. A strike was called and quickly settled, providing for an election under the supervision of the National Labor Relations Board (NLRB).

On June 8, the outside AFL union won and a number of changes took place: wages rose from a minimum of 40 cents an hour to 68 cents; also introduced were time and a half for overtime, job classifications, seniority rights, paid vacations, etc.

The election seemed to settle the matter, but Howard fought its results. Lengthy hearings ensued—filling eight volumes with 1,514 pages of testimony—after which the NLRB ruled in favor of Local 325.

Howard continued to fight. He might be forced to recognize the union, bargain with the union, and even come to a written agreement with the union, but no one could force Howard Heinz to sign an agreement with the union. For the next four years, the issue wended its way to the Supreme Court.

The struggle energized him. In 1937 Howard turned 60 and told his board that he "felt younger" than he had 10 years earlier. Nothing could diminish his good spirits. "There are lots of people who think we sell a hundred million dollars a year. We don't, but it is not very far off. . . . You have doubled the business in the last four years."[14]

The largest selling products were, in order, soups, strained foods, beans, and ketchup.

The company kept growing: a new factory in Medina, Ohio; a new tomato products plant in Fremont, Ohio; a fresh pickle plant in Holland, Michigan; a new office building in Pittsburgh; new branch houses in Philadelphia, Miami, Los Angeles, and Oakland, plus three new branch houses in Canada, and two in England. Canada again expanded its manufacturing and storage facilities, and built a lakehouse pump to draw eight million gallons of filtered water from Lake Erie to its processing plants.

---

14. Managers Midsummer Convention, August 9, 1937.

Howard poured money into print ads and radio commercials, as well as something new, "market research." He'd been impressed by the Gallup polls in the last election. He authorized expenditures for a Heinz pavilion at the 1939 New York World's Fair.

To a convention of salesmen at Chicago's Morrison Hotel on December 12, 1938, he proudly announced the birth of a grandson, H. J. "John" Heinz III. That same month, famed business writer Merryle S. Rukeyser heaped praise on the man who had "endeavored to make his own economic cycle."[15]

Rust Heinz, an artist, preferred designing cars to making pickles. Howard's youngest son, with movie star looks, studied and lived in California, designed the personal car of Carole Lombard and Clark Gable, and also patented a design for "the car of tomorrow," the Phantom Corsair Coupe. The Heinz Company called its prototype truck (above), designed by Rust, "The Comet," and used it at the 1939 New York World's Fair for advertising purposes. Tragically, Rust died in an automobile accident in Pittsburgh in 1939.

---

15. Rukeyser newspaper column, December 12, 1938.

Heinz Chapel. Howard and his family generously supported a wide variety of causes, including the Pittsburgh Symphony and the Regional Planning Association. A founder, president, and director of the association, Howard brought Robert Moses to Pittsburgh to study highway and traffic problems. Though the Founder originally left a bequest to the University of Pittsburgh to build a memorial to his mother, Howard, with his sister, Irene Heinz Given, and brother Clifford, enlarged on their father's proposal and commissioned the French-Gothic Heinz Memorial Chapel, dedicated in 1938. A city landmark, its architect was Charles Klauder, who also designed the university's Cathedral of Learning. The chapel's 23 famous stained-glass windows by Charles Jay Connick took seven years to create and revived the "lost art" of medieval-style stained-glass craftsmanship. The chapel receives over 100,000 visitors a year.

On December 28, 1939, thousands of Heinz employees again sat down in the United States and Canada, to celebrate the 70th anniversary of the House of Heinz. In Howard's telephoned address, he looked toward the future by reminding everyone that his father used to say, "A real leader does not wait for opportunity, but makes one himself."

On January 6, 1941, in a five-page decision written by Chief Justice Harlan Fiske Stone, the NLRB decision was affirmed. Howard had lost his battle with the union. One month later, at the age of 64, he unexpectedly suffered a stroke while recovering from a routine operation, and died in Philadelphia.

Howard left a huge organization of close to 17,000 employees and a brand name whose "57 Varieties" (in fact, there were hundreds of varieties, ranging from calf's-foot jelly and walnut pickles to mincemeat, lemon curd, and stuffed mangoes) were known around the world.

Through the Howard Heinz Endowment, the bulk of his personal estate—estimated in excess of $52 million—was to be distributed to civic, church, art, and philanthropic organizations in Pittsburgh and western Pennsylvania.

By anyone's definition, Howard Heinz proved to be "a real leader."

Henry John "Jack" Heinz II, age 23, in 1931.

Henry John Heinz II:
The Internationalist

———

(1908–1987)

The full burden of leading "the old firm" fell upon the shoulders of Henry John Heinz II—Jack to his friends, Mr. Heinz or H.J. to employees—when he was 33, making him "one of the youngest men in the U.S. to head a major company."[1]

His 25 years as chief executive spanned enormous changes in America, the food industry, and the H. J. Heinz Company. A linchpin between the old and new Heinz, he presided over its transition from a family-run to a professionally managed company with dignity and charm, thus ensuring its survival as an independent firm still bearing the family name.

Jack shared many family traits: enormous energy and curiosity; an international vision; devotion to civic and philanthropic causes; a lifelong interest in nutrition; a variety of nonbusiness enthusiasms, for photography, architecture, art (three Gauguin paintings hung on his office wall), skiing, wine; and, of course, an unquenchable thirst for travel (by the mid-1950s he was averaging 90,000 miles a year).

---

1. Arthur Baum, "In Grandpa's Shoes," *Saturday Evening Post*, June 1949. This major article on the family and company was written with the close cooperation of Ed Parrack of Ketchum, McCleod and Grove. Jack Heinz hired Parrack to handle public relations in 1946.

77

Handsome, trim, athletic, a bit of a romantic and adventurer, he swam the Bosporus; toured Soviet Russia at 22; married three times; at one point, owned 12 homes in America, England, the Caribbean, and France; and socialized with the English royal family. A devoted Anglophile, in 1979, he was knighted for his contribution to British–American relations.

He was an exquisite host and boon companion. "Of all my friends," recalled James "Jaz" Laughlin in his funeral oration, "Jack Heinz was the most fun to be with."

Jack's good spirits, according to Laughlin, were a reaction to "a rather stern bringing up." Morewood Heights was an austere and formal home. Nevertheless, unlike the self-made Founder with callused hands, Jack was raised with every advantage. As a *Saturday Evening Post* story noted, "Jack Heinz is . . . excessively educated and exceedingly articulate. By education—Shadyside, Choate, Yale, Cambridge—and by rearing in a family of considerable elegance and great dignity, his tastes have been elevated to the impeccable in music, literature, social behavior, and above all in food." Decades later, Tony O'Reilly described him as a man of "stratospheric elegance."

Part of his education involved following in his father's footsteps and learning the family business from the bottom up. On that point, Jack loved to tell the following story. "Before my father died, we were talking to Winston Churchill in England. Churchill looked at me and said, 'Knowing your father, I suppose he will insist on your starting at the bottom of the ladder. This is nonsense. Start at the top and work your way down.' "

Jack spent summer vacations in various parts of the company, beginning with the pickle-salting station in Plymouth, Indiana, where Howard had begun, and, during the summer of 1930, on a five-week tour with the English sales force.

A lifelong friendship sprang up between the great Hellen and Jack. According to Jack's widow, Drue Heinz, Hellen "looked after Jack" and "taught him about the world." She added, "My husband talked about him up to the day he died."

After a year of postgraduate study in economics at Trinity College, Cambridge, Jack again worked with the U.K. sales force, then returned to the United States, moving up from salesman to

Mrs. Howard Heinz (Elizabeth "Betty" Granger Rust), with sons Jack and Rust. An uncommonly beautiful woman, raised in Michigan and heir to a lumber fortune, Betty graduated from the Ogontz School for Young Ladies in Philadelphia, and first captured Howard's attention at a skating party given by a mutual friend. They courted for five years. On the afternoon of the wedding, work at the Main Plant stopped for several hours and 1,500 Pittsburgh employees attended a reception and dinner in the auditorium, courtesy of the bridegroom.

Future chairman Henry J. Heinz II (right) spent three years in England at the company's Harlesden factory after Yale and a postgraduate course at Trinity College, Cambridge. Here young "Mr. Henry," as he called himself on sales calls to hide his famous name, stands in the doorway of a typical 1930s grocery store, with East London branch manager A.E. Cutliffe. Like all formally dressed salesmen, with homburg, stiff collar, and sales satchel, he is suitably dressed for the part. Partly as a result of his happy years in prewar England, he became a lifelong Anglophile.

branch house manager to headquarters' sales and advertising, to Howard's assistant, and, in 1936, to the board of directors.

In 1934, Howard sent him to Australia to locate the company's first manufacturing plant. On the train to Canberra, he met and impressed the future prime minister, then Attorney General Robert Menzies. Jack found an old piano factory in Richmond, Victoria, and jumped over a fence in his business suit on a Saturday to inspect the place for himself.

By then he had already married Joan Diehl, the individualistic young woman he'd been courting since Yale. An aviatrix, on the weekend of Jack's senior prom at Yale, she rented an airplane, made three attempts to land in New Haven, and finally did so, "rolling right into Jack's new yellow Packard roadster. . . . He thought it was fine. I made quite an impression."[2]

Jack and his bride lived at Rosemont Farm, built as a summer cottage by Howard and his wife, Betty, and their wedding present to the couple. Henry John Heinz III was born in 1938.

JACK AND WORLD WAR II

Jack took over the firm in the midst of immense wartime challenges. In London, the blitz was on. German bombs had already hit Harlesden's soup building and had killed two Heinz employees. Between rationing and food import restrictions, especially tomato products from Heinz Canada, many varieties disappeared. Heinz U.K. came up with new varieties based on homegrown ingredients, worked overtime to turn out a key wartime protein, baked beans, and under government supervision led the supply and distribution of beans to British citizens from all manufacturers.

Jack traveled to England five times during the war: three times at the invitation of the British Ministry of Food, which sought his advice and cooperation; once when Harlesden was bombed; and

---

2. WQED interview, 1992.

Jack Heinz confers with members of the Harlesden factory's World War II Home Guard at the fortified plant. In 1940, with isolationism rampant in the United States and many Americans opposed to entering the war, Howard sent an $80,000 check to Lord Beaverbrook on behalf of employees of the London plant, to purchase two RAF planes. After Howard's death, Jack Heinz traveled to England five times during World War II. German bombs hit Harlesden's soup building twice.

once on an official inspection tour of food needs in England, Belgium, and the Netherlands.[3]

In the United States, Jack turned to an elderly partner at McKinsey & Company for advice, especially when it became clear that company finances were less rosy than Howard had publicly intimated. Sales were closer to $60 million than the $100 million *Fortune* and other magazines thought. Guided by McKinsey, Jack created the company's first controller and personnel divi-

---

3. *Tide*, the news magazine of advertising, marketing, and public relations. July 26, 1946.

sions. In 1943, he also promoted Bill Hogan, a bright, tough Irish-American, to the post of treasurer-controller. Overall, Jack embraced wartime challenges, such as the impact of rationing on food production, with youthful vigor and enthusiasm.

Of major concern was a wartime tin order that prohibited the packaging of soups in ready-to-serve form (its competitive advantage over Campbell). That order immediately put the company out of 23 varieties of the soup business, and 1,000 employees out of jobs. Baked beans were transferred from tin to glass containers, and baby foods, whenever possible, went into paper containers. Heinz stopped producing cereal rice flakes, which left it with idle machinery and excess capacity. What to do?

According to Junius Allen, then secretary to Jack Heinz, and Karl Lang, who transferred quality control principles from food to war production, the idea of making CG-4A military glider wings in the Cereal Building originated with W. M. Gardner, president of Pittsburgh's Gardner Display and a key Heinz supplier. About to be put out of business by the war, with know-how and connections in the wood business, Gardner proposed a joint venture to Frank Armour, then head of advertising, who proposed it to Jack. It's easy to see why the idea of "making parts for bombers . . . pursuit planes . . . and gliders . . . struck Jack's fancy."[4]

To fellow industrialists in Pittsburgh, planes were more impressive than food. The press applauded Jack's leadership and the company's ingenuity. His prestige rose. Suddenly, like his father during World War I, he became a highly visible civic and business leader, chairing the United War Fund. In 1942, Jack received Pittsburgh's "Man of the Year" Award for his leadership and delivered speeches promoting food allocation, conservation, and rationing. Demonstrating, too, the family instinct for public relations, he beat the drum for the company's War Products Division and sponsored the country's number-one quiz program, "Information Please," with Clifton Fadiman and Oscar Levant.

The company threw itself into the war effort, converting to condensed soups and rehiring employees to manufacture and produce huge quantities of K and C rations. From "beans to bomb-

---

4. WQED Karl Lang interview.

ers," from "pickles to pursuit planes," were the slogans. The Pittsburgh factory went from one to three shifts. Frank Armour headed up war production, conferring almost daily with Jack. The company designed and manufactured canisters for shells, plastic and wood parts for planes and bombers, pontoons, cone sections, and seats for airplanes, as well as glider wings. Each glider was capable of holding 40 people. They played a key role in the Normandy landings on D day.

The company undertook a massive advertising campaign to recruit new workers, many of whom were housewives and mothers trained by a federally funded public-school course in plane construction.[5]

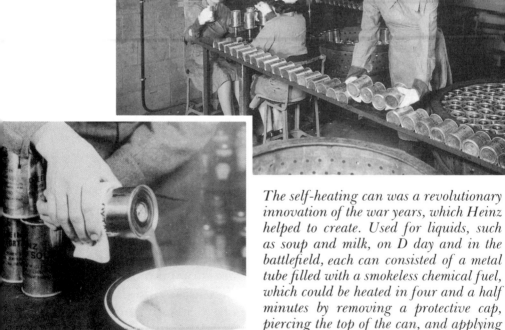

The self-heating can was a revolutionary innovation of the war years, which Heinz helped to create. Used for liquids, such as soup and milk, on D day and in the battlefield, each can consisted of a metal tube filled with a smokeless chemical fuel, which could be heated in four and a half minutes by removing a protective cap, piercing the top of the can, and applying a lighted cigarette to the fuse.

5. *The 57 News*, June 1942.

As a wartime edition of The 57 News *reported, "A group of 60 women answered Uncle Sam's call to prepare themselves to join the job army in war work." They received technical training in airplane construction at Pittsburgh's South Vocational High School, and were then eligible to apply for "positions with the newly organized Heinz War Production Division to assist in the making of plastic plywood parts for military airplanes." Federal funds paid for the national defense training program. Altogether, 2,800 men and women received vocational training for war work from 100 teachers in 12 Pittsburgh schools.*

The moment World War II ended, Jack's ambitious expansion plans filled the employee newsletter, *The 57 News*. However, profits were down and taxes were taking a greater bite of revenue. To finance growth (as well as to make family estate-tax valuation easier, according to Junius Allen and Burt Gookin), in September 1946 he announced the company's first public stock offering in its 77-year history.

Investment bankers Morgan Stanley & Company headed a large group of underwriters. *Time* magazine observed, "Prospective investors, getting their first look inside the Heinz door, saw an appetizing sight." On October 15, the company went public. Some 200,000 shares of common stock at $25 per share and 100,000 shares of preferred stock at $100 per share were snapped up. "The entire amount was oversubscribed within twenty-four hours."[6]

6. H.J. Heinz Company Annual Report, April 30, 1947.

In the late 1940s and 1950s, Jack married twice. In 1947, he married the daughter of one of Morgan Stanley's partners, Jane Ewing. They divorced in 1952. In 1953, he married Drue Maher, born in England of Irish parents, and widow of Dale Maher, U.S. chargé d'affaires in South Africa. They led a jet-set life, entertaining and being entertained by Onassis, Churchill, Aly Khan, Truman Capote, Agnelli, etc. Drue described herself as FBI—foreign-born Irish. Devoted to writers and literature, she founded a distinguished publishing house, Ecco Press, in 1971, and also established a literary prize for short stories, administered by the University of Pittsburgh Press, which bears her name. A renowned hostess, she threw a lavish costume party for Jack's 57th birthday. For his 75th, she closed off New York City's 57th Street, arranged for a fireworks display over the East River, and had a band play in front of their elegant Sutton Place town house.

JACK AND POSTWAR RECOVERY

In addition to running the company, Jack led an increasingly international life. During an era when much of America turned isolationist, he devoted a great deal of time to European recovery and food programs, as well as world trade issues. Like his father, Jack testified in Congress on trade issues, worked with public–private groups supporting international cooperation, attended International Chamber of Commerce and Bilderberg conferences in Europe, assessed an economic assistance program to Pakistan for Eisenhower, and continued to contribute to British recovery programs. In Pittsburgh, he became a leading member of the Allegheny Conference and Community Chest. During his chairmanship of the Community Chest, a woman in the Heinz art department designed the organization's (later the United Way) enduring "red feather symbol."

In 1947, the company pioneered a national campaign to help feed "the hungry children of Europe." It donated one million packages of baby food and pledged, in coast-to-coast print ads, to donate "another package for every package of Heinz baby food

Henry John Heinz II visiting President Harry S. Truman in connection with the Community Chest's national campaign. While Jack Heinz was chairman of the Community Chest, which later became the United Way, a woman in the Heinz art department designed the organization's red feather symbol.

bought by mothers throughout the United States"[7] during one week in April. Between three and six million food packages were turned over to the Quakers for distribution. The humanitarian gesture brought enormous goodwill to the company.

The idea was suggested to Jack by Parrack, with whom he had begun to work closely since 1945. That year, when Jack attended, as a spectator, the first United Nations meeting in San Francisco, he roomed with Pittsburgher Parrack, an executive at Ketchum McCleod and Grove. Parrack attended as acting assistant to E. R. Stettinius, Jr., Truman's secretary of state. Jack was so impressed by Parrack's abilities that he agitated to have the Heinz Company switch from another advertising and public relations shop, Ket-

---

7. *The 57 News*, April 1947.

chum Inc., to Ketchum McCleod and Grove. KMG later acquired substantial segments of its advertising business.

Parrack's idea instantly appealed to Jack, who, at times aloof and demanding, had a notoriously warm heart for the less fortunate, especially when it came to matters of nutrition. For example, Tony Beresford, ex-managing director of Heinz U.K., vividly recalls how, in 1951, when rationing in England was at its worst, "Mr. Heinz was thunderstruck, appalled, when he saw what the British people lived on." He arranged to "make up a big food parcel so that every single employee in England had a good Christmas dinner. It contained absolutely everything you could think of, a canned chicken, vegetables, Christmas puddings in cans, and even sweets for the children. It was absolutely amazing. Each case was addressed in Pittsburgh to the employee it was going to in England ... and all the American people wrote little notes and popped them in. Its effect on the employees in England was absolutely overwhelming." Jack's personal generosity was not always on the public record. Retired corporate technical director Lee Harrow recalled how Jack provided an anonymous college fellowship to a hard-working African youth who'd impressed Harrow while working with him on a temporary assignment in South Africa. The young man needed funds to live and study in the United States and Jack provided them.

Between 1945 and 1965, the company still operated much like an extended family. As ex–board member Lewis Lapham put it, "In the U.S. everything—salaries, jobs, promotions, new products, advertising—depended on Jack."

J. Wray Connolly, senior vice president, recalls that when he joined the company's law department in 1961, "H.J. was more than president and CEO. He was the lord and master in many respects. And he involved himself in all kinds of decisions which someone like that shouldn't have ... like picking the baby food labels and deciding whether the recipe of a particular product tasted right. It didn't matter what a million consumers might think, it mattered only what he thought was right. . . . It was not only paternalistic, it was like a sole proprietorship."

When Lewis Lapham, a friend of Jack's from Yale who became the company's first outside director, joined the board in 1958,

"Heinz sat at a desk on a little platform and we sat in a little semicircle in front of him. And everyone called him mister."

It should be remembered, however, that Jack operated much like other scions of family-run businesses, such as his friend Henry Ford II, to whom he was often compared in the press, especially since both Henry Ford and Henry John Heinz were "named and numbered" after their illustrious grandfathers, and "each had inherited control of his business from a father who had died before his time."[8]

Even under Howard, this style of leadership had its limitations. Junius Allen, who joined the company as a clerk in 1934 and retired from the board in 1973, recalls hearing tales about H. C. Anderson, Howard's treasurer, pulling out a piece of paper, showing it to Howard, then tearing it up. Nevertheless, such practices were not unusual for that era.

After the war, the company slowly emerged from its primitive financial structure. McKinsey & Company, consultants, and treasurer-controller Hogan, under the direction of Jack, began to bring a modern cost-accounting system to the company. In 1945, to help him implement the system, Hogan recruited a former colleague from Firestone, R. Burt Gookin, the company's first M.B.A. who, 20 years later, would become its first non-Heinz CEO. According to Gookin, the company's accounting practices were so inadequate, he sensed the opportunity of a lifetime.

"I'd really be able to do something," recalled Gookin. "And we did it, too." He and Hogan, replaced in 1947 by Frank Cliffe, built a first-rate financial team and, over a 10-year period, inculcated cost-accounting principles and practices into every factory in every Heinz affiliate. That's when the company first understood how much each product cost to produce and how poor their margins really were.

In 1946, Fred Crabb, then chief U.K. cashier and a decade away from becoming Heinz U.K. managing director, spent six to eight weeks in Pittsburgh, taking the McKinsey-led course on the ele-

---

8. Arthur Baum, "In Grandpa's Shoes."

ments of budgetary control and standard costs. A close friendship developed among Crabb, Hogan, and Gookin, who had only been in the company six weeks.

During that visit, Crabb also heard financial horror stories. "The government still owed Heinz money," said Crabb in an interview, "but the company didn't have the ability to invoice their subcontractors and suppliers, so the government didn't pay. At one point, Heinz literally ran out of cash."

The postwar U.S. company operated much as it had before. As the 1948 Annual Report shows, its executive team (who formed the company's inside board of directors) was mainly a roster of aging men, many of whom dated back to the days of the Founder. They included H. N. Riley, manufacturing and research (with Heinz since 1912); A. L. Schiel, executive vice president (1914); I. M. Melius, foreign sales (1909); J. H. Letsche, sales and distribution (1913); Franklin Bell, advertising (1928); J. B. Holcomb, general manager of sales (1925); J. G. Bennett, purchasing (1905); T. B. McCafferty, secretary (1920); Charles Heinz, personnel (1926); Frank Armour, Jr., manager of manufacturing (1927); and Frank B. Cliffe, treasurer and controller (1947).

"The directors were gods," recalled George Greer, who joined the company in 1959, "and they all had their little empires. Every day at noon when we were all on the North Side, the directors would go to the garage, load into a limousine, drive to the Duquesne Club, all sit together at one round table at lunchtime and it was 'there go the directors.' " This ultimately proved to be a serious limitation for the business.

However, between 1945 and 1965, the company expanded and appeared to prosper. Pent-up demand for food and the baby boom dramatically increased sales in the United States, Canada, the United Kingdom, and Australia.

In the United States, key figures in maintaining quality and leading growth were C. Lee Rumberger, vice president of research and development (and later, corporate development); P. Kenneth Shoemaker, vice president of manufacturing; John D. Scott, vice president of sales; and Ross E. Jones, vice president of distribution.

Major new factory and administration buildings were built: a new head office in Leamington, Canada, in 1948, and a $5 million factory expansion in 1956; the Kitt Green factory in 1959 and the Hayes Park headquarters and research center in 1964 in the United Kingdom; a $15 million Pittsburgh building program that involved tearing down the Printing Building and Box Factory and removing, in 1952, "The House Where We Began" to Greenfield Village; the Pittsburgh Research and Quality Control Center in 1958.

For the Research Center opening, Jack Heinz, emulating Howard, organized two weeks of dedication activities, whose key event brought together 4,000 dealer and distributor customers and their wives at 29 simultaneous sit-down dinners across the United States. A closed-circuit television tour of the facilities was hosted by NBC's "Today Show" star Dave Garroway.

INTERNATIONAL GROWTH

The company's worldwide sales (including exports to over 200 countries) boomed. Encouraged by Jack's vision of international growth, Heinz planted seeds in foreign countries that ultimately bore rich fruit. In 1957, it entered the European market by acquiring the Taminiau Company, a Dutch family jam-and-jelly preserve business in Elst. (It also sold a Spanish olive-growing and manufacturing subsidiary, largely forgotten during the war.) It set up a distribution center in Belgium. In 1960, capitalizing on its million-dollar export business to Venezuela, it built a plant in Valencia and set up headquarters for Alimentos Heinz in Caracas.

"Foreign affiliates were essentially on their own," recalled Allen, who became vice president, international, shortly after the war. "I headed up a department with one assistant and secretary, while General Foods had an international department of 200."

That was so because, in most American companies, U.S. headquarters had to approve all decisions made abroad. Heinz company affiliates were autonomous. Local managers only needed Pittsburgh approval for major capital investments and board-level appointments. After 1958, each affiliate budget had to be approved in Pittsburgh. Out of that evolved an annual executive budget meeting in April, the end of the fiscal year. In this environment of minimal interference, affiliate business flourished.

In the United Kingdom, for example, Heinz brands dominated the marketplace and the culture. Many Britons believed (and still do) that Heinz was an English company with an American branch. Under an outstanding succession of managing directors—including W. B. Cormack (who also helped set up the Australian company), Fred Crabb, and Tony Beresford—Heinz U.K. contributed huge profits to the company.

Allen traveled the world investigating foreign acquisitions and acting as liaison between company headquarters and the affiliates. "I always thought I had the best job in the company," said Allen. "It wasn't a job, it was a way of life."

In 1962, Heinz entered into a joint venture with Nichiro Fisheries in Japan. In fiscal 1963, it acquired Societa del Plasmon, a baby-food business in Milan. In fiscal 1964, a new Heinz affiliate formed in Mexico with the merging of six established Mexican food-processing companies into Heinz Alimentos S.A. de C.V. Heinz never turned a profit in Mexico, and sold its last Mexican business in the mid-1980s. In 1965, a Portuguese company bought by the British for its tomato-processing facilities, IDAL, technically transferred ownership to the U.S. company. There seemed to be no end to non-U.S. expansion.

Unfortunately, Heinz U.S.A.'s poor profit performance dimmed the company's overall luster. As early as 1950, it was clear that the company's highest ratio of net income to sales—7.4 percent—was recorded in 1941 during Howard's last year as head of Heinz. By fiscal year 1950, "its ratio was $4.3 million on $170.5 million or 2.5 percent of sales."[9]

Matters did not improve significantly over the next decade.

Jack, with his love of travel and increasing number of public and private interests, spent less time on the nuts and bolts of the business.

"Jack was not as fascinated by business," said Parrack, "as he was with international affairs."

Moreover, as Allen observed, "H.J. was not a financial man. He

---

9. *Sales Management* magazine, December 1950.

learned primarily through personal contact rather than through digging through statistics or reading a lot."

On the other hand, judging him by the standards of his era, when there was less focus on the bottom line and more on jobs and growth, Jack's expansion of the business internationally and his ability to grow and maintain full employment domestically were impressive accomplishments and considered hallmarks of his successful stewardship.

New, young managers may have found his management style old-fashioned, but the average employee enjoyed being part of a family-run business, and felt great affection for the man who personified its successful past and, presumably, healthy future.

As George Greer recalled, there were generations of employees on both sides of the Atlantic who every night before dinner would say, "Thank God for Mr. Heinz and the great Heinz family."

Even though the post-1946 company was, technically, a public company, employees from Kitt Green to Fremont still viewed it as a family company, which presided over their lives with familylike values. Thus there were company dances, picnics, clubs, sports teams, and company gifts for weddings, birthdays, and other special occasions. Lillian Weizmann (general forewoman, who joined the company in 1902 and retired in 1953) and her counterparts were viewed a bit like dormitory "house mothers" who chaperoned and looked out for their "girls." Eden Hall Farm embodied all that was best in the company's familylike culture. It was a different world, and one in which Jack's attentiveness to both big and little matters—from company picnics (with son Johnny) and service awards to sales conferences and plant openings—was applauded.

JACK'S STRENGTHS

Jack's strengths were advertising and public relations, and, in fact, he focused more on issues of quality, taste, nutrition, and aesthetic design than the bottom line. He prided himself, for example, on the Heinz tradition of having fine chefs who made

German-born Sebastian Mueller (1860–1938), the Founder's brother-in-law, arrived in Pittsburgh at the age of 24 and presided over the company's worldwide manufacturing operations for the next 54 years. The Founder's "right-hand man," according to a biography written by a former Heinz employee and Eden Hall Farm trustee, Richard F. Herr, he was recognized in the food industry as "a leading authority on the commercial preparation of food products."

Mueller also "practiced his own brand of personal paternalism, directed primarily to the hourly paid female workers of the H.J. Heinz Company's Pittsburgh factory." For example, he personally paid for countless operations and medical needs of female workers and strove to create optimal health conditions in the factory. Perhaps that is why Howard Heinz eulogized him as "a disciplinarian with a great heart," as well as "the man who had made the greatest impression on the Heinz business with the exception of the Founder."

Tragedy dogged his family life: his father abandoned the family; his mother died when he was nine; his brother mysteriously disappeared; his two daughters, Elsa and Alma, died in infancy within five days of each other; his only son died at 18. After his wife of 46 years (the Founder's sister) passed away, Heinz colleagues became Mueller's family, and the company his ruling passion. He left most of his estate in trust to maintain his country home, Eden Hall Farm, as a free vacation retreat for female employees of the H.J. Heinz Company.

Eden Hall Farm, about 20 miles northeast of Pittsburgh, beautifully landscaped and with ample recreational facilities, has continued to benefit Heinz working women. (For many years, it even provided bus transportation to female employees visiting for a week or weekend, as seen above.) It has speeded recovery for those recuperating from illness and provided vacation opportunities to thousands of women, some of whom might not otherwise have been able to afford them. Sebastian Mueller believed that "work and health are the big things of life," and he did his best to help Heinz women improve their lives in these areas.

quality products. This had its pluses and minuses, depending on one's perspective.

For Lila Jones, who joined the company in 1950, in 1958 became its first woman manager, and remained with the company for 24 years, Jack's sophisticated knowledge of food and "educated palate" were a definite plus. He personally interviewed her for the job of top home economist, during which they talked a great deal about mutual food tastes and nutrition.

In 1940, Jack established the Nutrition Foundation (later known as the International Life Science Institute) to promote understanding of health, nutrition, and safety issues facing government, industry, and the public. Over the years, his interest deepened, as did his recognition that poor nutrition often stemmed from inadequate knowledge. In the 1930s, the company first began to tabulate and publish nutrition information for physicians, dietitians, public health workers, and home economists. It continues to do so to this day. The seventh edition of *Heinz Nutritional Data*, published in 1990 and edited by the company's corporate nutrition coordinator, Dr. David L. Yeung, is one of many ongoing programs devoted to improving worldwide nutrition knowledge and feeding practices.

In Lila Jones's day (the fifties and early sixties), the home economics department played a significant role in marketing and promotion, especially for the institutional food-service market, and reported to Franklin Bell, head of advertising.

Jones oversaw five home economists, a publicity writer, photo studio, test kitchens, factory tours and guides. She and her staff devised new recipes for Heinz products, worked with grocery and institutional salespeople, and planned elaborate lunches and dinners for food editors and national restaurant groups, over which Jack Heinz personally presided. "He was the host," Jones recalled. "Invitations always went out in his name," and Jack paid infinite attention to the menu.

There are endless stories about Jack's refined and discerning palate, especially when it came to soup.

"One time," recalled Junius Allen, "a fellow from Japan brought over a sample of soup to taste. H.J. tasted it and said, 'It tastes like old whale meat.' And to everyone's amazement, that's exactly what it was."

Lila Jones, senior home economist, between takes with Joel Aldred, a studio announcer in early Heinz television commercials. Jones represented the Heinz Company to magazine and newspaper food editors, and, to her amazement, the Heinz board selected her over professional actresses to represent Heinz on a series of television commercials made for "Studio 57" and other programs during the 1954–55 season. They thought the average housewife could more easily identify with Jones. Whisked to Hollywood, girdled, made over and coiffed by Hollywood's Bud Westmore, for five weeks she filmed at Paramount Studios, received Screen Actors Guild wages, and felt like a star.

Another time, according to his secretary, Loretta Oken, she had to call the company's top chef, Ferdinand Metz, at home to find out how he made vegetable soup. Mr. Heinz's New York chef "couldn't make a proper pot."

However, his tastes and those of the average American could not have been more different, which may partly explain a succession of soup failures with the American public. Another typical soup story involves a cream-of-spinach soup he tasted in a Paris restaurant. When Jack got back to Pittsburgh, he insisted that the company whip up a similar version and put it on sale. "It was so wonderful," Jack told a reporter, "but it didn't sell." He finally walked into a grocery store and asked the manager why it wasn't moving. "Mister," the grocer told him, "it says spinach."

Jack was even fussier about wine. As a company pilot on one of the old Heinz planes (four-engine Lockheed Jet Stars), painted ketchup red, told Bill Johnson, then head of Heinz Pet Products,

In 1962, Heinz executives actively participated in final tasting sessions of baby food. From left to right: B. Dent Graham, executive vice president, Heinz U.S.A.; Frank Armour, Jr., president; Henry J. Heinz II, chairman of the board; and C.L. Rumberger, vice president—development.

"The plane could be on the verge of crashing, it could be flying upside down, Mr. Heinz wouldn't say a word. But if we had the wrong bottle of wine on the plane, he would come totally unglued."

While Jack could be a perfectionist with architects, chefs, and home economists, he could depart for a social lunch in the middle of a business presentation.

At some level, making money didn't interest him. That, too, was typical of "gentlemen" who ran family businesses and focused more on "doing the common thing uncommonly well" than on the actual rewards. "Mr. Heinz never worried about the stock or the price of the stock," said Gerald Voros, former head of Ketchum Communications. He remained, as Crabb observed, a "gifted amateur," as were many of his business peers at that time. But it was an era of change, when professional managers were taking over the food business.

Instead of hiring outside professionals to modernize management, Jack continued to promote from within and to rely on, as had his father, a group of strong bosses—loyal, self-made men who "got things done"—to operate the day-to-day business.

An Era of Self-Made Men

"Management by personal loyalty" still dominated American business. It was an era when most companies resembled feudal empires, and departments were run like personal fiefdoms.

Frank Brettholle, who joined the company in 1948 and rose to become chief financial officer, heard and witnessed countless stories about the impregnable walls between departments. This had increasingly negative effects on the business. No one, for example, could find out which factory produced the lowest-cost ketchup or verify the accuracy of anyone's manufacturing figures. Procedures and equipment varied from factory to factory. Control was all; secrecy the rule. "I recall a day," said Brettholle, "when Mr. C. L. Rumberger told me he wasn't allowed in the Pittsburgh factory. And he was in charge of research and quality control!"

As late as 1963, when Frank Sherk, who had worked his way up from salesman to first president of Heinz Canada, came down to replace B. D. Graham, then head of Heinz U.S.A., Pittsburgh managers closed ranks. They conspired to keep him out of the factories and shared little information at Heinz U.S.A. board meetings. He quickly returned to Canada and soon retired.

Of all the self-made men, Frank Armour rose the farthest. A high-school graduate who joined the company in 1927 as a factory-tour guide, he moved from managing company exhibits at fairs to running the Heinz Pier, then to advertising, and to war production. After the war, his career took off. In 1947, he was elected to the board of directors. In 1950, he became vice president and general manager of sales and distribution. Totally devoted to Jack, loyal to a fault, he may have cared too much about people and not enough about their performance. Armour became president and chief operating officer of the H. J. Heinz Company in 1959. (In 1960, he actually received "The Horatio Alger Award," conferred upon him by the American Schools and Colleges Association, Inc.)[10] No nonfamily member had ever risen so high.

Armour was "a very enthusiastic individual . . . a man in a

---

10. *The '57' News*, May 1960.

Frank Armour, president and chief operating officer, the year he received the 1960 Horatio Alger Award.

hurry," said Brettholle. "I never saw Frank Armour walk down a hall in my life . . . he was always at a dog trot."

Lewis Lapham agreed. "Armour was an honest-to-god, hard-working Airedale. He lived, breathed, ate, and slept Heinz. He was smart doing what he was doing, but what he was doing, as it turned out, wasn't quite right." That is, he needed to be more strategic in a shifting economy.

CHANGING TIMES

In the United States, the food business was dramatically changing. (Similar changes would come later to the U.K. company.) Thousands of family-run groceries were being replaced by fewer but larger self-service stores and supermarket chains. That, in turn, altered sales, distribution, and marketing strategies. Food companies were switching and slimming down from a direct sales force to brokers. They were becoming more marketing oriented and less production and sales oriented.

But for a variety of reasons, partly its aging leadership and lack of new blood, and partly the weight of its successful past, Heinz U.S.A. changed too slowly.

Forbes, in a frank profile of the company, "57 Varieties of Trouble," in its April 1, 1964, issue noted, "In the early fifties, the sweet smell of success turned somewhat sour. . . . Heinz is not doing nearly as well as most of its competitors in the U.S. and, without the European market, it would barely be getting along." The article went on to point out, "As late as 1959, Heinz still was selling much of its 57 varieties directly to grocers. Armour has stopped this practice almost completely. Like its competitors, Heinz now bypasses the grocer to sell to wholesalers, chains and voluntaries. The company lost precious years, however, by clinging to Founder Heinz's ways—and the job of modernizing the marketing set-up is still only half-completed."

But the company had more than distribution problems. "Heinz was basically sales oriented," Brettholle recalled. "It had the philosophy that only volume produced profit." Again, it was hardly alone in viewing business from this perspective. However, there were limitations to this philosophy.

Also, Heinz's national pricing policies bore little relation to transportation costs, and marketing techniques remained primitive. "The company didn't even have Nielsen tracking market shares until the late fifties," recalled Don Wiley, former senior vice president, general counsel, ex-board member, and vice chairman of the Heinz Company Foundation. "They were just looking at volume without understanding the market." Soup, baby food, ketchup, pickles—the company's key products—were losing market share to competitors.

"The hair on the back of my head stood up," said Lapham, "because you knew it wasn't going well, but you didn't know why."

Also, until 1960, there were no domestic acquisitions. "We started 15 years too late," said Gookin, who, in 1960, became a member of the board, as well as vice president of finance. He persuaded the company to change its policy. In 1961, he engineered its first U.S. acquisition, Reymer & Brothers, a Pittsburgh company manufacturing fruit-based drinks under the trade name of Blennd. In 1962, it made another local acquisition, Hachmeister, a Pennsylvania producer of wholesale bakery ingredients. Neither ultimately amounted to much, but they paved the way for the company's first major acquisition, which proved to be a stunning success.

In 1963, Gookin found StarKist—in the tuna, pet-food, and fish-meal business—led by the ebullient, entrepreneurial Joseph J. Bogdanovich. By then, people peddling companies were beating a path to his door. Gookin and Armour negotiated the deal. In 1965, spearheaded by Armour and William D. Mewhort, vice president of finance and treasurer, they entered the frozen-food business by buying Ore-Ida Foods. These were major accomplishments whose value has only increased over time.

Although Gookin found StarKist "through sheer luck," the truth was that the Heinz Company needed to bolster profits.

Indeed, within the company, matters came to a crisis in fiscal year 1963. Though consolidated sales set a new high, consolidated net income declined. England, Canada, and Australia set new sales and profits records, while U.S. earnings plummeted. In fact, that year Heinz U.K. supplied close to 85 percent of the company's profit! Without StarKist's numbers, the picture would have looked even bleaker.

Something had to be done about Heinz U.S.A. management and the domestic profit picture.

Management Changes

After joining the board in 1958, Lapham, president of the Grace Line (who later became president of Banker's Trust), persuaded Jack to bring in more outside directors. They included John A. Mayer, president of Mellon Bank; John T. Ryan, Jr., chairman of Mine Safety Appliances; and William P. Snyder III, president of the Shenango Furnace Company. They, too, were dismayed by

October 1963 photograph from The 57 News *shows the four-person law department of the H.J. Heinz Company: (standing, from left to right) George Greer, J Connolly, Don Wiley, and (seated) P.M. Duff. Wiley joined the one-man Heinz law department in 1956, transferred into the corporate executive offices in 1960, and moved back to law as general counsel in 1965, expanding its scope. In 1972, he became vice president, general counsel, secretary, and a member of the board. Though retired in 1990, Wiley remains on the board and is vice chairman of the Heinz Company Foundation. Today, a staff of almost 20 attorneys is headed by senior vice president Lawrence J. McCabe.*

the situation. With their approval, Lapham convinced the namesake and grandson of the Founder that it was in his best interest and that of the company to appoint professional managers for the day-to-day management of the company.

"My impression," recalled Lapham, "was that Jack wanted to be a distinguished businessman; he wanted to be an art collector; he wanted to go everyplace, see everything, do everything. He was generous; he was honest, but there wasn't enough time in the world for him to pursue all these interests."

"You be chairman in the British sense," suggested Lapham. According to Gookin, "Lapham was a very good diplomat." After a long evening of discussion in Lapham's Greenwich, Connecticut, home, Jack agreed to move upstairs.

"It wasn't an easy decision for him," said Lapham. "My respect for him grew that night."

The changes initiated that evening took several years to fully unfold. Ultimately, they freed the company to become its best self, which, as it turned out, was beneficial to both the company and the family. As Bill Genge, former chairman of Ketchum, observed, "H.J. had a lot at stake in the company's success, being the company's largest shareholder by far. He had the good sense and good judgment to recognize that it was time for a change."

Jack's move to nonexecutive chairman also freed him to devote more of his time to his many interests and passions, chief among them the city of Pittsburgh and its renaissance. As chairman of the Howard Heinz Endowment, he disbursed "more than $300 million in grants to Pittsburgh and Pennsylvania organizations in the arts, social services, health, education, urban and international affairs."[11]

The endowment helped to fund, among others, the Pittsburgh Symphony, the Carnegie Museum of Art, nutrition education programs, and one of Jack Heinz's most stunning contributions to urban restoration, Heinz Hall.

Between 1966 and 1987, Jack remained an active and beloved chairman of the board. He and Tony O'Reilly developed an especially warm relationship. O'Reilly followed Gookin's tough job of separating family and company. Gookin stayed completely away from the family so as to make the decisive break.

By the time O'Reilly became CEO, he was freer to enjoy H.J.'s friendship, and utilized the chairman's experience and considerable charm for the benefit of the company. Nothing pleased Jack more, for example, than his trip in 1986 to China for the opening of the baby-food factory. A lifelong nutrition advocate, he was thrilled to witness the introduction of Heinz's nutritionally enhanced cereal product in China. At the same time, the Chinese,

---

11. Heinz Quarterly Report, 1987.

Jack Heinz and his wife, Drue, at the 1971 opening of Pittsburgh's elegant new performing arts center, Heinz Hall. Under the chairmanship of Jack Heinz, the Howard Heinz Endowment contributed more than $1 million to acquire the old downtown Penn Theater, and some $10 million more to renovate it. Jack Heinz personally monitored and supervised the design and execution of the transformation, which resulted in a performing arts center of the highest quality. Heinz Hall continues to serve as the permanent performing home of the Pittsburgh Symphony Orchestra and the Pittsburgh Youth Symphony. The nation's press praised the hall as "an acoustical gem" and "a dramatic example of the best kind of urban renewal."

who venerate age and family, were honored to have Mr. Heinz at the opening.

John Heinz III worked briefly for the company in the sixties as product manager, but was drawn to public life early in his career. His father basked in his son's political success, first as a member of Congress, and then as a U.S. senator—the only Republican since 1932 to carry the Democratic city of Pittsburgh.

Over the years, the family has remained loyal to the city, and the people of Pittsburgh have returned that loyalty. That is why, as Bill Genge aptly put it, when Senator H. John Heinz III died so tragically in a plane accident in 1991, "It was just the most sorrowful thing for this town. The city basically closed down."

Today, Teresa Heinz, widow of Senator Heinz, continues the family's deep commitment to Pittsburgh and western Pennsylvania as chairperson of the Howard Heinz Endowment.

Senator H. John Heinz III

(1938–1991)

In an age marked by cynicism and distrust of politicians, Senator H. John Heinz III was a unique figure. Respected for his integrity and compassion, for voting his conscience and not just the party line, he was one of Pittsburgh's most beloved sons. His premature death at the age of 53 sent Pittsburgh, Pennsylvania, and the U.S. Senate into mourning.

Nowhere was the loss of John Heinz felt more acutely than on the North Side of Pittsburgh among Heinz U.S.A. employees where young John had worked after graduating from business school. "He was a man of the people," a tearful employee explained to a local television reporter. "When he died, it was as though a member of my family had gone."

At the funeral, Tony O'Reilly underscored the private and public loss. "Senator Heinz was a great American and a wonderful friend . . . he personified the civic spirit and generous compassion inherent in the American character. . . . Even though John Heinz was not involved in the management of the H. J. Heinz Company, as a major shareholder he took great pride in the extraordinary legacy of the Heinz family. . . . We will miss him greatly."

Throughout his political career, the heir to the Heinz fortune, who never had to work a day in his life, championed the disadvantaged and underprivileged. He may best be remembered for his advocacy of issues relating to improving the environment and helping the elderly. First elected to the House of Representatives in 1971, and to the Senate in 1976, his popularity and margins increased the longer he served.

His unique spirit may have been best summed up by Senator John Danforth, a close friend, who at his funeral said, "John Heinz was a giver . . . John Heinz made a gift to the people he wanted to serve. He made a gift of his life. He literally gave his life to public service."

Senator Heinz in the early 1980s with his wife, Teresa, and sons, Andre (left), Henry John IV (center), and Christopher (right).

John Heinz in August 1971 on the campaign trail. Running for a seat in Congress, he stopped to chat with members of Local 325 of the United Food and Commercial Workers, employees at Heinz U.S.A.'s Pittsburgh plant.

R. Burt Gookin in March 1964.

R. Burt Gookin:
The Professional Manager

～～

One day in 1963, CEO Jack Heinz and his president, Frank Armour, strolled into J Connolly's small, sixth-floor office and made an astounding request: find a management consultant—a neutral party—to examine the company and "make a decision as to who should be captain of the ship."

As Jack Heinz put it, "A ship can have only one captain."

Connolly was "stupefied by the experience." He didn't know why H.J. participated, "because he *was* captain of the ship," and had no idea why they had chosen him to help resolve the issue. Young, inexperienced, low man on the executive totem pole as assistant corporate secretary, it's something he's never understood to this day.

Nevertheless, off Connolly went on his assignment, interviewing prominent management consultants, including the famed Peter Drucker. (H.J. ruled out McKinsey & Company because of its previous company ties.) He hired Cresup, MacCormick and Pagget, and Willard MacCormick undertook the two-month study.

"The upshot of it was that, ultimately, neither captain was left on board," said Connolly.

For starters, in February 1964, Burt Gookin became executive vice president of the troubled U.S. operations. He faced an enormous task. As the 1964 *Forbes* article had bluntly asked, "Can they

109

effect radical changes quickly enough in spite of the dead weight of tradition?"[1]

They can and did because of R. Burt Gookin, the company's secret weapon. A workaholic numbers man and brilliant manager, Gookin possessed precisely the right skills, temperament, and experience for the job. He had been waiting in the wings for over 20 years and quickly bettered the bottom line. As the 1964 Annual Report stated, "Consolidated earnings improved materially over those of the previous fiscal year."

Heinz U.S.A. was on the march, and with it the overall company. Nineteen sixty-four marked the beginning of an over thirty-year rise in corporate earnings.

A year and a half later, in 1966, the board appointed Gookin president and chief executive officer of the H. J. Heinz Company. He moved into a large corner office. Jack Heinz relinquished control, and moved into a suite of offices at the opposite end of the hall. Armour became vice chairman of the board. Norman E. Daniels replaced Gookin as head of Heinz U.S.A. In a transition remarkable for its smoothness, lack of public rancor, and finger pointing, the professionally managed company was born.

Gookin, whom *Fortune* described as "a striver—suitably vinegary,"[2] proved to be a strong leader. Tough, competitive, frugal ("An accountant first and last," according to O'Reilly), utterly devoted to the company and to improving bottom-line results, it took just that mix of strength, will, loyalty, and determination to transform a culture, peel away decades of entrenched bureaucracy, and turn around, as Tom McIntosh, ex-vice president of corporate communications, called Heinz, "the lovable old lady of the food industry."

An Iowa farm boy, Gookin's road to the top reads like a Hollywood script, beginning with his 1930s depression-haunted childhood: short on cash, but rich in family affection and talent. Gookin excelled not only in school (his parents were teachers who farmed in the summer and moved back to town in the winter), but also in sports. His father, a one-time "professional baseball player," lost

---

1. "57 Varieties of Trouble," *Forbes*, April 1964.

2. "Heinz Battles for Space on a Worldwide Shelf," *Fortune*, October 1971.

Burt Gookin receiving Pittsburgh's 1976 Man of the Year Award, with Don Wiley and Tom McIntosh. McIntosh worked on the Heinz account with Ketchum, McCleod & Grove for 11 years, then moved to the client side of the business in 1965, hired by Jack Heinz as director of public relations, a newly created position. During his 23 years with Heinz, McIntosh transformed and upgraded the company's image by producing some of the most sophisticated and best-designed annual reports in corporate America. He also inaugurated elegant presentations for securities analysts at the Four Seasons restaurant in New York City.

most of his capital "in the farm depression of 1925–26," but encouraged Burt in "every form of athletics"—especially golf. When Burt was six, his father cut down a regular-sized set of clubs and said he could play with him if he kept up. Burt, a fierce competitor, more than kept up. At the age of 13, he beat his father for the town's club championship. "He pretended to be mad about it," said Gookin, "but he was extremely pleased." He also won high-school letters in football and basketball.

Gookin, also a Golden Gloves boxer, went to Northwestern University on a scholarship, made the golf and boxing teams, and put himself through college. He graduated with a B.S. degree in accounting and finance. It was the depth of the depression. He sent his laundry home every two weeks and made ends meet by waiting tables, working afternoons for the Firestone Company, and getting between $3 and $5 a night "boxing three rounds in all the dirty little boxing clubs in Chicago."

But it was golf that provided the biggest break for young Gookin. Indeed, it would always help him in the business world. ("I have a lot to thank golf for in my life.") After college, already married and working full-time as an accountant for Firestone, he became a star at the Firestone Country Club, winning its golf championship three years in a row. That drew the attention of a group of Firestone Harvard Business School alumni who decided to give Burt a scholarship.

In 1940, M.B.A. degree in hand, Burt moved to Los Angeles ("I didn't like cold weather"), where he worked for Forest Lawn Memorial Park as assistant to the controller. During the war, rejected by the army and navy because of poor eyesight, he contributed to the war effort by working in the systems and procedures department of the Los Angeles Shipbuilding & Drydock Company, which built and repaired naval vessels. He then spent a year as assistant to the treasurer at the Consolidated Steel Corporation.

GOOKIN ARRIVES IN PITTSBURGH

In 1945, Hogan recruited Gookin to the Heinz Company as executive accountant. Gookin still recalls how, one fall day, he left sunny Los Angeles; took a two-day, three-night train ride east; and arrived in Pittsburgh at 11 A.M. to discover that the city "was absolutely dark and all the street lights were on. I thought, good heavens, I certainly have made a mistake."

Pittsburgh's day-into-night smog was infamous, and the air so dirty that executives regularly took an extra white shirt to the office if they planned an evening out. Often, one couldn't see across the street at high noon, and, according to Parrack, the local postwar joke was that "Pittsburgh was behind the Steel Curtain."

Gookin rose slowly through the ranks, and, courted by other

companies, almost quit. (Gookin's first wife died and he married Mary L. Carroll after joining Heinz. Their two children are Cristy and David.) However, head and shoulders above most of his Heinz peers, and with farm-boy habits that brought him to the office at 7 A.M., it was clear the company desperately needed his skills and that, with patience, he would find room at the top.

Gookin's long apprenticeship, especially the introduction of cost accounting into Heinz factories and offices, taught him the nuts and bolts of the business. "Measurement of any sort, even as to whether advertising was producing sales, didn't exist." It also exposed him to the company's wealth of "bright people at the second and third levels of management" who lacked a unifying focus. "They didn't have a mission statement or any real idea what the purpose of the business was." Gookin, a relentlessly analytic thinker, would change all that.

In 1951, he became controller of the company. In 1959, he was elected a director and vice president of finance (a newly created position), and also appointed to the executive committee. (That same year, Ralph W. Hunter became secretary of the company.)

Gookin's exceptional financial and strategic skills were immediately visible to the company's outside directors. They realized that the company needed professional management. He represented the future.

When Gookin first tackled Heinz U.S.A.'s problems in the early 1960s, America was being transformed by the Beatles, miniskirts, rock music, freedom rides, and a panoply of other cultural changes. Yet, at the corner of Heinz and Progress Streets, bells still rang four times a day: to start and end work, before and after lunch. Smoking was still forbidden in offices, which meant that everyone chain-smoked during lunch or descended to a basement lounge called "the hole" to light up. It stayed that way until Gookin became chief executive officer of the company.

The culture changed in big and little ways. "The bells stopped ringing," said Connolly. "You were allowed to smoke at your desk, partly because Burt was a smoker, but partly because it dramatized that this was the new Heinz."

Management by loyalty disappeared. Why? Because, as Connolly characterized it, Burt put the focus on "performance, profits, and results." Indeed, his single-minded focus on profitability made other agendas and attitudes intolerable and obsolete. "When you hurt the business," said then-attorney Wiley, "you were in trouble with Burt Gookin."

So Heinz went from being, said Wiley, "a paternalistic company with a bunch of people protecting their little fiefdoms to a company that was committed to being a major player in the food business."

Gookin broke other taboos. Most important, he began to bring in outside talent. One of his first moves as head of Heinz U.S.A. was to recruit as vice president the first professionally trained marketing person in the company's history, a Procter & Gamble hotshot, Paul D. Townsend, who in turn quickly hired away other rising stars from P&G. They included Paul I. Corddry, product manager, beans, spaghetti, macaroni, canned meals, applesauce, mustard, chili con carne, barbecue sauce, and horseradish; and Charles M. Berger, product manager, ketchup and chili sauce. Corddry and Berger would have long, successful careers with the company.

Townsend reorganized and focused product management. He separated institutional and grocery sales. He oversaw advertising and sales promotion and ended the U.S. company's 30-year marriage to one advertising agency, Detroit's Maxon, Inc., making a partial switch to New York's hot shop, Doyle Dane Bernbach. By March 1965, the Beatles were working with Heinz on a youth-oriented consumer promotion for eight product lines.

Gookin did not solve all of the company's domestic problems. That would take until the mid-1970s. But he did well enough to be handed the job for which he had been grooming himself for 25 years—president and chief executive officer.

CEO GOOKIN

In 1966, CEO Gookin hit the ground running with a fix-it list that ranged from bringing in more outside directors to the board and forming a separate acquisitions group to redefining the company's objectives in terms of earnings on invested capital. To help

Happy Soup, a nutritionally fortified line of children's soups, was adver-
tised with Disney characters. Launched by Heinz U.S.A. in the mid-1960s,
sales zoomed, but eventually plummeted, for the ill-fated but highly promot-
able Happy Soup line.

him implement organizational change, Gookin brought in-house
as senior vice president of corporate development Donald C.
McVay, a Harvard Business School classmate (and best man at
his wedding). McVay, with McKinsey & Company from the mid-
1940s, was a consultant to Heinz for 20 years, then joined the
company in 1966 as corporate senior vice president and board
member. He worked closely with Gookin and O'Reilly until his
retirement in 1981.

During his reign, Gookin, with unwavering clarity of vision and
purpose, methodically transformed the organizational, financial,
and management structure of the H. J. Heinz Company; tripled
sales; and moved Heinz to the number-one spot in investment
appreciation among the country's then-leading 17 major food
processors.

Architect of the modern Heinz, what he wrought became—and remains—the foundation upon which his successor built a truly global marketing-driven food company. O'Reilly gives Gookin full credit for bringing order, structure, and a cost-cutting consciousness to the company, which he still strives to emulate. In addition, said O'Reilly, Gookin created "two important things we really haven't changed in 25 years. First, he introduced a standard job analysis and compensation structure . . . which breaks a job down into problem solving and dollar-volume accountability, with points attached to every job so that people are transferable between functions and there is equity to the process of paying people. Second, he brought in the business-planning system with McVay."

In 1967, Gookin also created, under McVay's direction, a separate World Headquarters management group. It included compensation, technical services, and corporate planning. "Burt wanted a very small corporate staff," McVay recalled. "That way, they couldn't stick their noses into everything." Besides, with autonomous affiliates operating profitably, why add to overhead? "You didn't add bodies easily under Gookin," said Wiley. "Everything had to be cost justified."

Heinz Restructured

Then, in 1968, Gookin restructured the company and senior corporate management along geographic lines. Instead of two blurred financial groups, U.S. and international, each major business affiliate became a profit center. This changed everyone's mind-set. As Chuck Berger put it, "Now each profit center was as important as its profits."

By 1971, U.S. operations accounted for over half of company profits. Five senior vice presidents reported to Gookin: three headed up staff functions (finance, corporate development, and corporate services, such as legal and public relations); two senior vice presidents (North America/Pacific, Europe/Latin America) oversaw worldwide lines of business, with each affiliate CEO reporting to his area senior vice president. Together, these key employees presided over the decentralized Heinz empire and, ultimately, competed to succeed Gookin.

This flexible system has evolved and changed over the years according to the personality and strength of each CEO and his "college of cardinals." (In the late 1960s and early 1970s, Gookin's college of cardinals included Don McVay, John Connell, Don Wiley, Junius Allen, Bill Agnew, John Crossen, and Tony O'Reilly.) The system continues to surface and test the executive capabilities of rising executives to this day.

McVay installed the company's first worldwide three- and five-year planning process, which meant, for the first time, setting financial and marketing objectives, and then meeting them. It also meant producing a corporate planning manual and training executives, such as Chuck Berger, to go into the field and instruct affiliate managers on how the system worked.

Gookin and McVay further revolutionized the culture by installing a modern incentive system linking senior executive compensation (for about the top 100 managers) to management performance. (This move did not meet with universal acclaim, especially at Heinz U.K. However, as McVay put it, "When the U.K. saw that others were really making a lot of money out of it, they decided, well, yes, we want to be in on that." Some, philosophically opposed to the system, left.)

Gookin ploughed more money into advertising ($10 million in 1970, mostly into television), cut the sales force, and refocused sales efforts on chain and organization buyers. He also consolidated operations, invested in high-speed machinery, pared product lines, and focused much of his time and talent on customers in the food industry, creating mutual alliances for growth.

For example, he launched an annual golf competition to which the top brass of every major food company, grocery and institutional, was invited. He served as chairman of the Grocery Manufacturers Association and received an award for improving relations between suppliers and distributors. In 1974, he led the development of the Universal Product Code, which he still considers one of his greatest achievements.

Gookin took great pride in his unpretentious, one-of-the-boys' style and liked to call himself "just a shiny-assed accountant." Clearly, he was far more than that, a forceful and, by all accounts,

Plant tour guides in the 1920s (left) and 1960s (below). Plant tours, another inspired idea pioneered in 1899 by the Founder, promoted the company's name, products, and spotless facilities. The tour became a "must-see" stop for visitors to Pittsburgh, as well as for schoolchildren in the region. In January 1972, when food processing became more mechanized and less interesting visually, plant tours quietly ended. Over two and a half million people passed through the Pittsburgh factory's doors during those 73 years.

eminently fair leader. The systems and strategies imposed by Gookin and his executives were logical, reasonable, objective, and fit together like the parts of a well-designed clock. Indeed, they reflected the orderly, punctual man who was never late for an appointment. As Ralph Johnson, Gookin's assistant, noted, "You could set your watch by Burt Gookin."

Within a relatively short time, Gookin's fingerprints—his character, temperament, and goals—were visible, especially in the quality of people he promoted and attracted to the company. The private, low-key Gookin did indeed possess one of the true hallmarks of a great leader—the ability to recognize, motivate, and manage talent. Gookin didn't mind intelligent mistakes. "The freedom to fail," he once said, "means there is also freedom to succeed. . . . It is important to allow people to establish their own goals. . . . The ultimate aim is to create an entrepreneurial spirit and keep it alive."[3]

Gookin's self-confidence and decisiveness became evident when trouble developed in various parts of the company. For example, when accounting problems arose in Italy, Gookin flew to Milan and fired Dr. Oscar Pio, the man who had brought the Italian baby-food company to the attention of Heinz. With Pio out of the way, Plasmon gradually turned into one of the company's crown jewels.

By 1971, the business press was beginning to notice Gookin's achievement. That year, in a lengthy *Fortune* article, Judson Gooding wrote: "Gookin has transformed Heinz from a genteel participant in the food business to a driving competitor by a sophisticated mixture of meticulous planning for internal growth, acquisitions, and management changes. In the process, he has opened up the constricting atmosphere at Heinz's crenellated brick headquarters on Pittsburgh's Progress Street—an atmosphere that visitors used to liken to that of a Prussian boot camp."[4]

Many of the people whom Gookin promoted, moved around, or brought into the company became key leaders over the next

------

3. Judson Gooding, "Heinz Battles for Space on a Worldwide Shelf," *Fortune*, October 1971.

4. Ibid.

20 years. Among the standouts were Agnew, Berger, Brettholle, Connolly, Connell, Corddry, Herrick, Patton, McVay, Wiley, and O'Reilly. Especially O'Reilly. McVay believed that bringing Tony O'Reilly into the company, then moving him quickly up the management ladder, would be one of the achievements for which Gookin would be best remembered.

No doubt Gookin will forever get high marks for picking his successor and for creating a meritocracy where performance, not age or country of origin, counts.

In 1967, Tony O'Reilly was managing director of the Irish Sugar Company. It owned, among other things, Erin Foods, a subsidiary whose greatest asset was the patent rights to an accelerated freeze-drying process. O'Reilly was looking for a business partner for the food company, and talked to 18 major food processors between December 1966 and February 1967. The company most interested in the process was Heinz U.K., then being run by Tony Beresford. In April 1967, a joint venture, Heinz–Erin, was formed. As it turned out, the company's real asset was O'Reilly, not its freeze-drying process. He charmed and impressed Beresford and Crabb, who encouraged Gookin to invite O'Reilly to Pittsburgh. It was a seminal event.

In July 1967, O'Reilly spent four days crossing the Atlantic (reading *The Life of Harold Macmillan*) on the *Queen Mary*. He flew from New York and arrived in Pittsburgh without a change of clothes because the airline had lost his luggage. O'Reilly loves to tell the story of how, the first two times he visited Pittsburgh, not only was his luggage lost, but his hotel room was occupied, in each instance, by a man and woman in bed.

Gookin threw a party attended by "all of the high command," including McVay and Connell, as well as up-and-coming managers, such as Chuck Berger. It was already clear that this 32-year-old Irishman was someone special. Indeed, Fred Crabb had already recommended to Gookin that O'Reilly be brought into the company. Gookin visited O'Reilly in Ireland twice. O'Reilly tells a wonderful story about Gookin's "famous trip to Ireland with his great golf bag, which had a black shroud on it. When the luggage moved down onto the baggage floor, people blessed themselves as his golf bag went by, thinking it was the body of a returned Irish-American coming home to be lodged in the old sod."

On Gookin's second trip, in October 1968 (on his way to Italy to fire Dr. Pio), he offered O'Reilly the top job of U.K. managing director.

It was an astounding move. It took courage and nerve to inject a 32-year-old Irishman into an inbred, hierarchical English management group, which, though beginning to slow down, still contributed about 50 percent of total company profit to Heinz.

"I take credit," said Gookin, "for having the good judgment to take on the good judgment of Fred Crabb."

Another key figure in the decision was McKinsey consultant Karl Hoffman. He'd seen O'Reilly in action; talked to General James Gavin of Arthur D. Little Consultants, who had worked with O'Reilly at the Irish Sugar Company for two years; and persuaded Gookin to go with O'Reilly.

O'Reilly, already a father of six children (including a set of triplets), said he then "had a very definite career in mind, which was to go into politics in Ireland." In fact, his old friend Jack Lynch offered to make him minister of agriculture. But O'Reilly, feeling "the economic imperative," reasoning that financial independence would eventually make him a better politician, and challenged by the offer "to run one of the great companies of Great Britain," agreed to go for three years.

Two years later, in 1971, while on a remote moor in Scotland, O'Reilly got a transatlantic phone call from Gookin asking him to become senior vice president in charge of North America and the Pacific. This meant overseeing the heart of the business—Heinz U.S.A., StarKist, Ore-Ida, Heinz Canada, Australia, and Japan. John Connell would return to Heinz U.K. and replace O'Reilly as managing director.

Again, O'Reilly told himself he'd spend three years in America. A year later, at just 36, he became executive vice president and chief operating officer (COO). By 1973, he was president and chief operating officer. In 1977, the board designated him heir apparent to Gookin. In 1979, Gookin, having reached the retirement age of 65, passed the baton to his hand-picked successor. He remained on the board until 1984, resigning after close to 40 years with the company.

Gookin will be remembered for far more than his inspired choice of O'Reilly. First, for his financial performance, guiding

Heinz from a less than $600 million company in 1966 to, in 1979, when he retired, a $2 billion sales giant. In addition, between those years, net income increased fourfold and earnings per share became three times greater, as did dividends on Heinz stock.[5]

Also, during his reign, the balance of profitability shifted back, for the first time since the 1930s, to the United States. "In fiscal 1979," according to that year's Annual Report, "domestic sales accounted for 62 percent of the consolidated total . . . domestic earnings rose to 73 percent of the total. We reinforced, more than ever before, the description of Heinz as an American company with profitable offshore operations."

As O'Reilly later acknowledged, "Gookin essentially shaped the company in its modern form. Through consumate leadership, he took the company from its paternalistic, family-based mode and made it a thoroughly professional company."

An impressive achievement, it didn't quite fulfill every Gookin goal. Once asked by O'Reilly if he'd ever entertained another ambition, "Yes," said Gookin, "I would have preferred to be a professional golfer."

At the age of 80, he still plays a mean game of golf.

---

5. *57 News*, May–June 1979, vol. 8, no. 3.

From left to right, Don Wiley, Frank Brettholle, Burt Gookin, and Tony O'Reilly at a 1973 Heinz Italy business plan meeting held at the Villa d'Este on Lake Como, north of Milan.

Golf has been a valuable ally to Burt Gookin. A gifted and competitive athlete, he won his first club championship at the age of 13; entered Northwestern University on a sports scholarship, where he made the golf and boxing teams; and also earned pocket money during the depression as a Golden Gloves boxer. Gookin's championship play as a golfer later brought him to the attention of Firestone alumni, who secured for him a Firestone scholarship to the Harvard Business School. During his long career at Heinz, Gookin's industrywide reputation as an outstanding executive was matched only by his extraordinary reputation as a golfer.

The 33-year-old Tony O'Reilly.

Anthony J. F. O'Reilly:
The Global CEO

~~

World-class is an adjective often used in conjunction with Tony O'Reilly and his activities. The press not only has acclaimed him a world-class athlete, chief executive, press baron, and entrepreneur, "the consummate business-statesman," according to Henry Kissinger, but it also has credited him "with transforming the H. J. Heinz Company into a global player,"[1] delivering to its shareholders world-class rewards.

When O'Reilly became CEO, the Heinz company's market capitalization was $908 million. By the end of 1989, with no addition of shares, it was $9 billion. And shareholders who reinvested dividends from the beginning of fiscal 1984 through fiscal 1993 have realized a 10-year total return of 551.5 percent, equivalent to a 20.6 percent compounded annual rate of return.

O'Reilly, an Irish national, has gathered about him people who reflect his ability to live, work, and do business in world capitals. There's no room at the top for provincial or parochial thinking. Heinz is increasingly training its people to be global managers.

O'Reilly has been crisscrossing the globe since the age of 19,

---

1. Joann S. Lublin, *The Wall Street Journal*, May 21, 1992.

when he became the youngest member of the championship British Lions, an all-star international rugby team. Indeed, rugby brought the large man from a small country onto the world stage. It gave him a taste of (and for) international life and stardom, which forever marked him. So while fiercely devoted to Ireland, where he remains "unquestionably its best-known businessman,"[2] he has long understood that "you have to play the big game elsewhere."

As a rugby winger, O'Reilly was incredibly fast—especially for a man well over six feet tall. As a player in the fields of business and finance, he has been equally swift. Today, still embedded in O'Reilly's towering frame is the tough, fearless, decisive, and driven athlete's love of action and need to excel.

Gookin and O'Reilly, while vastly different personalities, shared the lessons and language of competitive sport. Inwardly driven achievers from modest backgrounds, smart "jocks," they respected in each other the drive, discipline, focus, leadership ability, and ambition that brought success.

However, as practically everyone knows, O'Reilly and his background are unique.

Nature and nurture favored O'Reilly from the start. A gifted athlete from a young age, the Dublin-born O'Reilly was an only child of doting parents, vivacious Aileen (whom he clearly resembles) and John Patrick O'Reilly, a civil servant and customs officer who rose to become Ireland's Inspector General of Customs.

The gregarious O'Reilly home overflowed with young Tony's teammates and friends. His mother's warmth and hospitality made it everybody's second home. Tony's parents, not wanting to overprotect their only child, encouraged his fearlessness (by age six he was playing the violent game of rugby) and independence (he traveled alone, often by rail and bicycle, from a young age). In fact, Tony O'Reilly had an idyllic youth. As he put it to one interviewer, "I was a happy boy, at a happy school, coming from a happy home."[3]

---

2. Thomas O'Hanlon, "The Long Reach of Tony O'Reilly," *Fortune*, December 1973.

3. "I Remember, I Remember," radio interview in Ireland with Peadar O'Donnell on the "Education of Tony O'Reilly," August 1992.

Belvedere College, a famous Jesuit day school for boys in Dublin (attended by the likes of James Joyce) where the curriculum included French, Latin, and Gaelic, became almost a second home. Tony trooped in and out of the unprepossessing jumble of redbrick buildings—a gated, urban enclave built around a concrete courtyard—from age six to 18, his formative years. His natural exuberance was expended on a variety of sports (rugby, tennis, cricket, soccer, cycling—excelling in all of them) and on the stage. He loved to perform, sing, play the piano, and participate in all forms of public speaking. "He had a great gift in the art of communication," said Father Michael Reidy, one of his mathematics teachers at Belvedere. Focused more on sports than on books, he was a child prodigy at rugby.

RUGBY, THE GREAT TUTOR

Belvedere nurtured the boy and his great gift. "We were quite sure we had a player of great class in the making," said Reidy. He quickly became a star on the famous Belvedere team, which meant being a national figure in Ireland. When the school understood that O'Reilly was about to become a national rugby figure, and therefore open game for the press, one of Belvedere's priests took the 15-year-old O'Reilly aside and informed him that his parents were not married. O'Reilly's father had left his first wife and family and, as a Catholic, could not remarry. O'Reilly maintains that this did not upset him, but rather strengthened his view of his parents' devotion to each other and their "love match." The subject was never mentioned in the house, nor was O'Reilly present when his parents eventually were married in 1973 in Belvedere College's chapel by the same priest who had broken the news to young Tony so many years before.

O'Reilly's outstanding play led, in 1954, to a spot on the touring Ireland team, and, in 1955, to everyone's astonishment (because of his youth), an invitation to play with the British Lions in South Africa. In 1959, while playing in New Zealand and Australia, O'Reilly established a scoring record still unequaled.

To O'Reilly, as he expressed it to Cyert's M.B.A. class on leadership at Carnegie Mellon, "rugby football was the great tutor and the best training for business I ever had. It teaches you all of the basic elements that are necessary." These include discipline, teamwork, determination, collegiality, learning to live with defeat, win with grace, fight back from adversity, and survive "a pressure cooker of epic proportions."

O'Reilly learned as much off the field as on: how to handle the press and the podium, and not lose one's head to an adoring public. The press often took great pleasure in his gaiety and charm. Also, like many travelers, he learned more about himself. On long plane rides, for example, he discovered "the great companionship in books," which has never left him.

O'Reilly continued his formal education. After the touring season was over, he put in five months of 12-hour days studying law at University College, Dublin (four hours before lunch, four after lunch, and four after dinner), his mother in constant attendance. That's when he discovered another great gift: his photographic memory.

"I don't think it was of any concern to me until I went to law school. Then I found I could remember all the cases. I think it had to do with being interested."

O'Reilly's memory—his command of facts, figures, names, dates, places, and people—is legendary. Even more impressive, as one of his closest advisors, Ted Smyth, vice president of corporate affairs, well knows, is "the judgment that comes with his memory. Remembering what's important and what isn't. He reads very carefully and he listens very carefully. He's constantly seeking the kernel of truth or the significant detail. You can become a victim of paperwork and too much briefing if you don't have that attention for the real detail of the business."

O'Reilly's memory, energy, need for only four or five hours of sleep, and disciplined, orderly temperament that, as Smyth put it, "enjoys problem solving and creative solutions," partly explain a key aspect of his life that most distinguishes O'Reilly from his corporate peers: his ability to run Heinz—a global $7 billion enterprise and myriad companies, each of whose businesses is under constant competitive pressure that requires close attention—and to be a successful investor in other companies. Asked how he

Rugby transformed Tony O'Reilly (right) from provincial youth to cosmo-politan young man and forged a lifelong network of international friend-ships. He still has a special fondness for those countries and continents he visited as a young rugby player, including Australia, Africa, and New Zealand. Nelson Mandela, for example, president of the African National Congress, whom O'Reilly brought to Pittsburgh and with whom he has developed a rapport, recalls seeing O'Reilly play rugby on his 1959 tour. The British team, vocally antiapartheid, were considered heroes by the nonwhite community. In 1982, during negotiations to establish a joint venture in Zimbabwe, O'Reilly and Prime Minister Robert Mugabe (cen-ter, with Jack Heinz) discovered that they had been educated by the same Irish Jesuit priest.

juggled his time, O'Reilly quipped, "I don't play golf." The reality is that he is never off-duty at Heinz. He uses the phone at all hours of the day and night, seven days a week, to brainstorm with and motivate Heinz managers around the world.

O'Reilly is non–executive chairman of Waterford Wedgwood. He is non–executive chairman and controlling stockholder of Independent Newspapers, Ireland's largest publishing group, with businesses in France, the United Kingdom, South Africa, and Australia, and a market capitalization of $750 million. He is also a director of the New York Stock Exchange, the *Washington Post*, and Georgetown University, having resigned from a number of other companies to focus his time and energy. Still and all, it's not unusual for a visitor to be greeted with the phrase, "Dr. O'Reilly is running a bit late."

Through law school O'Reilly received a broad grounding in finance. He was an apt pupil. Among other talents, he has an exceptional financial mind. As one of his former CFOs, Karl von der Heyden, put it, "O'Reilly doesn't really need a chief financial officer. He is well-rounded . . . and has the combination of a very good marketing mind, tremendous antennae for financial plans, and the cautiousness of a lawyer."

O'Reilly received his B.C.L. (bachelor in civil law) degree with honors in 1958 from University College, Dublin, and qualified as a solicitor. But in 1958, opportunities were better abroad, so he joined a management consultant firm, Weston Evans & Co., in Leicester, England (playing rugby for Leicester as well). He worked as a trainee for two years, spending dreary 12- to 14-hour days on factory floors learning a great deal about accounting and standard unit costing. Not very exciting work, for O'Reilly it provided a personal test. "Life," he believes, "is about trying as you go along to better yourself and conquer yourself."

Since so many things come easily to O'Reilly, he has always been "suspicious of those activities that did come easily and rather aspired to those that didn't." Law school was another test. "I didn't want to sit down and study five years to be a lawyer, but I forced myself. It was a personal battle . . . between the natural hedonistic, fun-loving extrovert instincts that I have, with an inner sort of austerity that I think is a function, perhaps, of my Catholic upbringing and my Jesuit background."

O'Reilly's Career in Ireland

In 1960, O'Reilly returned to Ireland as personal assistant to the chairman of Sutton's, a family-owned company in Cork. It dealt with the agricultural cooperative societies and their products, and plugged him into the nascent cooperative movement. At night, he lectured on industrial management at Cork University. A talented speaker, his classes were standing room only. To help him manage his increasingly active life, he hired a personal secretary, Olive Deasy, who has been his right arm ever since. (O'Reilly has a reputation for exceptional loyalty and generosity to old friends, colleagues, and employees, while still expecting and receiving extraordinary levels of performance.)

O'Reilly's knack for knowing—and impressing—everyone worth knowing helps explain why, in 1962, the relatively inexperienced 25-year-old was invited to become the first CEO of the Irish Dairy Board. His mandate was to develop foreign markets for Irish dairy products. An enormous responsibility and "one of the most exciting periods" of his life, it set a prophetically hectic pace. He was in charge of 120,000 milk farmers and their dependants, which O'Reilly estimates added up to about 600,000 people out of a total Irish population of three million.

O'Reilly began his new job on April 2, and on May 5, a day before his 26th birthday, he married Susan Cameron, the daughter of an Australian mining executive whom he had met on his last rugby tour. On July 7, he made the decision, "really one of the most important decisions in my life," to create a national brand of dairy products. In October 1963, he revolutionized the export marketing of Irish dairy products by launching the Kerrygold international food brand. (Even today, the Irish Dairy Board, with its Kerrygold brand, remains the largest single export organization in Ireland, and enjoys annual sales of about $2 billion.)

An instant success, it launched O'Reilly's reputation as a bold marketing man. In 1980, already CEO of the Heinz Company, and juggling entrepreneurial business interests in Ireland, he completed a lengthy doctoral thesis for the University of Bradford, England, supporting many of his Kerrygold marketing assumptions and theories.

In 1966, he was persuaded to apply his executive skills to the troubled Irish Sugar Company, where, a year later, Bob Norman suggested bringing Erin Foods and its freeze-dried process to the attention of Heinz U.K. management.

O'Reilly Joins Heinz

In May 1969, O'Reilly officially joined the Heinz family as managing director of its largest offshore affiliate. He moved with his wife and six children (Susan, Cameron, Justine, and the triplets, Gavin, Tony, Jr., and Caroline) to England.

Heinz U.K.'s immense profitability was largely due to its brand strength, which permitted premium pricing of its products. Pricing covered a lot of sins, including poor productivity, especially at the manufacturing level. As in the United States, the retail environment was changing and the company's weaknesses were beginning to show. Retail chains were supplanting family-owned stores. Private-label competition was emerging.

Gookin brought in O'Reilly to shake up the hierarchy, improve margins, and inject modern marketing practices into the business. O'Reilly kept a close watch, receiving daily sales reports nationally and by region, reduced overhead, increased profits through a reduction in buyers' discounts, introduced a number of new products, and brought over U.S. marketing man Chuck Berger.

According to Berger, O'Reilly was focused on improving margins from the first day they met. "I'd been to Harvard, the West Point of American capitalism," Berger recalled, "where they didn't teach us one thing about the rest of the world and I thought marketing drove the entire business."

On a plane ride between Pittsburgh and New York, during one of Tony's first trips to the United States, the two men chatted about the business, and O'Reilly posed the question that became one of his driving themes. "Couldn't you get more marketing money if, while sustaining quality, you could find a way to reduce

Group shot of five distinguished Heinz U.K. managing directors who helped to create one of the most successful affiliates in the Heinz family. Collectively, they led Heinz U.K. to ever-increasing levels of success during its "golden" era, and turned Heinz into one of the most beloved brand names in Britain. From left to right: Tony O'Reilly, Fred Crabb, Willie Cormack (whose 80th birthday the group is celebrating), Tony Beresford, and, with back to camera, John Connell.

the cost of the product, get a bigger margin, and then use that margin for marketing?" It forever changed Berger's perspective.

Derek Finlay, a U.K. McKinsey consultant to Heinz who had long been urging change within the U.K. company, recalled meeting O'Reilly for the first time. "He was a very energetic, charismatic character . . . who brought a breath of fresh air and creativity to that company." Finlay finally succumbed to O'Reilly's entreaties and officially joined the company in 1979, when O'Reilly became CEO.

George Greer, who joined the company as an attorney and served as U.K. product manager in ketchup and soup between

1968 and 1972, also had a front-row seat to O'Reilly's two years as U.K. managing director. "He came in with great stature. He knew what he was doing. I think he shook up a lot of people. But he was very good with older men. Very respectful. Tony has great interpersonal talent. He doesn't get his power from putting people in their place; he elicits support. The old-time British people resented some of the Brits who were ahead of him, but never resented O'Reilly. Tony brought a new style of running the business. He gave them direction and they got on with it."

He got on with a number of other things as well, including training, at the age of 34, for his last international rugby game at Twickenham, and planting the seeds of his entrepreneurial empire by forming Fitzwilliam Securities, an Irish venture capital firm, with a number of friends.

Gookin, to his credit, never had a problem with O'Reilly's active investment life. As long as he did his job, he could do what he wanted on his own. But O'Reilly has always made clear that he is a manager of Heinz first and only an investor in his other business interests. He is helped in this by his choice of very able CEOs for his newspaper and other investments.

Tony arrived in Pittsburgh in August 1972. His chief mission as senior vice president was to turn Ore-Ida and Heinz U.S.A. into profit-making operations.

On his first visit to Ore-Ida, instead of taking the traditional plant tour, he said to Paul Corddry, vice president of sales and marketing, "I don't want to hear all about that. I want to know why your cash flow has been so poor." Corddry was astonished. "We thought he'd come out to say hello, and he knew our total business."[4]

"He figured out the whole business in about 15 minutes," Connolly agreed. "We'd been there for five years and weren't sure we had it figured out yet, but he knew where the levers were right away."

Corddry also recalls that O'Reilly "could just sort of take a look at our reviews and zero in on the one or two things that really

---

4. O'Hanlon, *op. cit.*

O'Reilly in top rugby form. An international rugby star as a young man, O'Reilly loves to recount the tale of his last, infamous 1969 rugby game at Twickenham, which was thoroughly (and amusingly) covered by the press. As the Sunday Telegraph *put it, the 34-year-old O'Reilly "scarcely covered himself in glory, but the match supplied him with one of his best stories." It seems he was delivered to the game in the company's chauffeur-driven limousine. A placard in the crowd read: Heinz Meanz Haz Beanz. According to former coach Mick Doyle, Willy John McBride, no ban-tamweight himself, said to O'Reilly, "Jesus, you're so huge . . . your best attacking move today is to shake your jowls." As O'Reilly tells the story, "I dive on the ball and receive what centuries of Irishmen have received from passing Englishmen—a boot on the back of the head. I came to after about 30 seconds and I can hear this great cacophony of sound. Out of it, quite clearly, came one Irish voice shouting, 'And kick his bloody chauffeur while you're at it.' "*

mattered. That was clear from the outset. The other thing that became clear over time was that he remembered everything you said."

Ore-Ida was poised to take off when O'Reilly arrived on the scene. He helped it happen a bit sooner by deciding to write off a disastrous 10,000-acre investment and convincing World Headquarters to invest big bucks into marketing and plant automation.

In retrospect, there is a certain glow to those turnaround times. "He was young, and we were young," said Connolly. Bonds were forged that would last over 20 years.

Ore-Ida's turnaround was O'Reilly's first big success. Heinz U.S.A. took longer.

In 1973, 77 percent of domestic profits emanated from StarKist. (Earnings were about $26 million on sales of $705 million.) Heinz U.S.A. earned $4.5 million on sales of $375 million. Only ketchup and vinegar were brand leaders. StarKist remained the most profitable domestic affiliate throughout the 1970s, until Heinz U.S.A. became the solid profit center it remains to this day. In fact, one of the central—and largely unheralded—dramas of Tony O'Reilly's reign is that when he arrived in Pittsburgh in 1972 to oversee, among others, Heinz U.S.A., its volume was about 110 million cases, and the business was losing money. Today, Heinz U.S.A.'s case volume is approximately the same and it is the company's most profitable affiliate.

If leadership is about getting people moving or, as Dick Cyert, a board member, once said, "a leader determines what is important and is able to inspire people in the organization to think about those things that the leader thinks is important," then O'Reilly has proved to be a superb leader. He turned Heinz U.S.A.'s potential into reality by reorganizing its structure, bringing in a more rigorous low-cost-operator philosophy, reducing and changing the product mix, and continuing to import fresh marketing and management blood.

As one *Fortune* reporter later noted, "Tony was managing for the new economy before there was a new economy."[5] A leading

5. Arthur M. Louis, "How to Manage in the New Economy," *Fortune*, June 23, 1986.

apostle of cost-cutting, he also "shut down 16 major plants" between 1980 and 1986.

In 1978, O'Reilly shook up Heinz and the food industry with a
bold acquisition. For $100 million, he acquired Weight Watchers
International (the meeting operation) and Foodways National, to
which Weight Watchers had licensed the manufacturing of its
frozen-food entrées. O'Reilly shrewdly detected a lifestyle change;
correctly anticipated the 1980s' obsession with health, wellness,
and fitness; and stuck to his game plan when problems developed.
It eventually proved to be a home run.

O'Reilly's ability to turn the domestic picture around guaran-
teed him the top spot at Heinz. As Cyert noted, "He is just brighter
than every other businessman . . . and has provided extraordinary
leadership to the group of people he has brought around him."

TEMPEST IN A TEAPOT

There are pluses and minuses to decentralization. One of the
minuses became embarrassingly evident in April 1979 when allegations were raised about the existence of certain affiliate accounting practices that had resulted in a limited transfer of income
between fiscal years. In those days, little information was shared
among affiliates. Each company more or less ran itself, and that
included its accounting practices.

What had taken place was the result of too much success rather
than not enough. With compensation partly based on achieving
profit goals, too much income in one year had the potential to
throw off executives' annual bonus levels for the next year. This
could be offset by paying invoices in one year for services to be
rendered in the following year.

The audit committee of the board of directors investigated the
allegations for a full year, during which, to management's acute
embarrassment, no 1979 Annual Report or proxy statement could
be issued. In the end, however, the affair turned out to be something of a tempest in a teapot.

While it was clear that such practices had been carried out between the years 1972 and 1979, the committee report stated: "The amounts involved in such practices were not material to consolidated net income or shareholders' equity. It is further noted that the audit committee found no evidence that any member of the board of directors or any officers or personnel at World Headquarters planned, participated in or directed any of the income transferral practices nor that any individual employee obtained any direct financial benefit from the practices uncovered." No one had been stealing. No one had been lining his or her pockets. No one was fired.

Nevertheless, it was a serious wake-up call. As a result of the painful public inquiry, new auditors were brought in, the company's inside corporate audit team was substantially beefed up, a new Code of Conduct was issued, and, most important, uniform accounting practices were established for all affiliates, to be closely monitored and controlled by World Headquarters. Corporate reporting structures permanently changed, and for the better.

O'REILLY AS CEO

In July 1979, the 43-year-old O'Reilly—with "the old pickle company" a scant 10 years—became president and CEO, ushering in an unprecedented era of growth.

Upon Gookin's modernized and professionalized foundation O'Reilly built a company that, during the 1980s, soared. It became one of the premier stars in the food firmament.

O'Reilly brought about growth through a clear and consistent five-point strategy. First, to expand geographically and establish joint ventures in developing areas of the world, particularly in Africa and Asia (Zimbabwe, Egypt, Thailand, Korea, and China, as well as Greece, Spain, Hungary, and New Zealand), where Heinz products had no presence and the population was growing twice as fast as that of the rest of the world. As Thomas MacMurray, vice president of corporate technical services, said, "We are driven by where we are not." It was Derek Finlay who, at a memorable executive meeting in Greenbriar, West Virginia, said, "Heinz

Heinz continues to extend its geographic reach. For example, it recently entered a strategic joint venture with Kuwait Foods Company. On February 18, 1992, Tony O'Reilly and Jassim M.A. Al-Kharafi officially opened a new factory, southwest of Cairo, to manufacture Heinz ketchup, sauces, and, eventually, other products. Egyptian production of fresh tomatoes is the second largest in the world, with California the first, and Heinz's agricultural research team led by Dr. Ben George is already beginning to introduce new varieties of processing tomatoes to its joint-venture partner.

products are sold to 15 percent of the world's population or, to put it another way, 85 percent of the world's population has not been exposed to a Heinz brand."

Although each affiliate has its own research and development group, when the company contemplates joint ventures in new parts of the world, MacMurray, among his other duties, pulls together a task force to investigate a range of issues that directly impinge on the likelihood of a successful operation. They range from evaluating growing and environmental conditions to assessing manufacturing facilities and processing technology.

Second, to add new products and services to the company's familiar product line. Third, to commit more dollars to marketing big brands (marketing expenditures went from about 2.5 percent of sales under Gookin to 9 percent). Fourth, to further rationalize the structure by cutting costs and achieving low-cost-operator status. Fifth, to continue to pursue acquisitions in the food business. As *Dun's Business Month* noted, "The company has made some 20 acquisitions over the past decade, all of them in or very close to the food business. It is an article of faith not to overpay for corporate buys. $370 million since 1976 for acquisition is now worth $1 billion."[6]

Since then, the company has also purchased JLFoods, a $540 million acquisition that substantially strengthened the company's fast-growing food-service business, and, for approximately $300 million, Wattie's Ltd. in New Zealand, a processor of canned and frozen foods under the leadership of David Irving. It expects to expand from New Zealand's low-cost base into the Asian–Pacific market.

Leadership, like teaching, is more art than science. Strategies alone cannot explain why one company soars and another muddles through. One of the keys is empowering people and picking the right people to empower. O'Reilly, like Gookin, has always given senior managers great freedom while remaining a tough and demanding boss. The nature of O'Reilly's expectations can be glimpsed through written excerpts from letters he wrote to those directly reporting to him, a tool of leadership he initiated when he first came to the United States.

"I felt the best compliment I could pay as an area vice president," said O'Reilly, "was to sit down, lock myself in a room, and, a bit like an exam, go page by page through business planning presentations, and really take a lot of time to examine the hypothesis . . . conclusion . . . contradictions . . . and to give a signpost to the weight of the future. The chief executive . . . was left in no doubt whatsoever where I wanted him to take the company. I don't think there's any way you can wriggle out of those letters. They're about as detailed as you can get."

When he became CEO, O'Reilly continued the practice, writing

---

6. "The Five Best Managed Companies," *Dun's Business Month*, December 1986.

"a series of essentially personal letters at the beginning of each year, setting out my expectations for my senior vice presidents as to what they will do and what I think are the shortcomings of their performance the previous year." Not simply a performance review, they were "more a career review."

Overall, these letters illuminate O'Reilly's strengths as commander-in-chief, which include his: strategic intelligence and razor-sharp antennae about people; instinct for danger and ability to move quickly; recognition of top performers and willingness to pare away nonperformers, be they people, products, or assets; and the degree to which he defines the overall mission for his senior management and the entire business. In other words, within the philosophy of decentralized management and mutually agreed-upon goals, O'Reilly—like any first-class coach—is exceedingly attentive to the details and timetable of the tactics. There is no ambiguity. As O'Reilly puts it, "Leadership is about conveying what the guidelines are."

More specifically, they reveal his management ideas ("An area senior vice president is not a Mr. Nice Guy, but a change agent") and sense of humor ("I am dictating this letter to you slowly because I know you can't read fast"). They pull no punches ("I have just reviewed the second quarter financials . . . to say that I am disappointed is an understatement") and are enormously educational ("Welcome to Pittsburgh and to the new world, that of the area vice presidency. . . . The job is both strategic and tactical and the risk exists of either trying too little and therefore having little influence over the scheme of things or attempting to supersede line management in the discharge of their functions and hence becoming unnecessarily interruptive in the day-to-day running of the affiliate concerned").

Deep down, O'Reilly is a teacher who loves to impart his insight and knowledge to those who follow. One new area vice president, for example, received a single-spaced nine-page letter that not only assessed his positive and negative performance over 10 years, but laid out in considerable detail O'Reilly's assessment of the people, products, and affiliates he was about to oversee, what battles had to be won, what trips had to be taken, what tough decisions had to be made, what potential acquisitions needed to be examined, and so forth.

"In leadership," said O'Reilly, "the hardest thing is to find out what precisely you need to do to achieve given ends. That's the analytical process . . . a curious mixture of inspiration and perspiration where you have to slave your way through a vast amount of data and then you make your mind up. Right or wrong, this is what I want to do. Then you have to take the consequences. None of us can call it right all the time, but if you hit it six out of 10, you're doing pretty well, provided one of the four is not of a terminal nature."

The 1980s were a period of unparalleled success for the Heinz Company. Yet, along with the dramatic success of Ore-Ida, Heinz U.S.A., Weight Watchers, and many of the non-U.S. affiliates, there were the requisite number of product failures and some disappointments in terms of return. These included, among others, La Pizzeria frozen pizzas, Mrs. Goodcookie frozen cookie dough, dry baby food, Nadler, a chilled-salad business in Germany, plus wine and restaurant businesses in Australia.

O'Reilly's collegial style of leadership, which has led to a genuinely apolitical, all-for-one environment, works well for two key reasons. The first is that, among other things, O'Reilly has the rare ability, according to Smyth, "to sort out issues directly and up front without acrimony." As Cyert noted, "Tony likes people. Even somebody he is firing, he knows good things about them and continues to let them feel good about themselves." The second reason is that the compensation system is extremely generous toward those who have served the company well.

By 1986, securities analysts like John McMillin of Prudential Bache were pointing out that "Heinz has boosted its gross margins from 27 percent to 40 percent in 10 years," and calling the company's management the best in the industry. "It is no exaggeration to call it brilliant,"[7] said McMillin.

The public accolades began to pour in. *Dun's Business Month* designated Heinz one of the five best-managed companies of 1986. In 1990, *Chief Executive Magazine,* via a committee of peers, anointed O'Reilly "Chief Executive of the Year." What set O'Reilly apart in their minds "was the degree to which vision, leadership,

---

7. "H. J. Heinz: Power in the Pantry," *Dun's Business Month,* December 1986.

skillful marketing, and an empowered employee base can execute strategy on a consistent basis."

However, as the recession began to take its toll on U.S. business in the early 1990s, the press and security analysts began to pay attention to the overall issue of executive compensation. In particular, many focused on Heinz and O'Reilly, whose total 1991 compensation, tightly linked to the outstanding performance of the 1980s, made headlines. That year, O'Reilly exercised stock options valued at $71.5 million (or about $7.1 million per year), which represented the rewards of a decade of leadership and profitable growth, amply reflected in the company's stock market rise.

Significantly, he did not cash in the stock options, but held on to them, making him the shareholder with the largest single personal investment in Heinz. (Teresa Heinz has shared beneficial ownership of the largest bloc of shares—33,426,451, or 13.2 percent—in trust. She has sole voting power and sole dispositive power over 735,922 of the shares.) However, the exercise of stock option gains accumulated over a decade was represented in some quarters as annual compensation, which it clearly was not. Since then, the press has become more discerning in distinguishing between company compensation tied to performance and that which is not. Today, the Heinz Company's compensation philosophy and system—which continue to be based on strict performance requirements—is generally regarded as a sound model for rewarding and motivating management.

O'REILLY, THE GLOBAL CEO

O'Reilly's management style may well point the way to what will be required of all world-class executives whose companies succeed or fail in the universe of global competition.

Indeed, what many once considered were unusual O'Reilly traits—not sitting behind a desk at headquarters for long stretches of time, delegating much responsibility to others, mixing entrepreneurship with corporate stewardship, hopscotching around world capitals—may actually add up to exactly what is required of a new category of manager, the global CEO.

Among those requirements are a nonparochial vision of opportunities and markets (including how Heinz and other companies can help, not just reap profits from, less-developed parts of the world); a profound sense of history and empathy for many cultures; a keen instinct for future trends; a respect for the power of public opinion and global communications—in short, a multidimensional character.

Multidimensional may be an understatement when it comes to O'Reilly. As Don Wiley has pointed out, "There are so many Tonys."

There's the entrepreneurial O'Reilly and the corporate O'Reilly. "In Ireland, I'm an investor; in the U.S., a manager . . . I am much more conservative in my role as trustee, which is what I am for the shareholders of Heinz, than I am as the owner of my own business." The reality is that he has brought a great deal of entrepreneurial risk taking to Heinz, enabling it to grow. The purchase of Weight Watchers, JL Foods, and Wattie's are outstanding examples. He urges his managers at Heinz to perform as if they owned the company: to be exacting about cost, to be entrepreneurial about growth, to balance risk taking with corporate stewardship.

Then there's the Irish O'Reilly ("There's no fireside like one's own"), who expends much of his free time raising money and cultivating support for his country through a nonprofit organization he cofounded, the American Ireland Fund. The Fund, dedicated to peace, culture, and charity, is now the largest private organization raising finances for Ireland overseas, contributing over $50 million during its first 15 years.

There's the citizen-of-the-world O'Reilly. Recently, for example, as chairman of the South Africa Free Elections (S.A.F.E.) fundraising campaign, he raised millions of dollars for voter registration and education in South Africa. O'Reilly, one senses, would get restless if he had to remain in one house or in one city or on one continent for long.

There's the gregarious O'Reilly who has always integrated work and social life, whether hosting Fox Chapel pre-Christmas touch-football games for senior managers and their families or inviting customers, associates, and colleagues to Ireland for working week-ends. "I have always felt that the social opportunity to get to know your fellow workers is at least as important as the workplace," said O'Reilly.

There's the private, reflective O'Reilly ("We should all work ceaselessly to enjoy the bliss of solitude. That notion has great attraction"[8]), who has a literary bent, and increasingly longs for "the lovely homes I don't live in," the books he doesn't have time to finish, and the quieter rewards of success with his children, some of whom are working in O'Reilly's entrepreneurial businesses, and his second wife. O'Reilly and his first wife, Susan, divorced after almost 30 years of marriage. In 1991, he married Chryss Goulandris, a member of a Greek shipping family.

There's O'Reilly the politician, musician, publisher, Irish-art collector, pedagogue, stand-up comedian, tennis player, country squire, cattle breeder, land investor, etc. An unusually complex personality, the contradiction and pull between the reflective and active man remain the central tension within his life to this day.

Above all, there's the man who never stops working. And perhaps, in the fast-moving 1990s, nothing less will do for the leader of any company. As Walter Schmid, Asia-Pacific director, noted, "I think the whole notion of a company in transition is a hallmark of the success of the company. Those that are successful are able to change with the times."

As the history of Heinz amply illustrates, a company must constantly renew itself to remain on top. Ongoing success can never be taken for granted. O'Reilly observes, "When people say, well, of course, everyone has to eat, I always feel grossly insulted by that. Because they sure do have to eat, but they don't have to eat your products. They can change their diet quite dramatically and . . . within that diet pattern they can eat 40 other brands just as easily as yours. The food-product life cycle may be slower than, say, a new computer software game. Nevertheless, it's a highly competitive market . . . and a more difficult industry to make money in now."

In truth, it's always been a difficult business in which to make

---

8. Closing line of O'Donnell interview.

money, but during the 1980s, O'Reilly and his senior managers made it look easy.

In recent years, there's been a changing of the guard. Those who guided the company through the late 1970s and, as O'Reilly termed it, "the rather splendid and glorious eighties," are passing the baton to a new generation.

Indeed, those who have already achieved substantial success "in battlefield conditions" will lead Heinz into the 21st century.

O'Reilly is the second-longest-running chief executive officer in the food industry. Still motivated by "a fierce pride in the Heinz Company," still energized by the player–coach role, Tony O'Reilly is still playing to win.

Section III

A Basket
of Groceries

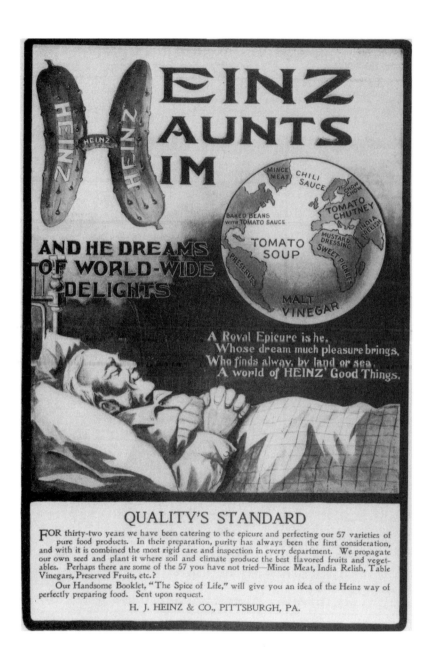

The Founder's vision and famous motto, "The World Our Field" are trumpeted in a 1901 "Heinz Haunts Him" advertisement. Note the product names written on various countries around the globe.

Introduction

~

Although most people think of ketchup, soup, beans, baby food, gravy, pickles, and vinegar when they think of Heinz, the fact is that Heinz makes food in almost every product category somewhere in the world; sometimes with the Heinz brand, often without it. In fact, 65 percent of annual sales comes from products that do not bear the Heinz brand. As O'Reilly has often said, "Heinz is a world brand, but it is to a greater extent a world of brands."

For example, in Italy, Heinz makes soft drinks; in England, salad cream and canned meats; in the Netherlands, canned salad; in Zimbabwe, cooking oil and soap; in Korea, margarine and chocolate; in Canada, maple syrup; in Venezuela, puddings; in New Zealand, ice cream; in the United States, frozen snacks and pocket sandwiches.

Also, tucked away in restaurant kitchens in North America, Britain, Central Europe, Japan, and Australia, Heinz offers restaurateurs, fast-food chains, and institutions specially packed varieties of ketchup, tomato products, condiments, soups, "signature" sauces, breads, sweet goods, pastas, potatoes, appetizers, tuna, pickles, pizzas, frozen coated vegetables, cheeses, lake fish, seafood, and juices.

Under other brand names, it sells an incredible variety of canned, dry, and frozen products. Those brands include Weight Watchers, StarKist, Ore-Ida, Plasmon, Nipiol, Dieterba, Misura, Guloso, Olivine, Orlando, Petit Navire, Amoré, Jerky Treats, Meaty Bone, 9-Lives, Recipe, Reward, Skippy, Kozy Kitten, Skippy Premium, Tomattina, Chef Brillante, Chef Grand, Teo, Cardio-Fitness, Greenseas, and many others.

From an investment point of view, the company's diversified portfolio of products and brands is a big plus since, as John M. Mazur, assistant treasurer and head of investor relations, has pointed out, "It gives us more flexibility in managing the business . . . and that enables us to have a steadier growth pattern."

At the same time, divestiture is as much a part of managing a business as are acquisitions, and Heinz has been remarkably successful in its use of divestitures both to strengthen its product portfolio and to free up capital for more profitable investments. The company has divested itself of successful businesses, such as Hubinger (corn sweeteners and syrups) and Chico-San (rice cakes) in the United States, Sperlari (candies) and Liven (eyeglass frames) in Italy, and Frutsi (juices) in Brazil, either because margins did not prove to be as high as expected, economies changed, or products turned out to be too different from the company's basic branded recipe businesses. Heinz believes it does best by sticking fairly close to processes it already knows.

The rewards of this strategy are self-evident. As O'Reilly observed to shareholders at the company's 1993 annual meeting, "The good news is that approximately 60 percent of Heinz's worldwide sales are in number-one brands." Often, too, these brands are number one by a wide margin.

EIGHT MAJOR BRANDS

If there is a single thread linking the eight major brands described in this section, it is that each has gone through periods of difficulty, challenged by competitors and/or unanticipated external circumstances, and each has rebounded with renewed strength. World War II, to take but one example, built the Heinz U.K. bean business, realigned the baby-food business, and put StarKist's tuna business on the map.

Moreover, while the opportunity to improve a brand always exists, frequently, as one former senior vice president, Dick Patton, observed during Heinz U.S.A.'s mid-1970 reorganization, "Only when we were up against a crisis did we act. *So crisis is the opportunity.*"

In fact, if the history of the Heinz Company's major brands teaches us anything, it is that no matter where the crisis has taken place—in pet food or weight-control food, potatoes or ketchup—it has spurred innovation and risk, forging new solutions to old problems, even renewing so-called "mature" brands, launching them on new life cycles.

In the early 1990s, much has been written about the private-label challenge to brands. Heinz has seen it all, and dealt with it all, before. In the 1970s, for example, when Heinz U.K. was challenged, it propelled its number-one brands to even greater market share, while private labels picked off the weaker brands. The same shakeout is occurring in the United States, where Heinz brands in 1993 increased their market share and had their highest volume in seven years.

Perhaps it's fair to conclude that brand renewal and product innovation are the twin signs of a company's vitality and capacity for growth. Clearly, that has been true for the H. J. Heinz Company, as the following stories demonstrate.

The Ketchup Story

~

Today, ketchup and Heinz are virtually synonymous. It's the company's flagship product, used around the world as a condiment, sauce, and cooking ingredient.

In the United States, ketchup is an enormous business—one of the most broadly used products in the grocery category. It is found in 97 percent of all U.S. households, and four out of five restaurants.

Ketchup is only one of several hundred tomato-based products—sauces, pastas, condiments, juices, purées, paste, beans in tomato sauce and other food combinations, such as chili, that use quantities of tomatoes—produced for the retail and food-service market.

As former corporate vice president Don McVay told an international Tomato Technology Conference in 1974, "red tomato pins instead of pickle pins" could well be the company's worldwide symbol.

"Heinz is the world's largest buyer of tomatoes," said John Dryer, retired general manager, quality assurance and research at Heinz U.S.A. The company purchases just under two million tons a year, and knows more about this edible fruit, a succulent member of the nightshade family (*Lycopersicon esculentum*), than anyone else. At various times in history, the tomato was thought to be poisonous, hallucinogenic, and an aphrodisiac, hence its French name, *pomme d'amour*, or love apple.

The company has led the way in agricultural research and revolutionized tomato growing, harvesting, processing, storage, and packaging. Today, Heinz remains on the cutting edge of agricultural and tomato-paste-processing innovation. It is the world's largest producer of ketchup, and has been at the job for 118 years.

"Blessed Relief"

Ketchup, introduced in 1876, seven years after the founding of the company, was one of the first bottled condiments in the Anchor brand line. Other early products included horseradish, sour spice gherkins, sour mixed pickles, chowchow pickles, sour onions, prepared mustard, vinegar (Heinz, according to *Modern Packaging* magazine, was the first to put vinegar in a bottle), green pepper sauce, and red pepper sauce.

An arduous, time-consuming product for the home cook to prepare, Heinz's thick, spicy ketchup was marketed as "a blessed relief for mother and other women in the household."

From the beginning, Heinz ketchup, like horseradish, was a natural, pure product, never adulterated, as it was by many others, with benzoate of soda or other artificial preservatives that eventually were banned by the Pure Food and Drug Act.

By the turn of the century, most of the packaging hallmarks were in place: the octagon glass bottle (an all-time classic, on a par with the Coca-Cola bottle), keystone label, neckband, and screw cap (which gradually replaced corks and wax). According to Frank Kurtik, Heinz family archivist, the keystone image appeared in May 1878, and was legally registered as a trademark in 1926 by H. J. Heinz.

Love Apple Pie

1/3 cup HEINZ TOMATO KETCHUP	1/3 cup granulated sugar
2 teaspoons lemon juice	1 teaspoon cinnamon
6 cups sliced peeled tart cooking apples (about 2 pounds)	1/3 cup butter or margarine, softened
2/3 cup all-purpose flour	1 unbaked 9-inch pie shell

....

Blend ketchup and lemon juice*; combine with apples. For topping, combine flour, sugar and cinnamon; cut in butter until thoroughly mixed. Fill pie shell with apples; sprinkle topping over apples. Bake in 425°F oven, 40 to 45 minutes or until apples are cooked. Serve warm with ice cream, if desired. Makes one 9-inch pie.

*If apples are very tart, add 1 to 2 tablespoons granulated sugar to ketchup mixture.

A 1962 creation from the company's Consumer Test Kitchens, Love Apple Pie was first served to the nation's food editors at their annual conference in New York. Though pie purists initially shuddered, it turns out that ketchup's function in the recipe is to heighten the apple flavor. It remains a Heinz classic.

PIONEERING AGRICULTURAL PRACTICES

The company's obsession with quality, and its belief that the best way to make high-quality processed food was to locate production near high-quality farmland, led to a string of "branch factories" supported by an agricultural research department to develop improved varieties for each location.

"The importance of tomatoes in our business was recognized early on," said Ogden Perry, retired general manager of manufacturing. "That's the reason our predecessors supported research and development as energetically as they did."

In 1916, the company ran its first tomato-yield trials. In 1920, it hired its first full-time agricultural-research specialist. To maintain its high standards of quality, Heinz grew its own tomato plants (until 1936, plants were grown either in Heinz greenhouses or under direct supervision), and became a leader in developing new and improved varieties. In 1936, Dr. J. J. Wilson began a tomato-breeding program.

Over the past 50 years, the yields of tomatoes in the United States have gone from three to five tons an acre during the 1930s, 1940s, and 1950s, to between 30 and 60 tons an acre in the 1990s. By the 1950s, breeders were manipulating plant hormones to increase flowering, as well as to regulate the time and type of flowering.

Also in the 1950s, Heinz became known as the "founding father" of Portugal's modern tomato-culture industry. The company's agronomists worked with local growers to perfect a genetically stable plant with the right yield, color, consistency, and mold resistance. In a 10-year span, land cultivation grew from 5,000 to 50,000 acres, yield per acre tripled, and volume rose from 24,000 tons to 790,000 tons.[1]

Tomatoes from Portugal were sent to the U.K.'s Standish factory, which, in 1948, first began production of ketchup, as well as to, in 1958, the company's Central European manufacturing facility in Elst, Holland (near the battle of Arnheim during World War II). Between 1928 and 1948, the U.K. received supplies, shipped by boat, from Leamington, Canada.

Heinz agronomists exploded the myth that it was impossible to grow tomatoes commercially in the Mississippi delta, the wet fields of Venezuela, the Australian outback, or the California desert. They also pioneered disease-resistant varieties that increased productivity with fewer and fewer pesticides.

Heinz first located U.S. branch factories in Pennsylvania, New York, New Jersey, Ohio, Michigan, Indiana, and Iowa. When state and federal water projects brought irrigation to the desert, the company expanded tomato production to California. Today, the industry is primarily centered in California, where nearly 90 per-

---

1. McVay speech, November 9, 1975.

cent of processing tomatoes (as opposed to salad tomatoes) are grown.

In 1910, Canada turned out its first bottle of ketchup, and two years later, started to produce cooked spaghetti. (The Canadian operation officially became the H. J. Heinz Company of Canada Ltd. in 1940.)

In the old days, thousands of seasonal laborers swelled the Heinz ranks during tomato season, both in the fields and factory. All work was performed by horse power, human power, and, as the Founder used to say, heart power. Plants were set by hand. Fruit was picked by hand as it ripened, and delivered by wagon, which meant short hauls to receiving stations. Heinz field men covered their territory by horseback, by buggy, or by bicycle.

Horse-drawn wagons waiting to load tomatoes onto barges for processing at Heinz U.S.A.'s Salem, New Jersey, plant, circa 1912.

It was a labor-intensive business, and the harvested tomatoes, according to Dryer, who joined the company as a microbiologist in 1961, were much like those grown in a home garden. Big and soft, they cracked easily, which created tremendous waste, as well as quality problems. Heinz factories in different parts of the world processed fresh tomatoes for ketchup over a two- to three-month season, then bottled and stored inventory for labeling and shipment throughout the year. Marketing would try to estimate yearly demand, agriculture would estimate how much to plant, factories would try to turn out neither too much nor too little supply. It was an inefficient, expensive system with enormous amounts of capital tied up in underutilized factories, inventories, and a vast network of warehouses.

But those frenzied, labor-intensive days and nights during "the season" embodied a culture warmly remembered by many, including Ogden Perry, who, in 1949, began to work summers for Heinz. "It paid for my college education."

Perry moved up to personnel manager, factory manager, and then oversaw four factories from Pittsburgh. In those days, if the plant was short-handed, he and everyone else would pitch in, unloading baskets of tomatoes for five and six hours a night. "You felt good after having come through a tough time. There was a lot of camaraderie and support."

Perry also recalled the ketchup cooks. "They had to be men of steel, because they were cooking in banks of open 350-gallon kettles. It was hard to breathe in those kitchens because of the vinegar vapor and general steam level. Basically, it was a hellish job and the ketchup cooks were a revered bunch of people."

REVOLUTIONARY CHANGE BEGINS

Suddenly, in the mid-1960s, everything began to change. Heinz revolutionized the ketchup business—in the field and factory, from packaging to marketing. The dramatic story of the 1960s, 1970s, and 1980s is a complex series of interrelated agricultural, technological, and marketing breakthroughs that resulted in Heinz dominating the market as never before.

The revitalization of ketchup is inextricably entwined with the reorganization and turnaround of Heinz U.S.A., one of the great (and largely untold) success stories of the company. Indeed, the changes that ensued in the ketchup business partially explain the astonishing transformation of Heinz U.S.A. from perennial money loser and company stepchild to, from the 1980s on, largest profit contributor and company star.

To begin with, in the early 1960s, as already recounted, Heinz U.S.A. profits were at an all-time low and management decided to bring in Paul Townsend, marketing director of Procter & Gamble, France. Townsend got a call from Jack Heinz—how would he like to be vice president of marketing for Heinz U.S.A.?

Actually, Townsend had just accepted a job with the Lincoln Mercury Division of Ford, but, after a visit to Pittsburgh and meetings with Jack Heinz, Lou Collier, then vice president of marketing (who moved up to senior vice president of marketing and sales), and Armour, then president and COO of the company, he decided that the H. J. Heinz Company really needed him more than did Ford.

Townsend, voluble and fast-paced, came on board in January 1964, and within weeks got the bad news. "Everyone told me that the ketchup business was in trouble, but I didn't know how big the trouble really was until I got there." A barely profitable "mature" product, it was running neck and neck with Hunt's and Del Monte. Each had about 20 percent of the market. And ketchup wasn't the only problem. As Townsend recalled, the company was losing between $2 to $4 million on U.S. sales of about $180 million.

Townsend, in charge of both retail and food-service, proceeded to raid Procter & Gamble for talent. "The first guy I hired as product manager was Paul Corddry." Then he tapped John Hays, head of market research at P&G, France, to become general manager of marketing services; Ralph Lund, for general manager, product marketing; and Steve Fountaine for manager of consumer research. Chuck Berger was put in charge of ketchup.

"In terms of consumer marketing," said Berger, "P&G pretty much wrote the book." With a surplus of young marketing people, it was constantly being raided. Berger and Corddry arrived on July

8, 1964, and, within a year, had become group product managers.

Townsend and Berger moved fast on the ketchup front. "Heinz's share of market," said Berger, "was 23.6 and Hunt's was 23.4. And Hunt's was moving up like a rocket."

They quickly analyzed the product, package, pricing, promotion, and advertising, and discovered that, while the product and package were terrific, pricing was an immediate problem. They counterattacked with three key moves. First, they shocked everyone at the company by reducing the premium price of Heinz ketchup, narrowing the differential between Heinz and Hunt's from 5 cents to about 3 cents. Then they mounted a massive advertising campaign, and, taking a leaf from P&G's detergent book, added a 26-ounce "ketchup lover's ketchup" and wide-mouth bottle size, which brought more shelf space. Sales immediately began to climb.

According to a 1956 *Christian Science Monitor* profile of the company, a wide-mouth ketchup bottle had been tried before, but had been rejected by consumers. A decade later, the company learned the same lesson. The sugar in ketchup oxidizes and begins to darken when air hits it, and, in a wide-neck bottle, it turns black faster and deeper because more surface is exposed to the air. So while the wide-neck bottle was more convenient, it was eventually withdrawn from the market.

Townsend hired a hot New York shop, Doyle Dane Bernbach, for its advertising. "It was the smartest thing I ever did," said Townsend. Until then, the account had been with Maxon of Detroit. Maxon, according to James A. Gordon, who joined Heinz in 1946 and moved into advertising in 1952, had devoted "a major portion of its ketchup budget to outdoor billboards" pushing the theme, "red magic." (Perhaps, in part, because within Heinz, ketchup was long known as "Big Red," so that decades of salespeople in the United Kingdom called themselves "the Red Army.")

Forbes, in its bruising April 1964 article on Heinz, "57 Varieties of Trouble," noted that "Heinz has only begun to realize the importance of advertising in today's screaming world. For 30 years it potted along (almost solely) with a single agency, Detroit's Maxon . . . Heinz's failure to match its competitors in advertising has proved costly even in catsup." The article further noted and approved Townsend's arrival. (The article so shook Heinz that it finally agreed to bring in-house Tom McIntosh, who had been working on the Heinz account at Ketchum since 1953. He skillfully presided over the company's communications for the next two decades.)

Townsend, a "mover and shaker," said Gordon, brought a new level of sophistication to the company. He established marketing objectives, developed a five-year marketing plan, and used focus groups. "Bill Bernbach was violently opposed to focus groups," recalled Gordon, "but they were done anyway." Townsend also issued coupons for ketchup for the first time. "It became a very big promotion vehicle for Heinz."

Billboards were abandoned. Television became the company's primary advertising vehicle. In those days, TV advertising was mostly black-and-white one-minute commercials. To save money, Townsend went to a 30-second commercial, and shot in color (just emerging) to show off the product.

The collective creativity of the new Heinz marketing team and Doyle Dane wound up producing two revolutionary ketchup commercials. Townsend recollects that it cost only $8,000 for the two commercials, when the average cost in those days was $50,000 per commercial. They would become among the most successful and enduring ad campaigns ever devised, and included (1) the world's first ketchup race (showing only hands and bottles), which used the phrase "thick and rich," with nothing coming out of the Heinz bottle while the other stuff ran like water, and a narrator saying, "Heinz loses, Heinz always loses"; and (2) the world's first ketchup plate test, which again said, in effect, nothing is running out of Heinz ketchup because it's thicker and richer.

At the same time, new emphasis was placed on food service, long regarded as a stepchild to the retail business. The vice president of sales, Jim Hamilton, hired new people, such as Bill Costello, to set up area master distributorships (replacing direct sales). The program took three years to implement, and in the process, according to Costello, who in 1972 became vice president of food-service marketing and sales, Heinz went from 32 to 10 warehouses, eliminated a fleet of trucks, reduced the sales force (known as route men), and increased business from about $40 million to $80 million in three years.

To prevent retailers from selling to restaurants, Townsend set up a new pricing system and put a neckband on institutional bottles that said "Served by Fine Restaurants Everywhere." He shipped ketchup in huge railroad carloads, as well as by smaller truckloads. As Townsend put it, "We blew the roof off the business."

But Heinz U.S.A. was still losing money. In the midst of the ketchup wars, Jack Heinz and Frank Armour moved upstairs. Gookin, a cost cutter, never enamored of marketing, became head of Heinz U.S.A. Townsend slashed advertising costs, while maintaining increased sales and profit. Fueled in part by ketchup's turnaround, the Heinz U.S.A. picture improved and Gookin became CEO of the H. J. Heinz Company in 1966.

However, one of the ironies of Townsend's and Berger's success was that the company was running out of ketchup. At Heinz U.S.A. executive meetings, Townsend was flabbergasted to hear complaints from manufacturing and agricultural people. Demand was exceeding supply.

PIONEERING KETCHUP PRODUCTION FROM TOMATO PASTE

According to Berger, lack of supply was the chief reason Heinz pioneered the production of ketchup from tomato paste. In fact, it developed a recipe formula every bit as good as fresh ketchup, so good that no one could, and still can't, tell the difference.

Making ketchup from paste gradually improved the economics of the business. Paste has many advantages; among them, speed. Heinz can process a year's worth of tomatoes into paste far quicker than into ketchup. Another advantage is that the supply is no longer limited to the yearly harvest. Paste can be stored for year-round production. By 1968, according to Berger, "50 percent of the company's ketchup was being processed out of hot paste."

"Jim Anderson and Foster Crocker were the real unsung heroes of the company's conversion to paste," said George Greer. "They created methods for paste storage and bulk transport, and, in fact, hold patents on the processes."

Paste, in turn, gave marketing the flexibility it needed to, as Berger put it, "really start moving the needle in terms of volume." Up until then, Heinz didn't have enough factories to grow from five million cases per season, sold in the mid-1960s, to over 11 million cases, reached in 1969.

Heinz moved into brand leadership in most parts of the country. Berger also persuaded Gookin to raise its advertising weight. By 1969, the company was spending about 60 to 70 percent more on ketchup advertising, powering the brand into a bigger share of market and doubling the sales volume in five years.

Townsend, restless by nature, left in 1967. In 1969, Berger was promoted into corporate planning. By 1971, Heinz had captured about "34 percent of the $170 million ketchup market,"[2] where it remained until the mid-1970s.

After Heinz turned to paste, other revolutions followed that led Heinz to become expert in the agriculture, storage, and production of tomato paste. Ultimately, it led to closing seasonal factories and producing ketchup from stored paste 365 days a year.

First, Heinz agronomists began to develop tomatoes specifically suited for processing into paste. These firmer, crack-resistant varieties with thick skins, higher pectin, higher solids, and better color were also bred to mature at the same time so that they could be mechanically harvested.

Next, Dr. Ben George and his agricultural team—about 20 specialists—in Tracy, California, revolutionized the industry with their pioneering introduction of tomato hybrids. (World-class scientists, they included research station managers Drs. Sayed, Emmatty, Prend, Schroeder, and Marvin Schott.)

"Between 1980 and 1985," said Perry, "we didn't grow one variety we had grown five years before." In 1981, for example, new disease resistances were incorporated into breeding lines. In 1983, the first Heinz hybrids were commercialized. In 1990, a commercialized hybrid set new levels for ketchup yield. And in 1991, under corporate technical vice president Tom MacMurray, a formal process began for transferring breeding objectives to

---

2. *Forbes*, March 1, 1971.

Mechanical harvester near Heinz U.S.A.'s Fremont, Ohio, plant, the largest ketchup factory in the world, eliminates any need for harvesting by hand. First employed in the 1960s and 1970s, the harvester cuts the tomato vine just under the soil level, lifts the vine, shakes the tomatoes off, and then throws the vine back onto the ground. The tomatoes go up a conveyor belt, drop six feet into a truck, and are hauled hundreds of miles to a factory.

affiliates around the globe. Today, the company's tomato agriculture department is the envy of the world.

Before hybrids, non-Heinz growers would routinely steal Heinz varieties from the fields to keep up with the company's innovations. Hybrids do not reproduce themselves, which makes the imitation of Heinz varieties (they differ from location to location, depending on the weather, soil, and moisture conditions of each environment) more difficult, and gives Heinz a substantial competitive advantage.

Hybrid seeds are produced in India, Thailand, China, and Taiwan through a labor-intensive process of cross-pollination by hand. It takes about 12 years to develop a hybrid variety, which is utilized by growers for about five to seven years.

Dr. George and his team developed new hybrids for the company's contract growers to use. As hybrid varieties become mature, there are new, improved products to take their place.

Heinz does not own land or grow its own tomatoes. Instead, each affiliate contracts with growers, as it did when farmers, like John Dryer's grandfather, grew tomatoes for the company and delivered them to the Pittsburgh factory in a horse and wagon. In the United States, Heinz contracts for about 10 percent of the country's total supply of processing tomatoes.

The Heinz agriculture department decides which varieties to plant, and where and when to plant and harvest. It provides each grower with specific amounts of seeds or plants, with quality standards and delivery schedules to be met, as well as specific pesticide parameters.

"Our growers are the best in the business," said Perry. Some growers have 40-year relationships with the company, although contracts are extended only on an annual basis.

TOMATO PASTE: A WORLD COMMODITY

Bulk paste has now become a world commodity. Delloite and Touche has noted a seven-year price cycle. When tomato-paste prices are high, paste manufacturers produce more, and new manufacturers enter the business. In the late 1980s, due in part to a change in America's diet, which increased consumption of Italian and Mexican tomato-based food, demand for tomato products exceeded supply. Tomato-paste prices promptly rose and the industry expanded about 20 percent. Two years of tomato gluts then resulted in plummeting prices, a series of bankruptcies among weaker producers, and a 20 percent crop cutback. Gradually, tomato-paste prices have again begun to rise.

Today, Heinz U.S.A., with about 100 large-scale growers, operates three ketchup factories (in Fremont, Ohio; Muscatine, Iowa; and Tracy, California) and one for single-serve pouch ketchup (in Pittsburgh).

To ensure a steady supply of this vital ingredient, Heinz works with a global network of growers in Portugal, Spain, Greece, Venezuela, Australia, and New Zealand. U.S. plant breeders travel around the world to advise and work with growers, as well as to evaluate and select new breeds.

The tomato season is often called "the campaign." Basically, it's an ongoing battle with the weather. "It's you versus disease, heat, rain, early frosts, not enough sun, or, believe it or not, too much sun," said Perry. (Tomatoes won't turn red if nights don't cool down.) "I've looked at 35 tomato seasons, and not one is the same." Also, like a military campaign, the planning, timing, and logistics of synchronizing people, machinery, and packaging with midwestern and California weather—processing 140,000 tons in seven weeks in the Midwest or 800,000 tons in 12 weeks in California—require the skills of a first-class army.

It's a highly managed, specialized business and Heinz manages it at a higher level of efficiency than anyone else.

In California's San Joaquin Valley, the crop is now 100 percent mechanically harvested. No human hand touches the tomato throughout the planting, harvesting, and cooking processes. In addition to being planted and harvested mechanically, a sea of tomatoes is unloaded from trucks with high-speed flumes of water that move the tomatoes into factories where high-temperature scalding removes the skins. The tomatoes then continue through a sophisticated production and storage process, also pioneered in the 1960s.

Around 1970, factory kitchens changed from steaming open vats to enclosed batch cookers. With a push of a button, ingredients began to be added by weight. Today, a factory "kitchen" is a bank of computers with one or two people peering at charts, meters, numbers, and statistical analyses on a computer, and from time to time making an adjustment on a dial.

The frantic frenzy of the season has been largely transformed into a model of highly mechanized order. Amazingly, too, total production time—from harvest to bottle—now only takes two to four hours. During "the season," factories run 24 hours a day, seven days a week. It takes an average of 24 tomatoes to fill a 14-ounce bottle.

Leamington, Ontario, factory, mid-1920s, receiving tomatoes. Today, 75 Canadian growers plant about 12,000 acres, supervised by an agricultural team of about 15 specialists. Between August 10 and the first week in October, some 6,000 to 7,000 tons of tomatoes are processed daily at Canada's only ketchup production plant, in Leamington. Nonpaste tomatoes are immediately turned into fresh tomato juice (Canadian law forbids juice from paste). Tomatoes processed into paste are stored in the facility's six-million-gallon tomato-paste tank farm. Mechanical harvesting began in Canada in 1968.

Taste Differences Around the World

Heinz ketchup, though basically the same recipe worldwide, is spiced somewhat differently depending on the country in which it is made. John Dryer, one of the eight or 10 people in the United States who know the recipe, guards it like a military secret.

What varies, according to Dryer, sounding a bit like a wine taster, "are the background flavor notes of the spicing."

While products are increasingly global, taste remains tenaciously local. It's as true for ketchup as it is for barbecue sauce. One of the secrets of Heinz's international success is its respect for cultural differences and adaptation of products to the local palate.

The biggest difference between ketchup around the world is sweetness level. The English, with a 57 percent market share, and its Commonwealth countries (especially Canada, with a 70+ percent market share, and Australia, with 23 percent of the market) produce a sweeter ketchup than does the United States. So does Venezuela. On the other hand, Central Europe, half of whose business is ketchup, and where it's a market leader in Holland and Belgium, prefers a spicier ketchup. (These taste differences are equally true across the Heinz product gamut, from mayonnaise to beans to soup.)

Moreover, in direct contrast to the U.S. consumer who, until "salsa ketchup," never accepted ketchup variations, Elst produces hot ketchup, Mexican ketchup, and curry ketchup for 10 to 15 markets—including Holland, Belgium, France, Switzerland, Austria, Italy, Germany, and Scandinavia. In Europe, "tomato ketchup variants enjoy a 20 percent market share."[3]

---

3. "Heinz Shakes Up Condiments Fixture," U.K. press release, January 1993.

ASEPTIC PROCESS REVOLUTION

The tomato-paste revolution was itself triggered by a revolution in production technology, which began in Heinz Canada in the 1950s.

Basically, tomatoes off the vine are 95 percent water and 5 percent solids. Heinz takes tomatoes down to about 32 percent solids, which means, as many have pointed out, that being in the ketchup business means being in the "evaporation" business.

For decades, Heinz removed water from tomatoes as home cooks do, through hours of open-vat boiling. Then, according to Murray Pennell, general manager of research and development in Leamington, Heinz Canada bought and adapted two Buflovac evaporators, used in dairies, which rapidly pulled off water, about 20,000 pounds per hour, by a pioneering vacuum process. In 1951, tomato-paste manufacturing began with the installation of these evaporators. The concentrated tomato paste was then heated to 200 degrees (sterilized) and stored in 100-ounce sterilized tin cans for nonseasonal use.

It was not an ideal storage system: metal cans are difficult to handle, expensive, and inefficient to store and dispose of. This was a particular burden for Heinz Canada, which, until the 1950s, exported most of its tomatoes by boat to England. A bumper-crop season, for example, meant storing two million cans of tomato concentrate.

Wasn't there a more efficient way to store paste?

In 1950, an employee in the cold-storage area of Heinz Canada's Leamington factory (to this day, no one knows who) came up with the idea of going to bulk storage tanks (much like oil tanks) of tomato paste through an aseptic (sterile) process then used in the pharmaceutical industry. The idea wended its way through the plant's suggestion system to Ralph Rosen, Leamington's factory engineer. To his credit, Rosen jumped on it, visited a pharmaceutical house, and began to experiment with a team that included Ken Shaw, Bud Roberts, Walter Plum, Bob Marshall, and Conrad Beyer.

By the 1951 season, Heinz Canada had taken its first step toward revolutionizing the tomato-paste industry with aseptic processing.

It was pumping one to two gallons of paste a minute. Today, paste is pumped at about 200 gallons a minute.

Experimentation went on for about two years with increasingly larger tanks. In 1957, three new proprietary aseptic-processing technologies—cooling down paste through a flash-vacuum system, transferring paste aseptically, and sterilizing tanks—were transferred to Heinz U.S.A. But they were not problem-free.

In fact, the project was something of a gamble. Yet, over the next 10 years, according to Dryer, who became the U.S. company's chief troubleshooter in the aseptic area, "millions of dollars were invested in a technology no one was absolutely sure would work. There was a lot of guts involved with that call." Among those who made it were Frank Armour, Jack Heinz, and engineer Jim Theys (who later became general manager of manufacturing).

During the 1960s, a team of 15 to 20 Heinz U.S.A. engineers and microbiologists labored to "eliminate problems, commercialize the innovation, and bring it to major scale." The Tracy, California, plant scaled up to 125,000-gallon tanks. When Heinz switched to producing ketchup from paste, perfecting aseptic processing became even more critical to Heinz U.S.A.'s bottom line. Dryer, in charge of the microbiology lab in Pittsburgh, spent two and a half to three weeks each month on the road, mainly in Ohio, Iowa, and California, helping to solve problems as they arose.

Life on the road was without frills. "When I first started traveling," said Dryer, "you stayed in boardinghouses and took your own car. In Bowling Green, we stayed in Mrs. French's boardinghouse on Troop Street. You paid $10 bucks a week and brought your own towel." Dryer also trained the first women retort (huge sterilizers) operators in the history of the company.

Heinz U.S.A. pioneered the aseptic filling of railway cars with bulk paste, so paste could be moved from California to Ohio. In the late 1970s, it also came up with the next major technological and packaging breakthrough: the ability to store tomato paste in gigantic, flexible sterile bags (holding 300 gallons of paste) fitted with nozzles, supported by a plywood box, which could be shipped by rail to various factories around the country. The aseptic paste would be sucked out of the bag (made by the Scholle Company), the box folded down and shipped back to California for reuse. In short, Heinz pioneered a revolving tomato-paste tank farm.

The Scholle Corporation first brought the idea of an aseptic-bag process for paste to Heinz. It was the beginning of a long relationship. The two companies continue to work together to innovate equipment and technology. According to Dick Wamhoff, president and CEO of Ore-Ida, who, in the 1970s, presided over taking down costs on both the agricultural and purchasing sides of the ketchup business, "Heinz was the first to work with suppliers to develop reduced cost structures."

Since packaging is 60 percent of ketchup's total cost, Scholle bag technology significantly reduced storage, transportation, and production costs. By 1980, Heinz had completely converted its Stockton factory to 300-gallon technology, the first in the world to do so. Today, it is a standard for the industry, as well as other industries.

Heinz affiliates quickly recognized the advantages of the Scholle bag. Within two years, the technology was transferred around the company.

Since the mid-1970s, packaging changes have been one of the key drivers of increased ketchup usage and Heinz share growth. In 1978, Wamhoff oversaw the development of large-size Vol-Pak ketchup (a multilayer, metalized flexible bag) for food service, another idea brought to the company by Scholle and pioneered by Heinz. It replaced the use of costly, clumsy, and wasteful no. 10 cans of ketchup in restaurants. The first three-gallon Vol-Pak ketchup bag allowed restaurant operators to place the bag on a rack and refill plastic squirt bottles from the valve.

Instead of cannibalizing the million-and-a-half case can business, as feared, "every case of Vol-Pak became incremental business," said Wamhoff. Food-service ketchup sales zoomed.

Vol-Pak ketchup woke up a new generation of Heinz managers to the growth potential of food service. The company later introduced a one-gallon pouch, which again increased the restaurant and fast-food business. Today, it is selling about six and a half million cases of Vol-Pak ketchup. Since food-service sales growth does not entail expensive advertising or marketing, margins and profits are larger than on the retail side of the business.

In the mid-1970s, Heinz analyzed the single-serve ketchup and condiment business, and, working with a key supplier, American National Can, dramatically lowered the costs on its single-serve packaging. As the fast-food market began to boom, low-cost producer Heinz went from selling half a million cases of single-serve to five million cases in 10 years. Today, Heinz sells close to nine million cases.

Tomato Mafia

Clearly, the operations, technical, and manufacturing segments of the business deserve enormous credit for innovation and cost reduction. Over the years, a unique bond developed among those scientists, engineers, technicians, quality-control, factory, and production people who labored under enormous pressure to innovate up and down the line.

As Ben Fisher, former vice president, business development, put it: "They've been making ketchup for 30 years, built the new plants, changed the process, and are very close friends." In fact, they're known, affectionately, throughout Heinz U.S.A. as "the tomato mafia," because of the way they help each other out and stick together. "People would go the extra mile for you," said Dryer, "and I would go the extra mile for them."

Heinz U.S.A. Divisionalization

Despite improved ketchup sales, Heinz U.S.A. during the 1970s still was not profitable. Valiant attempts were made by Heinz U.S.A. leaders to shake up the organization.

Between 1970 and 1972, Heinz U.S.A. president Dick Grieb brought in new, highly qualified managers from the outside. Pay levels were raised. New accountabilities were developed. Management consultants led in-house finance teams to find new ways to reduce costs.

According to a Heinz U.S.A. "Reorganization History:

1976–1979," written by Stanley B. Henrici and commissioned by Dick Patton, then president of Heinz U.S.A., Grieb's successor, Ray Good (July 1972 to August 1976), a former McKinsey consultant and corporate planner, continued to bring in new people, including Ed Mertz, vice president of manufacturing, and Dick Patton. "Ray Good became convinced the company was still paralyzed in past attitudes," wrote Henrici, who worked in Heinz U.S.A.'s personnel department. "Despite the transfusion of new blood, it was still essentially the same network of old routines."

On December 31, 1975, Tony O'Reilly, then president and COO of Heinz, challenged Good in a 25-page letter and commentary on Heinz U.S.A.'s business plan. "Tell us," he said, "what you must do to get a 5 percent NPAT [net profit after tax] in your business." He encouraged Heinz U.S.A. to make a "radical change in existing fixed costs."

Until then, Heinz U.S.A., a centralized structure, had been organized along functional lines with separate manufacturing, marketing, sales, finance, agriculture, and technical divisions. No one person or unit was responsible for one product. Moreover, the product line had swollen to 1,500 varieties, many of which were not making money. Overseeing them had become a management and clerical nightmare. "The weekly computer printout on inventory at 11 warehouse locations ran to 45 pages," wrote Henrici.

In the spring of 1976, Good proposed a radical solution to the multiple problems of Heinz U.S.A. Restructure and divisionalize the company along product lines into three businesses: (1) tomato products and condiments (TP&C); (2) processed foods (soups, baby foods, entrées, frozen foods); and (3) pickles. O'Reilly agreed, provided profit targets could be maintained.

On Monday, April 26, 1976, the reshuffling of a $500 million company began. Some 8,000 Heinz U.S.A. employees were in for a shock.

To this day, to some old-timers the word "divisionalization" still brings a shudder. For while it was absolutely necessary, and launched the process that ultimately cured the patient, it took its toll. "It was a traumatic time," recalled Bill Springer, now president of Heinz North America, senior vice president, and member of the board. People's careers, lives, and jobs were turned upside down. A cradle-to-grave mentality and way of life were over. For some, it was the beginning of the end. For others, it was the day the sleeping giant, Heinz U.S.A., at last awoke.

Within six months, Heinz U.S.A. went from being a monolithic organization with diffused responsibility and accountability to one with product groups, profit centers, clear-cut goals and objectives. Each division had its own manufacturing, R&D, finance, marketing, and technical groups. For the first time, ketchup, soup, baby food, etc., had to grapple with their true cost structures.

Ray Good, architect of divisionalization, moved on to Pillsbury within months of launching the reorganization. Dick Patton, with a background in sales and marketing, implemented the massive changes. Named president of Heinz U.S.A. in July 1976, "Patton led the charge to turn Heinz U.S.A. around," said Springer. "He put every business under a microscope. Above all, Dick was focused."

Patton "was always looking for a good new idea," recalled Wamhoff. Guided, goaded, supported, and encouraged by president and COO O'Reilly, during the Patton years, a series of important new ideas emerged. They included switching from sugar to fructose in ketchup (a huge cost saving that prompted the acquisition of Hubinger) and Vol-Pak ketchup.

Patton energetically pushed his troops to strip down overhead; bring inventories under control; close factories (Salem, New Jersey; Bowling Green, Ohio; Chambersburg, Pennsylvania; Henderson, North Carolina); shrink warehouse space; eliminate unprofitable product lines; reduce volume; focus on growth areas; extend grocery ketchup market share; and introduce new products. Patton also revived a rigorous strategic planning process.

By 1979, a trimmed-down, energized, profitable company had emerged.

The reorganization also brought a new generation of management talent to the fore, people like Dick Beattie, general manager, operations and manufacturing, who, in 1977, replaced Patton as head of TP&C. (Patton moved up to become senior vice president and retired in 1989.) A hard worker, methodical and detail oriented, who thought about the company 24 hours a day, Beattie excelled in, among other things, cost cutting and turnarounds. He went on to fix problem situations at the Hubinger Company, Heinz U.K., and StarKist before retiring in 1988.

Beattie and others invariably recall the loyalty and goodwill that pulsed through Heinz U.S.A. employees. "The strength of the company was the quality of its middle management," said Beattie. "That was true wherever I went. Men like Dr. Dick Hein, in charge of research, and Burt Kleinsmith, in charge of Stockton manufacturing, epitomized the guys you could count on. There was a feeling of responsibility, dedication, and loyalty that was something special. It was like being part of a family."

Pittsburgh-born-and-bred Ben Fisher, who worked for Heinz for 17 years, agreed. "There's a great warm feeling about this company on the streets," he said, "which in Pittsburghese is called Heinz's, as in working over at Heinz's." Fisher took the plant tour and got his pickle pin when he was in the third grade and wanted to work for Heinz ever after.

"There was a lot of fellowship at Heinz," recalled Lee Harrow, the second corporate technical coordinator. ("One man, one job— hand a guy a set of blueprints and go do it.") He came up with the idea of tapping that fellowship by using experienced and devoted Heinz retirees for special short-term assignments. "They became known as Harrow's secret army" he said, and included men such as Bob Rolfe, retired from Ore-Ida, who worked for Harrow in China, Korea, and Thailand.

Harrow initiated the low-cost transfer of technology by moving surplus equipment from one affiliate to another. When Heinz U.S.A. closed its Salem, New Jersey, factory, he shipped its boilers, storage tanks, and evaporators for tomato paste to Venezuela. "With new equipment," said Harrow, "Venezuela was able to expand its business and become the leading paste processor and ketchup producer in South America." Today, in Venezuela, Heinz ketchup has about a 55 percent market share.

The remarkable turnaround of Heinz U.S.A., from a marginally profitable company in the early 1970s to its current position as the biggest profit contributor in the corporation, had its roots not just in the dramatic cost revolution from divisionalization. Equally important was the explosive growth of ketchup. Much of the marketing leadership in the mid-1970s and early 1980s came from David Sculley, who worked for Beattie in TP&C and later succeeded him. (It was Sculley who launched Homestyle Gravy in 1978, which turned into a home run.)

More important, it was the marketing moves on both grocery and food-service ketchup that drove the profit mix of the company. It was Sculley who brought back the great competitive ketchup plate demonstration commercials of the mid-60s. "I'm a great student of business history," said Sculley, "because history is the most accurate and inexpensive form of market research." This advertising, plus the addition of a larger 44-ounce glass bottle, powered ketchup forward to a new share high of 45%.

But the innovations in food-service ketchup proved even more significant. Sculley's team, with Bill Van Duzer as general manager of food-service marketing, and his successor, Jeff Berger, achieved dramatic growth by focusing on flexible ketchup packaging. They dropped prices on single-serve ketchup to competitive levels and expanded three-gallon Vol-Pak and smaller pouch-pack "bags" which were more convenient and economical, particularly for fast-food operators. In the 10-year period from 1973–1984, ketchup grew from about 20% of Heinz U.S.A.'s case volume to 40%. These moves set the stage for the 1980s.

HEINZ U.S.A., STAR PERFORMER

Heinz U.S.A. came into its own as star performer during the 1980 to 1985 Connolly years. "J took the company to a new level," said Springer. The hard work of the 1970s was paying off. Virtually every business moved ahead. Connolly, an excellent motivator, not only encouraged innovation, but, said Springer, also "put a very good team in place. He was an assiduous picker of talent."

A new generation of managers began to move up. Indeed, Heinz U.S.A., and the ketchup business, became the training ground for many who are now running major Heinz businesses or affiliates. In addition to Springer and Sculley, they include: John Crawshaw, president and CEO of Heinz Canada; Bill Johnson, CEO of StarKist, senior vice president and member of the board; Brian Ruder, vice president and area director—baby food; Jeff Berger, vice president of food-service for Heinz U.S.A.; Jack

Burley, president of the Heinz Service Company; and Dick Wamhoff, president and CEO of Ore-Ida.

PLASTIC PACKAGING BREAKTHROUGH

During Connolly's reign, another major technology revolution transformed the marketing of grocery ketchup. In 1983, Heinz pioneered a squeezable plastic ketchup container. Much easier to use, and less breakable, kids and parents loved it. As the employee newsletter *HeinzLine* summed up the packaging effort: "It took 15 years of development and testing before Heinz found the right 'marriage' of technology in a multilayer plastic container that met the needs of the customer and maintained the quality and integrity of the product at the right price."

A Heinz team worked with American Can for three years and introduced squeezable plastic ketchup bottles 18 months before its competitors did. Once launched, according to John Crawshaw, "it quite changed the dynamics of the product." The first 28-ounce version took the market by storm, and added about five share points to the business. It was followed by 64-ounce, 44-ounce, and 20-ounce sizes.

Combined with the growth in food-service and other innovative packaging, such as single-serve and flexible pouches, Heinz ketchup now commanded a 50 percent market share. Today, ketchup in 28-ounce plastic containers remains the company's biggest seller.

Canada, England, and Australia all wanted to get into plastic, and, according to Wamhoff, "came to Fremont, the biggest ketchup factory in the world, to see how we had done it."

Low-Cost Operator

During the turnaround years of the late 1970s, O'Reilly introduced the concept of "low-cost operator." As O'Reilly prophetically wrote to Patton in his 1978 year-end Business Plan review letter, "We want to become the *lowest-cost operator*. There must be a way to do it, and when it is done, there must be a system which constantly interrogates our self-satisfaction to ensure that the momentum is maintained."

In fact, a decade later, total quality management (TQM)—one of whose principal cost-saving ideas is "getting it right the first time"—became a new tool in the ongoing drive to take cost out of the system. Its language and principles have continued to "interrogate self-satisfaction" and "ensure that momentum is maintained" by empowering employees and fueling new practices, such as benchmarking, which provides an industrywide framework for measuring everything from price to productivity.

Automation, in the warehouse and factory, continues to reduce overhead. Today, for example, Fremont's hot-filling line can produce 650 14-ounce ketchup bottles a minute or 24,000 cases a day. Altogether, the factory can produce about 130,000 cases a day. In fact, in one week, it can make all the ketchup Canada consumes in a year.

In the United Kingdom, Kitt Green's Euro-factory is a high-speed, high-volume operation. This is in direct contrast to Elst, whose mission is different. The Dutch factory has 100 different label sets for different configurations of the same Heinz product. Thus its great strength as a production center is its enormous flexibility, which enables it to produce short runs for different countries, with short lead times between order and delivery.

The most labor-intensive part of any Heinz factory is still between the assembly line and warehouse.

With fewer but larger customers, the economics of distribution also have changed. For example, when Grant Jackson joined the company in 1948, a minimum delivery order was five cases, "and we'd break a case of soup in half." Many of the products would be shipped on Heinz-owned trucks. Now, a minimum order (for best price) is 44,000 pounds, or about 1,200 cases. And most products go out by common carrier.

Connolly and his Heinz U.S.A. successors, Sculley (1985 to 1988) and Springer (1988 to date), have all pushed the low-cost-operator concept, in terms of quantification and benefits. In 1985, O'Reilly accurately anticipated the pressures that, in the 1990s, would seriously bedevil the food industry, and launched "The Year of the Operator." It again meant doing more with less, while in no way lowering product quality. The message got through. For example, Heinz led the way, according to Ketchum media director Mike Walsh, "in moving from 30-second commercials to 15-second spots."

In 1990, with 60 percent of all U.S. ketchup sold in plastic, Heinz unveiled another major packaging breakthrough: the EnviroPet bottle, the first fully recyclable plastic ketchup bottle to be introduced. Supported by a multibillion-dollar research program developed through years of research with a division of Continental Can, Heinz took a leadership role in helping to solve the environmental problem of solid-waste disposal. Heinz sells 400 million bottles of ketchup in North America, Europe, the Far East, Australia, and South America every year.

FOOD-SERVICE GROWTH SKYROCKETS

During the Connolly–Sculley–Springer years, food-service growth skyrocketed. In 1980, it had about $183 million in sales. Today, with between 500 and 700 product varieties, its sales are closer to $700 million. Jeff Berger, vice president of food service and part of the business since 1974, is a high-energy fountain of new ideas. Committed to a close partnership with his largest customers, such as Wendy's, he expects to reach sales of $1 billion in the near future.

Nearly half of food-service sales is ketchup, all Heinz branded. "We have ketchup in every conceivable size," said Berger. That includes the classic 14-ounce glass and plastic bottles, little room-service-size bottles, single-serve ketchup, the no. 10 can, and various sizes of Vol-Pak bags up to 450 ounces (or 28 pounds of ketchup) hanging on a wall rack. In fact, food service sells more ketchup than retail, "about four to five million cases more," according to Berger.

Until 1989, all portion-control food-service products—including mayonnaise, salad dressings, jams, jellies—were manufactured under the Heinz brand. Then the company bought Portion Pak, which produces private-label products. It doubled sales. Heinz is now the largest supplier of single-serve condiments in the United States, a business approaching $200 million.

It also sells a vast array of premium-priced tomato products manufactured by Escalon, which it purchased in 1991, and has pioneered the concept and practice of creating "signature" sauces (mainly tomato-based proprietary spaghetti, barbecue, and pizza sauce recipes) for restaurants, created by Heinz's certified master chef Byron J. Bardy.

During Heinz U.S.A.'s Sculley years, Bardy innovated a food-service R&D department that now works with the national accounts sales force to create new business.

Food service, about 42 percent of Heinz U.S.A.'s business, brings in about 48 percent of its profit.

HEINZ U.S.A. RECENTRALIZES

Ironically, or perhaps inevitably, the intense drive in the 1990s to remove further costs from the system and become a global low-cost operator brought increasing pressure to recentralize operations, thus eliminating duplication of effort. In other words, divisionalization had come full circle. Under Springer, Heinz U.S.A. returned to a leaner, centralized organizational structure. By now, however, as Crawshaw and others have pointed out, each product is better understood and well established. What is required in 1994 is the exact opposite of what was required in 1974.

Regardless of Heinz U.S.A.'s organizational style, it continues to prove, as one former ketchup product manager, Mike Milone,

Two elegantly designed, award-winning 1993 print advertisements for food-service ketchup in the United States.

Heinz U.S.A. is renowned for its tradition of fine chefs who continue to test and create new retail, as well as food-service, products. In 1960, chefs worked diligently in the Pittsburgh research center, then the hub of all product development activity.

put it, "that the product life cycle doesn't need to exist." In fact, during the mid- to late 1980s, with heavy advertising to kids and teenagers, Milone and his team helped to further increase category consumption. Now marketing vice president of Heinz Pet Products, he still marvels at the ketchup story. "You can chart a series of steps and plateaus, steps and plateaus, continually upward. Innovations kept revitalizing and reenergizing the life cycle."

They still do. Heinz U.S.A. continues to produce new varieties, while not turning its back on the past. For example, in 1993, Heinz came up with a salsa-style ketchup, as well as a 70-ounce "real salsa" plastic jug geared toward warehouse clubs. And it returned to the 20-year-old Leo Burnett advertising theme, the most remarkable in the history of the brand, using the lyrics and music from the song "Anticipation," written by Carly Simon.

During an era when brands have been under attack, Heinz continues to fend off low-cost rivals and retain its allure. Heinz U.S.A.'s retail market share is more than 50 percent, and Americans continue to consume about 10 billion ounces of ketchup each year.

HEINZ PICKLES

From the beginning, pickles and Heinz have been as inseparable as peanut butter and jelly. Indeed, in 1875, their abundance precipitated the company's bankruptcy. But the Founder never lost his appetite for the humble cucumber or his appreciation for the sweet-and-sour humor it afforded poets and punsters alike. The jokes, as well as the pickles, made the company famous.

The Holland, Michigan, factory (at left) began processing pickles for Heinz in 1896. It was one of many such facilities. 1925 marked the high tide of plant expansion, with over 226 salting and receiving stations in the United States and Canada, and a harvest of over 900,000 bushels. However, pickles gradually diminished in importance.

Once the company's flagship product, pickles became a regional Heinz business in the late 1970s (although relish remains a national brand). The Holland plant, a high-cost operation, turned itself around and today is a model of quality and efficiency. Due to the steady decline of pickle consumption over the past 30 years, this largest pickle plant in the world is now the U.S. company's only pickle factory. It turns out 40 different types of pickles and over 20 million jars a year.

ADVERTISING AROUND THE WORLD

In America, category consumption has been increased by emphasizing "thick and rich fun" for middle America's families, and targeting teenagers. One Burnett ad, called "Rooftop," which ran in the United States in 1987 and won a variety of industry awards, has gone worldwide and been successful in other markets, such as Italy and Japan.

Interestingly, ketchup is consumed in quite different ways from country to country. In Holland and Venezuela, for example, it's primarily used as a sauce on pasta. In Greece, ads show ketchup on pasta, eggs, and meat. In Sweden, ketchup accompanies meatballs and fishballs.

In Central Europe, according to managing director Jean-Claude Jamar, the emphasis is on ketchup "magic," and its basic positioning and tag line are, "It's the real thing." Other ads promote Heinz as "the taste of the big world," or emphasize its healthy ingredients, totally free of preservatives and artificial coloring.

Few consumers in Europe realize that Heinz ketchup is American. In fact, the French think it's a German product. The Germans think it's Dutch. The Swedes think it's German because of its name. The English think it's British. And so on.

Therefore, themes that work in one country often are meaningless in another. However, with Europe alone representing a market of 40 million, more attention is being paid to creating ads that, with altered copy and messages but identical visuals, can be used around the world.

Heinz has long been recognized for defying the law of gravity by continuing to "squeeze more from food categories that seem to have no room left for growth."[4] How does it manage to grow so-called mature products? Basically, by rejecting the concept. "There is no such animal," said Bill Springer. That is particularly true for ketchup, his number-one product.

---

4. Alison Otto, "Heinz Processor of the Year," *Prepared Foods*, September 1990.

Clearly, in the United States, Heinz ketchup is a success story that not only has laid to rest the myth of the mature market, but has demonstrated the incredible power of the Heinz brand. In the years ahead, fueled by global satellite/cable communications, it may well become, as O'Reilly put it, "a citizen of the world."[5]

---

5. "The Brand: Citizen of the World," A.J.F. O'Reilly to the 34th Congress of the International Center for Companies of the Food Trade and Industry, Berlin, June 11, 1990.

The Baby Food Story

"The depression," Howard Heinz revealed to syndicated columnist Merryle S. Rukeyser on December 12, 1938, "woke us up to opportunities which we had hitherto neglected."

Chief among them was baby food. In fact, as *Fortune* noted three years later, "The big success of the depression was the baby food lines, which last year accounted for more than 100 million cans out of an estimated national production of 300 million."[1]

Howard Heinz did not invent the business. Gerber, Libby, and Beech-Nut were active competitors when Heinz entered the field, but Howard dramatically demonstrated the value of the Heinz brand.

"What Heinz did," according to *Fortune*, "was to put baby food in grocery stores everywhere and cash in on the Heinz reputation."

In 1931, Heinz introduced four varieties—strained peas, carrots, mixed vegetables, and spinach—in 4.5-ounce enamel-lined tins. The company merchandised them vigorously, employing 77 men to contact doctors, pediatricians, and retail stores, plus 44

---

1. "The House of Heinz," *Fortune*, February 1941.

women to visit new mothers "after the blessed event,"[2] and give them a free can of food.

In 1938, when another depression hit the United States, Howard added a line of junior foods featuring larger portions with a chunkier texture. A few years later, Heinz began national distribution of precooked infant cereal, an industry first.

By 1941, Heinz boasted 14 varieties on grocery shelves. "However repulsive they may be to adults accustomed to steaks and pastries," commented *Fortune*, with humor, "they are agreeable enough to babies and doubly agreeable to mothers who have neither to prepare nor to eat them."[3]

Heinz may not have invented the product, but Howard understood that everything the company stood for and excelled at—purity and quality, nutrition, dedication to preserving freshness and retaining vitamins in processed food—added up to the single most important ingredient required in the sale and consumption of baby food: confidence.

Consumer confidence—on the part of parents, grandparents, the medical establishment, the media, public opinion leaders—is the name of the game in baby food. Around the world, new parents want to be absolutely certain—reassured and convinced—that commercial baby food is as healthy and nutritious as, and often better than, the homemade alternatives.

Overall, baby-food sales worldwide for all manufacturers is a $7 billion business with four main categories: infant formula; wet baby food (in jars and cans), including juices and drinks; dry baby food and cereals; rusks and biscuits. Eighty percent of the world baby-food market is in North America and Western Europe, with a combined annual birth rate of eight million. Heinz has over $875 million of that market, mainly in wet baby food. On a worldwide basis, the company is number one in two categories: jarred baby food; and rusks and biscuits.

Heinz manufactures and sells baby food around the world, mainly in the United States, Canada, Australia, New Zealand, Britain, Italy, Venezuela, Hungary, China, and Thailand. (It ex-

---

2. Ibid.

3. Ibid.

ports to other countries, including Russia, Israel, and Saudi Arabia.) In most of these countries, especially where Heinz and its affiliates have long-established baby-food businesses, it has dominated major product segments of the baby-food market. Oddly enough, however, the place where it all began, Heinz U.S.A., is not one of them. A key reason for this anomaly is bound up with company history.

According to Ben Fisher, a product manager of baby food between 1981 and 1985, when Heinz U.S.A. converted one of its Pittsburgh factories during World War II to building gliders and devoted much of its food-processing capacity to war rations, the company stopped making baby food. "That gave Gerber a virtual monopoly for four years," said Fisher. "When we reentered the business after the war, we never got our market share back." This is in contrast to Canada, the United Kingdom, Italy, and Australia, where Heinz is the market leader.

POSTWAR BABY FOOD

Heinz U.S.A. fought its way back up to between a 15 and 20 percent share during the postwar baby-boom years, which stretched through the 1960s. Demand for baby food also exploded around the world: business soared in the ABC affiliates—Australia, Britain, and Canada.

Heinz constantly launched new baby-food products and remained at the forefront of packaging and processing innovation. In 1954, Heinz U.S.A. became the first company in the industry to market nationally a complete line of baby foods in glass jars.

Not all new ideas worked. In 1965, Heinz U.S.A. introduced a ready-to-serve senior-foods product line based on the baby-food model, with nutritionally sound requirements for those of "advancing years." The eight-and-a-half-ounce tins, featuring beef stew, lamb stew, etc., were high in proteins, calcium, and iron; were low in calories; and were packed without salt. They bombed. It turned out that people did not want to be labeled "seniors," and that they insisted on good taste. The product line quietly faded away.

In 1958, Heinz U.S.A. was the first major producer to put its baby food in jars with screw caps. "Sales took off," recalled Karl Lang, then responsible for the development of new packaging concepts.

In 1959, the company published its first *Handbook of Nutrition,* for mothers, pediatricians, nursery dietitians, and physicians. The 439-page handbook, available in bookstores, was the first complete compilation of facts known about the then relatively new science of nutrition, written under the direction of the Heinz research staff in collaboration with leading authorities in the field.

Heinz also pioneered steam-injection cooking for better nutrition retention, pop-top safety lids, open-code dating and kosher varieties. By 1972, it had become the number-two brand in the United States, and in 1974, the company could boast, "On a worldwide basis, Heinz sells more baby food than any of its competitors."[4]

Yet, the environment was changing. A confluence of factors—the end of the baby boom, new infant formulas, pediatricians pushing back the introduction of strained foods from four weeks to four months—added up to a contracting market. Dick Patton, head of Heinz U.S.A. during the reorganization years, shifted strategy. He made the difficult decision to reduce volume and market share to become profitable. Basically, that entailed exiting a number of markets, including New York. That profitable strategy continues. (In the early 1980s, Heinz U.S.A. tried to revolutionize the baby-food market by developing a range of instant baby-food products. Launched nationally and well received at first, it never took off and was a major disappointment.)

Today, baby food is the third largest retail business for Heinz U.S.A., after ketchup and private-label soup. Heinz produces more than 125 varieties in six categories and is positioned as the value brand, according to general business manager Bob Roussey, who has presided over the baby-food business for seven years: that is, it is lower priced and on a quality parity with the brand leader.

---

4. H. J. Heinz Company Annual Report, 1974.

Heinz is able to offer such "value" to consumers and retailers because the big story of the past 10 years has been the way in which Heinz has cut costs. It has done so through a total quality management philosophy, which has uncovered more efficient ways of producing, packaging, distributing, and marketing baby food. It also has done so through a $116 million capital investment, converting a Pittsburgh warehouse into a computer-controlled, state-of-the-art factory (manufacturing baby foods, soups, and beans) with twin high-speed baby-food lines capable of filling and sterilizing 1,800 jars of baby food per minute. For most baby foods, the entire production process now takes just three hours, ensuring maximum freshness.

Heinz works closely with its growers to maintain product purity and safety. The company is exceedingly proud of its record. "There are a lot of pesticides and herbicides we do not allow," said chairman O'Reilly, "and we test independently for those all the time. It's called a crop-screening program, and there are many technicians for Heinz who spend all their time monitoring and assessing. That was why, five years before Alar became a controversy, we already had it taken out of the apples that we used in our baby products."

Throughout the world, Heinz never adds salt, artificial flavors, artificial colors, monosodium glutamate, or preservatives. Only the minimum amount of an all-natural sweetener is added to the 10 percent of fruits and desserts that, without them, would be too tart or acidic for a baby's palate.

BABY FOOD AROUND THE WORLD

Outside the United States, the three great baby-food success stories are Heinz Canada, Heinz Australia, and Heinz Italy. Heinz is also the nutrition and market leader in Heinz U.K., China, and New Zealand.

A 1950s Pittsburgh soup line versus a 1993 state-of-the-art, highly auto-mated kitchen in Pittsburgh, with 1,000-gallon cookers and twin high-speed baby-food and juice lines capable of filling and sterilizing 1,800 jars of baby food per minute. Computer-controlled and operated, for most baby foods the entire production process now takes just three hours, ensuring maximum freshness.

Heinz Canada and Australia

For most of its history, Heinz Canada has been, as its president, John Crawshaw, described it, "the 57 Varieties exemplified." There are few other resemblances.

Geographically, Canada is larger than the United States and twice the size of Australia. Demographically, 85 percent of the population lives within 100 miles of the U.S. border. Until the recent free-trade agreement, Canada has always had an east–west orientation, with distinct English and French-Canadian cultures.

Also, unlike pre-1980 Heinz U.S.A., Heinz Canada has been an extremely profitable affiliate. (There have been unprofitable episodes that were the exception rather than the rule.)

In part, this may be because, as Ned Churchill, executive vice president of the affiliate from 1978 to 1981, pointed out, "Heinz has always been one of the biggest food companies in Canada," with a dominant brand presence. In some areas, Heinz product per-capita consumption was even greater than in the United Kingdom, remarkable in view of Heinz dominance on U.K. grocery shelves. It may also be because Canadians, like the English, feel that Heinz is a Canadian company with an American subsidiary.

Baby food was first produced in cans in Canada in 1934 (it began with nine varieties). Junior foods were introduced in 1938. Heinz Canada also began to export baby food to the United Kingdom in the late 1930s. In 1955, Heinz Canada's Leamington Factory installed the world's fastest baby food lines, capable of filling and capping 1,000 tins a minute. It switched to glass jars in 1965, and introduced tamper-evident packaging in 1989.

Australia, modeled on the U.K. affiliate, began local baby-food production in 1941. It was the first manufacturer to do so, but wartime tinplate restrictions forced it to stop. Baby food was re-launched in 1949, with varieties imported from the United Kingdom, by J. A. Ross, a Scot who arrived to take over sales and marketing. Local production in Australia did not resume until 1951, and by 1956, the newly built Dandenong factory was turning out 28 varieties.

Every affiliate that manufactures baby food has added tamper-evident packaging. It is a necessity because, with purity, safety, and confidence so critical to the baby-food business, over the years, baby-food producers have attracted extortionists on many continents who prey on new parents and their fears for their children.

Heinz has developed sophisticated crisis-management and security teams to protect the company and consumers. Whenever a threat, often false, arises, an experienced crisis team swings into action. One notable incident occurred in England when a former Scotland Yard detective tried to extort money from the company. Following a well-publicized drama, he was apprehended and sentenced to 17 years in jail.

In Canada, it was only after World War II, under the aegis of Frank Sherk, the first president of Heinz Canada (1958 to 1962), that the product line took off. Indeed, in both the United Kingdom and Australia, major consumer acceptance really began in the early 1950s.

In those years, Heinz Canada was a sales-driven organization, with salesmen six feet tall or taller, in hats and suits, on the road, operating from 12 sales branches, making sales calls, setting up promotional displays, and doing Saturday samplings in grocery stores. According to retired CEO Tom Smyth, even office people were sales oriented and challenged to develop new promotional ideas. "I recall walking down a street in Vancouver," said Smyth, "and seeing bottles of Heinz ketchup in the windows of hairdressers and real estate offices."

In the mid-1950s, the affiliate gradually shifted to a wholesale distribution system, but, unlike most other Heinz affiliates, it still sells through a direct sales force, over 150 strong, which works closely with the retail trade.

Although at one point there were 10 baby-food manufacturers in Canada, Heinz became the number-one brand in the 1960s, in part due to Sherk's strategies. According to Peter Neufeld, recently retired vice president of sales, Sherk's sales-driven philosophy was simple: "The more varieties, the greater the shelf space, the more you increase business." It absolutely worked. Supported by an active R&D team, new-product innovation soared, and by 1960, Canada boasted "the most complete baby food line of any company in the world"[5] with 178 varieties.

---

5. 1960 Annual Report.

In the mid-1960s, all affiliates went through similar experiences: rising consumer demand plus new competitors in the marketplace, which they met with similar strategies to retain brand dominance. They included the introduction of baby food in glass jars, expansion of the product line, and, when necessary, price reductions.

By the mid-1960s, the United Kingdom was producing over 100 varieties and enjoyed a market share of 86. As an advertising slogan boasted, "10 cans or jars of Heinz baby food are made and sold every second of every minute of every day."

By the mid-1960s, under managing director Frederick Vernon Kellow who led the affiliate through the mid-1970s, Australia was up to about 100 varieties and remained ahead of the market by being the first to introduce junior foods (1955) and toddler foods (1963).

In 1966, Canada took a downturn and John Connell moved from England to sort out some of the cost sides of the problem. Once that had been accomplished, Albert "Bunny" Forsythe, director of sales and marketing in the United Kingdom, became president of Heinz Canada from 1968 to 1977.

Andrew Barrett, who in 1968 also crossed the Atlantic from Britain to join Heinz Canada, recalls that Heinz already had about an overall 70 percent share. Barrett moved up in Heinz Canada through 1980, and eventually returned in 1989 as president and CEO.

Forsythe set up Heinz Canada's first marketing division and put brand management into place. He provided another serious boost to the baby-food business and "was a breath of fresh air to all of us," said Neufeld. "The biggest recollection we all have of Bunny is that he looked at sales salaries and immediately increased them all. He felt that Heinz salesmen should be the best and be paid the best."

In the mid- to late 1970s, throughout the world, the public's environmental and health concerns began to spill over into the area of manufactured baby food. New questions were asked, such as whether salt and sugar levels were too high, or what real effects added calories, vitamins, and nutrients were having on infants. The truth was that no one knew because no studies had been done in any country. Heinz responded quickly, ahead of the competition.

In 1976, Barrett, then general manager of baby foods in Canada, launched a four-year project that, for the first time, would study, survey, collect data, and publish clinical information on infant feeding practices in national and international medical journals. To lead the research project, Heinz hired as a consultant Dr. David L. Yeung, an academic who had received his doctorate in human nutrition from the University of Toronto and was an associate professor in applied human nutrition at the University of Guelph in Ontario, Canada.

The short- and long-term results of Dr. Yeung's work were illuminating for the public and medical community, and exceedingly positive for the Heinz Company around the world. For the first time, the beneficial effects of infant nutrition were verified and published. This not only confirmed Heinz Canada's role as a good corporate citizen and partner with the scientific and medical community in promoting good nutritional practices to parents, but also mobilized and further extended the company's commitment and resources to improving infant nutrition.

Product changes followed. Salt and sugar were removed from baby foods. New types of foods were added in Canada and other affiliates. In 1977, for example, Australia pioneered the introduction of infant yogurts, then adopted by other affiliates. Heinz U.K. brought to market a gluten-free range of baby foods and also added baby yogurt desserts. Those desserts now account for one out of three jar sales. The emphasis on health—a global trend for children and adults—has generally resulted in more nutritious varieties and more fruit desserts, such as Australia's fruit fingers (a world first), juices, and full nutritional labeling.

Dr. Yeung worked closely with Heinz Canada's longest-serving president, Tom Smyth (1977–1988), a highly visible executive with close ties to the trade who remains an excellent ambassador for the company, especially in the area of nutrition. As Neufeld put it, "Tom saw opportunities rather than problems."

It was Smyth, for example, who in the mid-1970s first suggested to Dr. Harvey Anderson of the University of Toronto the formation of a national organization, the National Institute of Nutrition (NIN), to develop and promote credible, independent information about nutrition for laypersons, the medical community, health professionals, and opinion leaders. In 1981, he backed the formation of the Infant Nutrition Institute, which is devoted to educating health professionals about new developments in this field. Today, supported by Heinz Canada and supervised by Dr. Yeung, it publishes a quarterly newsletter, supports conferences, pediatric nutrition courses, and other educational events.

It was Smyth, too, armed with independent information, who waged a campaign to convince the public that manufactured baby food was a healthy, nutritious weaning product, often better than homemade products.

At the same time, Heinz Canada made every effort to educate the public about the benefits of breast-feeding and other sound practices. Heinz affiliates around the world recognized that a key part of their mission was to become partners with new mothers eager for information on how best to feed and care for their infants. Heinz U.K., for example, has a home health-visitor program.

Dr. Yeung's temporary consulting job has stretched into a permanent and ever-widening mission. Today, as director of corporate nutrition, still headquartered in Canada, he is a companywide resource and consults with every Heinz affiliate. Indeed, Yeung and Heinz colleagues continue to support new clinical studies; annual symposiums in China, Hungary, Thailand, and Russia; nutrition newsletters in Australia, Canada, China, and Thailand; nutrition seminars and courses; literature; teaching aids; academic exchanges and new alliances in order both to raise nutrition awareness and increase technical knowledge.

Yeung was instrumental in establishing the Heinz Institute of Nutritional Services in China, as well as similar programs in Thailand, Russia, and Hungary. Australia, Italy, and the United Kingdom support similar institutes or advisory services. In the United States, the Heinz Institute of Nutritional Sciences was recently established as a nonprofit organization in Pennsylvania.

As a result of these activities, Canadian market share grew and margins improved with brand leadership.

Today, according to John Lewarne, vice president of food service, who joined the company in 1978 when the up-tick on baby food was in full swing, Heinz Canada's baby-food market share is 90 percent of the grocery business. It sells about 4.6 million cases a year, or about 110 million jars. In addition, it has the number-one share position, over 50 percent, in the infant-cereal business. (Infant cereal is an iron-fortified starter food.) Altogether, that adds up to about 15 percent of Heinz Canada's product-line profitability.

Today, Heinz Australia, led by managing director Terry Ward, manufactures 118 varieties, which give it enormous shelf space and visibility to 17.5 million Australians. Its market shares are impressive, with 89 percent of the wet-baby-food segment, 91 percent of baby drinks/juices, 100 percent of baby cereals, and 70 percent of baby rusks and biscuits.

Indeed, over several decades during which Heinz Australia entered and exited a variety of businesses, including wine and restaurants, baby food has remained a consistent core-product winner and marketing success.

In New Zealand, Wattie's-brand baby food entered the market in 1958. It is one of the leading baby-food brands in that country.

Trade concentration has steadily increased in Canada, the United Kingdom, and Australia. That is why a close alliance with major customers is one of the keys to success. In Canada, for example, where five retailers represent close to 65 percent of the retail business, the sales force not only is strongly customer focused, but is at the leading edge of technology. Heinz Canada recognized the information power that its customers were developing through scanning, so they developed a retail information group that has become a valuable resource for customers. Basically, it targets, down to store level, relevant demographics about consumers. Thus Heinz has become an important partner with retailers, adding value to the relationship by helping customers better target segments of market.

Barrett, now Heinz U.K. managing director, calls this "relationship marketing" approach the wave of the future. Not only does it add value for both the customer and the consumer, but it gives the entire marketing function more of a bottom-line business focus.

Heinz Canada continues to maintain its leading position through a strong product range—160 varieties—that covers all stages of infant feeding, constant innovation, and continual communication with new mothers and health professionals through direct-mail activity. As Lewarne put it, "Our communications provide added value to the consumer."

With competition on the rise around the world, either through private-label or new players, remaining a low-cost producer is equally critical to defending market share.

"Being proactive and ahead of the curve," said Crawshaw, "is a real mark of leadership." That is as true in Canada as it is in Australia, the United Kingdom, and the United States.

"There is no standing still," said Springer. "If you don't create a self-driven revolution, then outside events overtake you." Or, to paraphrase Dick Patton, change is the opportunity.

Heinz Italy

Internationally, Heinz Italy is the outstanding baby-food success story in the company. And it is a unique story as well. In fact, so successful is the company that when Italians talk about a healthy baby, they call it "a Plasmon baby." (Interestingly, between 1946 and 1966, the postwar average Italian became four inches taller, and today, the average Italian is even taller. Perhaps protein-laced Plasmon biscuits, baby foods, and pastas have made a difference!)

To understand this story, we must first look back briefly at the company's origins.

Malnourishment and protein-calorie deficiencies—with children and adults suffering from rickets, anemia, and stunted growth—were commonplace in 19th-century Europe. Next to nothing was known about nutrition. In 1870, a German scientist invented a process to isolate plasmon, a milk protein derivative, which he then used to enrich a variety of foods, especially for tuberculosis patients. In other words, he fortified foods with added nutrition and calories, and the results proved highly beneficial. Today, Heinz Italy is the only company in the world that can use the Plasmon trademark. Plasmon is produced in granulated form, pulverized into powder, and then added to various baby-food products.

In 1902, an Italian financial group, under the name Sindacato Italiano del Plasmon, organized a business to manufacture and market Plasmon-enriched products in Italy (as did other companies in other European countries). In one form or another, the company continued to manufacture products through two world wars. By the 1960s, owned and run by a lawyer as a small family business, it was turning out a quality line of plasmon-enriched baby-food products from a factory in Milan.

In 1961, Jack Heinz, bent on European expansion and seeking a toehold in Italy, asked Dr. Oscar Pio, a British-educated, Italian businessman from Malta, to find a suitable Italian company for acquisition. Pio found Plasmon, 80 percent of whose business was baby biscuits, plus pasta for infants and a few strained foods. In 1963, Heinz bought the company. The general idea was to introduce Heinz core products into Italy and install an up-to-date baby-food plant in the Milan factory.

Two years later, Lino Ghirardato, now president and general manager of Plada, Heinz Italy's dietetic- and infant-food division, joined the fledgling company as Milan factory engineer. He worked with the Heinz U.S.A. team—Ray Locke, Ray Preston, Bob Rolfe, and George Trebilcox—sent to install the baby food line, organize the company, and introduce to Italian management Heinz accounting and quality-control practices.

Heinz U.S.A. brought to Italy the essential technology of making strained baby foods. Baby food in Italy is pure strained fruit (including juices) and meat, baby biscuits, pastas, and baby cereals. There is a cultural bias against strained vegetables and food combinations, standard in other countries, for infants.

According to Chuck Berger, who joined Heinz Italy in 1972 as vice president, sales and marketing, "Initially it was a wonderful acquisition. The company had a wonderful brand name for its baby biscuits, and with added Heinz technology, Plasmon became the immediate leader in strained baby food."

It was the heyday of Heinz decentralization. Italy received perhaps one or two visits a year from executive vice president Junius Allen to discuss the annual budget, according to Dr. Peter Borasio, now a board member of Heinz Italy, then part of senior management.

"Gookin sent me a letter every year," recalled Luigi "Gigi" Ribolla, now head of Heinz Italy, who joined the company in 1967, and was then company controller. "Gookin asked us to increase results 6 percent."

To meet growing demand, Heinz Italy built a highly automated factory in Latina, south of Rome, three miles from the sea. A one-story, modular, Lego-like structure, the plant went into operation in 1969. A high-speed biscuit line was added in 1972 and further enlarged in 1982.

Latina manufactures about 70 percent of the baby-food line and, under the direction of plant manager Attilio Redondi and his TQM administrator, Daniela Bernardo, it is a model of efficiency.

In Italy, where babies are worshiped, according to Claudio Serafini, Plada's chief operating officer, baby food is treated with the kind of care Americans reserve for prescription drugs. Any new variety, for example, must be approved by the Ministry of Health in Rome. Government approvals, according to Alex Micardi, director of plant operations who joined the company in 1967, are extensive and ongoing. In addition to initial detailed documentation, 250 sample checks and tests are taken each year by regional and national inspectors in plants, supermarkets, and pharmacies. "Italy," said Micardi, "is more quality conscious in the area of dietetic products than anywhere else in the world."

Baby food is sold at premium prices in pharmacies (the U.K. also sells baby food in pharmacies), as well as in supermarkets, for somewhat less.

Overall, however, and in direct contrast to most other countries where baby food is usually a low-price, high-volume product, baby food in Italy is regarded as a complex, value-added product, and, therefore, an expensive, high-margin product.

So despite the fact that Italy, with a population of 58 million, has the world's lowest birth rate (which has been steadily declining since 1965), baby-food sales have constantly increased. Today, in fact, it is a $900 million market, or 25 percent of the total European market. (The United Kingdom, by contrast, with a similar population and family income plus a higher birth rate, is only a $650 million market.)

The 1960s were baby-boom years, and new competition jumped into the marketplace, including Gerber, Buitoni, and Erba. In 1968–1969, eyeing the growth in grocery sales, Plasmon em-

The Latina factory, south of Rome, boasts a high-speed biscuit line that is the biggest in Europe. The oven alone is 140 meters, or almost 500 feet long. This totally automated operation is so long, in fact, that it is monitored by a man who checks the ovens by riding up and down on a bicycle. Latina manufactures about 70 percent of Italy's baby-food line and is a model of quality and efficiency.

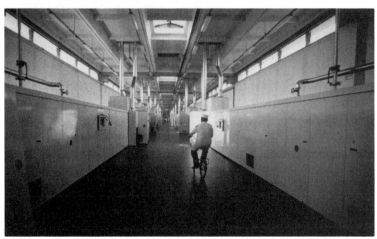

barked on an ill-conceived strategy: placing less emphasis on pharmacy sales and expanding distribution at the grocery level. Berger was called in after Plasmon's market share had plummeted from 70 to about 45.

Berger, who learned Italian from scratch, partly attributes his rapid fluency to the positive support of his colleagues at work. Delighted by his efforts, they would say, with typical Italian generosity, "It's a miracle, you speak like Dante." The entire family fell in love with Italy.

Berger edged market share up by emphasizing the high-margin biscuits and expanding the baby-food line. (The biscuits are enriched with about 12.5 percent of protein. According to Ghirardato, they once had 14 to 15 percent, but that was reduced because babies today are overfed rather than undernourished.)

Berger worked closely with Nick Pellizzati, then head of the company, and Ribolla. He discovered that antitrust laws work differently in Italy, making it possible to design a strategy that included buying a competitor. In 1974, they bought the dietetic division, Dieterba (a premium product sold only in pharmacies), from Carlo Erba. It launched Heinz Italy on its singular and remarkably successful path.

Basically, the company's baby-food strategy with its range of brands—Plasmon, Dieterba, Nipiol—has been to gain a market share in excess of all its competitors combined. Which it does with an astounding 93 percent share.

But there have been dramatic twists and turns along the way.

In 1975, Berger, much to his surprise, became the first non-Italian to head the company. He spent three more years carrying out the game plan he and Ribolla had devised. That involved, in addition to baby food, diversifying into other high-margin, dietetic-type foods, such as Misura, a line of low-calorie health products, which it launched in 1976, shrewdly anticipating the health and wellness market.

Berger, who expected to return to the United States within a few years, recognized Ribolla's exceptional qualities as a leader and manager. In 1978, Ribolla replaced Berger when he left to head the company's newest U.S. acquisition, Weight Watchers.

Ribolla drastically reduced fixed costs, increased return on investment, and looked around for new acquisitions. He recalls his first meeting with O'Reilly in Pittsburgh, to discuss a possible acquisition. "In 10 minutes he destroyed the reasoning behind the acquisition," said Ribolla, with a smile.

Since then, Ribolla's skills have come to be so highly regarded in the company that he keeps being given added areas of responsibility: first Portugal, then Spain and Greece, and, most recently, as senior vice president of Europe and a member of the board of directors.

Ribolla continued to strengthen Plada's presence in the baby-food market, without increasing fixed costs, by acquiring, in 1983, Nipiol (owned by Buitoni), a less expensive brand sold only in supermarkets. In 1991, Plada completed its baby-food line by entering the liquid-infant-formula business, again through acquisition.

Today, Plada has grown way beyond its infant-food origins. With nutrition the core of its business, it also manufactures Misura's products, isotonic drinks, artificial sweeteners, fiber-rich biscuits, as well as dietetic and therapeutic "medical" foods for those with special needs, such as kidney patients. These medical foods are endorsed by the Mayo Clinic and sold in the United States.

ECOLOGICAL OASIS

The baby-food business was growing by leaps and bounds when a crisis hit the industry in 1980. Traces of estrogen were discovered in strained meats because breeders were giving estrogens to their animals. Mothers simply stopped buying. What to do?

In one of the most brilliant examples of turning a crisis into an opportunity, Ribolla came up with a long-term solution to the overall problem of quality control in baby food by creating a model farm-to-factory program, called "ecological oasis."

Basically, it entails tight controls over suppliers and the conditions under which they grow or raise their food. Riccardo Laurita, head of quality, constructed the environmental-oasis plan.

There are rules and regulations for how animals must be housed and fed. There are complex prohibitions with regard to additives and pesticides in fruits and milk. A large laboratory in Milan, headed by Dr. Franco Taccani, constantly tests ingredients for

Heinz Italia's rainbow symbol for "Ecological Oasis Plasmon" elegantly conveys the message of farm-to-factory purity and quality; it was introduced in the mid-1980s.

metals, chemicals, parasites, viruses, and hormones. Two agronomists travel around Italy making surprise visits to Plasmon's environmental-oasis farmers and ranchers. "We had to completely reconstruct the market," said Micardi. And they did.

Ribolla bucked his marketing people, who wanted a quick fix. "No, I prefer to create the future," he said, and brought in a new marketing team, while investing time and money in creating and perfecting his sophisticated crop-screening program.

Plasmon did not begin to advertise and promote the purity of its products until the mid-1980s. However, the wisdom of Ribolla's decision was reinforced on April 25, 1986, the day the accident at Chernobyl awoke many in Europe, especially mothers of infants, to safety issues concerning fresh produce and milk and dairy products.

The company reassured the public that it was checking its products, and temporarily stopped the production of formula milk. Sales of Plasmon's "pure and nutritious" foods, protected by its renowned environmental oasis, increased. In fact, between 1987 and 1992, Plasmon doubled sales, and has continued to increase market share. Since Chernobyl, public opinion has changed 100 percent. Mothers now say to themselves, "If I give my child ready-to-use food, instead of pure and secure strained meat prepared by a pure and secure company, then I am not a good mother." And experts agree.

Today, like Heinz affiliates around the world, Plasmon works closely with mothers, pharmacists, and the medical community. Each year, for example, it sponsors a week-long nutrition course for 300 pediatricians, those just finishing their specialty training, and also sponsors a nutrition data bank.

In Italy, Plasmon has truly carved out a unique place for itself, as both a nutrition and a marketplace leader. In fact, guided by Ribolla and his team, Heinz Italy—with its high-margin foods— has become the most profitable food company in Italy and the most profitable affiliate in the Heinz family.

Heinz in China

Given the H. J. Heinz Company's leadership role in baby food and nutrition, it is not surprising that, in 1984, it became the first western company invited into the People's Republic of China to manufacture and produce dry infant cereal.

China, with an annual birth rate of 24 million and a fairly strict one-child-per-family policy, dotes on its infants. These pampered children, indulged by parents and grandparents, are called "little emperors."

On the other hand, according to Wah-hui Chu, former president of Heinz-UFE Ltd., who joined Heinz in 1985, a United Nations study showed that while Chinese newborns develop much like babies in the West until four months of age, their postweaning development drops off significantly because, one, they drink less milk, and two, there is a general lack of fortified weaning food in China. Therefore, a priority area for the Chinese government was to bring into China western technology to manufacture fortified products in the weaning food area.

The joint venture was proposed, negotiated, and signed in record time, roughly seven months, with Derek Finlay, senior vice president, heading the team.

Finlay, one of the few U.K. McKinsey types to make the trek westward from London to Pittsburgh, arrived at World Headquarters in 1981. He participated in a seminal study that pointed out that 85 percent of the world's population had not been exposed to Heinz brands. Moreover, those nations without the Heinz brand were in parts of the world that were growing twice as fast as Western Europe and North America. China, of course, was the largest example, and the decision was made to look for opportunities in Asia.

One day, a consultant from Hong Kong, Y. C. Wong, suggested by letter to Finlay that he could provide contacts for Heinz in China. It was a routine letter, but, on his way to Hong Kong for other Heinz business, Finlay followed up, bought Wong two gin and tonics at the bar of the Mandarin Hotel, and discovered that, indeed, he had papers to do business in Guangdong Province, the most entrepreneurial southern province in China, directly across the border from Hong Kong. The parties Wong represented were interested in manufacturing fortified baby food.

Finlay urged Roy King, a towering ex-U.K. salesman, with the company 40 years (the first 30 in the United Kingdom, the last 10 as area director in East Asia), to take a look. A few weeks later, Finlay got a call from King in Guangzhou saying, "You won't believe this, but these people want me to sign a contract to go into the baby-food business."

Well, it wasn't quite that simple. Finlay had a list of requests a mile long. Two days later, King called back and said, "You won't believe this, but they've agreed to everything you asked for in this province. If you want to talk about access to the whole domestic market, we'll have to go to Beijing."

And that is exactly what they did. Finlay, King, and their new Guangdong Province Chinese partners made the journey and presented their request to the appropriate ministers, "which was very strongly argued on our behalf," said Finlay.

China had only been open to the West for four years. Joint ventures were few and far between, and normally took years to negotiate. Living conditions, by western standards, were primitive.

Derek Finlay (left), Tony O'Reilly (center), and Jack Heinz (right) joined together in July 1986 for a ribbon-cutting ceremony at the opening of the first baby-food factory in the People's Republic of China. Corporate technical director Lee Harrow recalls that the dedication day of the Guangzhou plant was a "killer, hot humid day." He recorded the event with his camera and noted the endurance of ailing Jack Heinz, then in his 70s. "It was thrilling for Mr. Heinz, with his love of nutrition, to see the inscription on the building: The Heinz Nutritious Food Factory."

Western-style hotels were nonexistent. It was a moment of rapid change. John Mazur, then a lawyer with the negotiating team, recalls that during the year and a half he traveled back and forth to China, the population went from almost uniformly dressing in Mao outfits to, as he put it, wearing "brighter and brighter western clothes."

After a week in Beijing, and after the first banquet in the Great Hall of the People, Finlay got their piece of paper. A formal contract was signed on August 31, 1984. Construction of the factory began in September 1985, and 10 months later, on June 28, 1986, Heinz opened the factory, built from scratch, in Guangzhou (formerly Canton), capital of China's Guangdong Province, to produce four instant rice and soy cereal products.

Building and launching the factory was something of a bureaucratic nightmare. "The old-fashioned Chinese bureaucracy," said King, "was highly political in those days. There were party members, auditors, accountants, planning bureaus, municipal authorities, all kinds of approvals and licenses required."

Fortunately, Finlay could draw on experienced managers with Asian backgrounds, like Ed Tsang, already working at Heinz. Tsang, born in Hong Kong, fluent in Cantonese, and a Canadian citizen and engineer who had joined Heinz Canada in 1980, became the first factory manager in 1986.

The company's early logos and labels reflected the Founder's visual flair. Printed by lithographic stones, often with 20 colors, their registration and deep jewel-like tones are a marvel.

The H. J. Heinz Company on Pittsburgh's Progress Street, illustrated by the company art department in about 1895. Between 1890 and 1898, 17 structures arose around a green, open courtyard.
A model factory complex in every respect, including efficiency; the Baltimore and Ohio Railroad, for example, ran directly into the Vinegar Building.

GREETINGS FROM HEINZ OCEAN PIER ATLANTIC CITY, N.J.

In 1898, the Founder bought the Iron Pier in Atlantic City, New Jersey, and renamed it the Heinz Ocean Pier. Upon it he constructed an elegant environment in which to appreciate the company's products. Free to the public, it glowed at night with a 70-foot-high "57" sign on its roof. During the day, visitors could stroll on the boardwalk, lounge in the reading room or on the sun deck in rocking chairs, and visit several enclosed sections of the pier, including a glass pavilion with oriental rugs, ceramics, figurines, and a gigantic painting, "Custer's Last Stand." Other delights included a permanent exhibit of Heinz products, pickle pins and free product samples, daily organ recitals, community sings, lectures, motion pictures, souvenir postcards (like the 1902 edition above), and, during World War II, writing rooms with free stationery for servicemen and -women. Fondly known as the "Crystal Palace by the Sea," visited by millions of Americans, it was seriously damaged by a 1944 hurricane and dismantled the following year.

The Founder, who loved stained glass and became an important patron, employed Horace Rudy to carry out his commissions, which were completed in 1906. Still visible along the staircase of Heinz U.S.A.'s administration building and in the Sarah Heinz House are stained-glass windows inscribed with the Founder's inspirational mottoes, such as, "Our Field the Globe" and "Luck May Help a Man Over a Ditch If He Jumps Well." Charles Jack Connick, who later created the Heinz Chapel's stained-glass windows, apprenticed to Rudy, who moved to Pittsburgh in 1893 to complete a commission for the H. J. Heinz plant.

Elegant color drawings of Heinz products as depicted in the 1895 *Heinz Illustrated Catalogue,* a bound book—in itself a work of art—used by Heinz "travelers" to sell products, as well as the quality image of the company, to the trade. The products included Apple Butter (in stone jars), Strawberry Preserves (in wood pails), Preserved Sweet Pickles (octagon bottle), and Evaporated Horseradish. Illustrations from the 1910 catalog included such exotic products as Stuffed Mangoes (small melon mangoes cored and filled with finely chopped sweet pickle, spiced and seasoned, then preserved in Heinz sweet pickling liquor) and Euchred Pickle (preserved in a piquant sweet liquor made with Heinz malt vinegar, granulated sugar, and pure spices), as well as Pure Apple Cider Vinegar and Sweet Midget Gherkins.

Is there such a thing as "He-Ketchup"? Today's politically correct consumers might be horrified, but during the depths of the depression, when Howard Heinz increased his advertising blitz, he targeted the country's most desirable market segment: employed, white-collar males. The ad ran in a January 16, 1932, issue of *The Saturday Evening Post.*

HEINZ KETCHUP IS ALL KETCHUP

When you open a bottle of Heinz Tomato Ketchup and pour it on your food, notice how slowly it comes out of the bottle.

That's because Heinz ketchup is *all ketchup*— just the tomatoes and their own juice, thoroughly cooked, deliciously spiced, and sweetened with real

sound, luscious tomatoes raised from seeds developed by us and grown under our supervision—the water is cooked out of them. Otherwise it would thin down the rich tomato substance and reduce the flavor.

Real tomato flavor, nourishing goodness, and ... t you get

... MPANY

A 1926 U.S. Heinz ketchup food-service advertisement, the first in a 12-month campaign (a different ad each month) that not only depicted the thickness and taste of Heinz ketchup, but explained why it was so rich and thick: "The water is cooked out." Other ketchup manufacturers, by contrast, still used additives such as cornstarch to thicken their ketchup. Notice how the bottom copy emphasizes "how slowly it comes out of the bottle," and the top label, "free from benzoate of soda."

Howard Heinz fought the depression with a new product line, baby food. First introduced in 1931, vigorously merchandised and advertised, Heinz boasted 14 varieties by 1941. Here is a warm and cozy 1936 ad for the 10-product "quality" line.

Alimenti supermutritivi al PLASMON

BISCOTTI · PASTINE · CREMA DI RISO · FARINE · CACAO

"I know My groceries

—and I want the same quality of foods my parents demand. Three cheers for better tasting strained foods made by Heinz!"

MAYBE he can't talk yet, but give him Heinz Strained Foods and you'll see that he knows his groceries! He'll coo and crow with delight. For it does seem that children—even very small ones—definitely prefer the taste of Heinz Strained Foods!

And that's natural. Don't you prefer the fine "home" flavor of Heinz-made foods? Don't you enjoy how Heinz slowly simmered soups, oven-baked beans and the "pedigreed" goodness of Heinz Tomato Juice?

Baby deserves the same good quality in foods that tempts your appetite. Heinz Strained Foods for

infants and toddlers justare adapted by the American Medical Association's Committee on Foods. In most stores, these fine Heinz-made products cost only a few pennies more than "bargain" kinds. Your peace of mind is worth far more than this small difference! Order some today. Two kinds.

1. Strained Vegetable Soup.   6. Strained Beets.
2. Strained Peas.   7. Strained Prunes.
3. Strained Green Beans.   8. Strained Tomatoes.
4. Strained Spinach.   9. Strained Cereal.
5. Strained Carrots.   10. Apricots and Applesauce.

Heinz STRAINED FOODS

An Italian 1949 postwar Plasmon advertisement for biscuits, baby pasta, cream of rice, farina, and cocoa, which promoted the high nutrition of the brand.

The first 1964 ketchup plate ad, created by Doyle, Dane and Bernbach. The copy said, "Actual photograph of water running out of other catsup, 3 minutes and 39 seconds after both were poured. One reason you may pay a little more for Heinz." The print ad tied in with an equally effective television version of this depiction of Heinz thickness as compared with the leading competitor. In 1980, the Leo Burnett advertising agency updated the concept and created a similar print ad campaign.

Actual photograph of water running out of other catsup, 3 minutes 39 seconds after both were poured.

One reason you may pay a little more for Heinz.

In Japan, where Heinz first introduced ketchup in 1962, it is mostly used in cooking sauces. However, consumers are now being introduced to its uses as an ingredient in Western-style foods, for dips or on hot dogs. In 1993, Heinz Japan made a hilarious, award-winning commercial to launch the 14-ounce bottle—an open-cockpit plane turns upside down and the pilot holds a hot dog laden with ketchup that is so thick and rich it doesn't budge.

Henry John "Jack" Heinz II, in 1980, admiring a collection of early Heinz bottles and advertising art, now part of the permanent collection of the Historical Society of Western Pennsylvania.

Chairman Tony O'Reilly is fond of saying that "Heinz is a world brand and world of brands." It makes over 3,000 varieties of canned, dry, and frozen food in almost every product category. Sixty-five percent of annual sales comes from products without the Heinz brand name, such as Weight Watchers, StarKist, Ore-Ida, and Plasmon, and about 60 percent of the company's sales are in number-one brands—often by a wide margin.

Heinz ketchup containers used in company advertising from the earliest days of the company to the present. From left to right: circa 1876 (keystone bottle); 1887 (stone jug); 1888; 1890 (octagon bottle, first time used); 1895 (imperial bottle); 1920 (octagon bottle); 1993 (classic 14-ounce glass bottle).

The word ketchup is said to derive from *koe-chiap* or *ke-tsiap* in Chinese or the Malayan word *kechap,* spelled *ketjap* in Dutch, which meant brine or pickled fish or shellfish. During the late 17th century, the condiment arrived in England. English seamen discovered natives of Singapore using the sauce and tried to imitate it with mushrooms, walnuts, cucumbers, and tomatoes. It was first printed as "catchup" in 1690, and then as "ketchup" in 1711. In Mrs. Harrison's 1748 *Housekeeper's Pocketbook,* homemakers were told never to be without it. In America, a recipe for tomato catsup first appeared in 1792 in *The New Art of Cookery* by Richard Briggs. Maine sea captains began planting tomato seeds from Mexican tomatoes and enjoyed *kechap* on codfish cakes, baked beans, and meat. Today, the sauce is a combination of cooked and strained tomatoes with vinegar, sugar or corn syrup, salt, onion, garlic, and a variety of natural spices.

In the Founder's day, the Heinz Company used its magnificent Percheron teams and massive freight wagons as rolling billboards. Percherons were originally bred as warhorses to carry knights with 400 pounds of armor into battle. At one time, Heinz had over 150 teams of Percherons operating out of its Pittsburgh facilities. The Heinz stables, known as "equine palaces," were a showplace. They featured steam heat, electrically operated brushes, and the finest feed and care available. The horse operations were discontinued in the 1920s and replaced by trucks.

Today, John Dryer (left), a retired company executive, presides over the Heinz Hitch, which he drives, stables, and single-handedly re-created. Jack Heinz (center) only rode the Hitch once, at the 1980 opening of the Heinz museum at Heinz U.S.A. headquarters in Pittsburgh. It was the last company event in which he participated before his death, the following year.

The Hitch, an eight-horse wagon team of pure-blooded Percherons, performs at county fairs, parades, and on special company occasions. Fifteen million people have enjoyed the Hitch during its round-the-year schedule of appearances throughout the United States.

Chinese children who participated in the opening ceremonies, in July 1986, of the first baby-food factory in the People's Republic of China. The Heinz plant, located in Guangzhou (formerly Canton) in the entrepreneurial southern region of China, manufactures nutritionally fortified dry infant cereal. China, with an annual birth rate of 24 million and a one-child-per-family policy, dotes on its infants.

In 1970, Ann Miller danced on top of a Great American Soup can. Producer Stan Freeberg conceived and created this technically complex and costly television ad, which included a huge can rising through the floor and a large cast of dancers. At the time, the commercial, shot in Hollywood's Sam Goldwyn Studios, was deemed the most expensive ever made in the United States. Despite the lavish campaign and an excellent ready-to-serve product, Great American Soup never caught on with the public and was discontinued as a retail product. Today, the name is reserved for the company's line of food-service soups.

The Founder was a great believer in the power of expositions to promote the Heinz name and its products. Howard carried on his father's tradition, making certain that Heinz and its 57 Varieties had a prominent location in two 1939–1940 World's Fairs on opposite sides of the country: New York and San Francisco. Pickle pins were plentiful, and the Heinz animated Mr. Aristocrat Tomato Man greeted visitors.

In 1961, Tom Rogers created Charlie the Tuna for Leo Burnett's newest client, StarKist. The public immediately loved Charlie, but only when the campaign went into its second phase, emphasizing that "StarKist doesn't want tunas with good taste, StarKist wants tunas that taste good," did the product take off.

Morris the 9-Lives Cat first hit the airwaves in 1969, another Leo Burnett invention. Morris became such a celebrity that when the original Morris died in the late 1970s, instead of quietly switching cats, Burnett and Edelman Public Relations did a public star-search replacement, which created further favorable attention and publicity. Morris appeared on talk shows, was featured on network television's "Lifestyles of the Rich and Famous," ran for president in 1988 and 1992, and continues to do promotions and publicity, from broker and veterinary conventions to food-shows and philanthropic sponsorships.

Members of the H. J. Heinz Board of Directors: (*front row, left to right*) Donald R. Keough, Herman J. Schmidt, Eleanor B. Sheldon, Anthony J. F. O'Reilly, William P. Snyder, III, Samuel C. Johnson, Albert Lippert; (*back row*) Lawrence J. McCabe, Luigi Ribolla, David R. Williams, William C. Springer, William R. Johnson, David W. Sculley, Joseph J. Bogdanovich, Edith E. Holiday, S. Donald Wiley, Nicholas F. Brady, Richard M. Cyert.

The factory is a mini–United Nations, housing the best technology from China, Japan, the United States, Holland, and France. It is also sensitive to local practices. Then-president Wah-hui Chu canceled the original lunchroom design based on western models and had wok stations installed so that workers could cook their food. "The Chinese hate cold food," he said.

While the food business is not regarded as a high-tech business, it requires across-the-board chemical, biological, mechanical, and electronic technology that is complex to operate.

Wah-hui Chu brought western marketing, advertising, and pricing practices into China, using television (98 percent of the urban population owns a TV set), billboards, and radio. As a matter of fact, Heinz was one of the first companies to use television, and the campaigns were most successful.

Heinz also pioneered new methods of sales and distribution since, at the time, the very concept of sales—versus allocation—was quite foreign. Products are distributed to about 25 cities and, geographically, cover about 45 percent of China.

After some difficult bumps in the early stages, the company did so well that, in 1988, the factory expanded twice, doubling and tripling its original capacity.

A unique aspect of the joint venture is that Heinz also established the Heinz Institute of Nutritional Sciences (HINS), a nonprofit organization funded by the H. J. Heinz Company Foundation and the local company. Its sole purpose is to support research and disseminate nutrition information and education. In other words, its basic aim is to help the Chinese—academics, parents, the health profession—better understand and improve nutrition practices. Chaired by Dr. Yeung, it runs annual symposiums in different Chinese cities, bringing in experts from around the world.

The joint-venture model, in one form or another, is being replicated in places like Thailand and Hungary, where Heinz is already manufacturing baby food and other products.

Clearly, baby food is a high road into less-developed nations and an investment in the future. As Roy King said, "You have to take a long-term view. We need to put our roots down now. In 20, 30 years' time, we'll be glad we did."

The Weight Watchers Story

The story of Weight Watchers—how it began and grew into a multimillion-dollar business—is both a classic Cinderella story and legendary business story. Frank Capra could have written the script.

Jean Nidetch has told her inspirational tale many times, and in 1970 published a book, which became a bestseller, about the founding of Weight Watchers and its program.[1]

Nidetch's personal transformation never fails to move and inspire people: how perpetually fat, perpetually dieting Jean, a 40-year-old Queens, New York, homemaker, confided in and talked to a bunch of friends about her problems sticking to a New York City Department of Health Obesity Clinic diet. And how, by adding a group self-help dimension to the regime—that is, generous doses of empathy, understanding, compassion, encouragement, and love—she lost 72 pounds.

Parenthetically, according to Dr. Barbara Moore, nutritionist

---

1. *The Story of Weight Watchers* by Jean Nidetch, as told to Joan Rattner Heilman, W/W Twentyfirst Corporation, distributed by New American Library in association with the World Publishing Company, 1970.

and former general manager of program development for Weight Watchers International, the Obesity Clinic diet was developed in 1953 by nutritionist Dr. Norman Joliffe for the Bureau of Nutrition of the New York City Department of Health, which ran free obesity clinics. In 1963, the bureau was directed by Dr. George Christakis. When word got back to the bureau that Weight Watchers was charging a nominal fee and offering a service based on the diet, Dr. Christakis said he thought the diet belonged to everybody and believed Nidetch was doing a public health service by helping people follow it.

Nidetch's story is also about a woman with a mission: how this charismatic speaker and personality, through a genuine commitment to helping others win the same battle, went on to lead more meetings in more living rooms, and eventually created, with Albert and Felice Lippert, a unique weight-loss program and service.

Today, Weight Watchers is considered a world megabrand and, in the United States, Weight Watchers International is the largest of the weight-loss programs, with a 40 percent share of the market.

Eating to Lose Weight

From the beginning, Jean Nidetch emphasized a fairly startling and, to perennial dieters, counterintuitive aspect of the program, eating a lot of food. Starving was a no-no. Crash dieting was anathema.

"You really had to eat in order to lose weight," said Carol Morton, who became a member in 1970, lost 49 pounds, and spent much of the next 20 years working for Weight Watchers International in the United States and overseas. "This is a program that really teaches you how to eat . . . it changes the way you have to eat for life."

The first diets emphasized, in capital letters: NEVER SKIP A MEAL! As nutritionist Moore said, "Weight Watchers is working very hard to remove the deprivation mentality that people walk in the door with."

Today's program has four components: a food plan, a behavior-

Before and after: Jean Nidetch, spiritual founder of Weight Watchers, who remains its best worldwide spokesperson.

modification guide, exercise, and group support. According to Dr. Moore, it remains a respected model for weight loss in the professional and academic nutrition, health, and medical communities. That is one of the reasons it endures.

In 1993, more than 15,000 leaders held more than 30,000 weekly meetings in 24 countries around the world. Every one of those leaders must have lost weight on the Weight Watchers program and successfully maintained their weight loss to lead meetings. They are living proof that Weight Watchers offers an effective and healthy method of weight control.

Thirty years after revolutionizing the weight-loss field, Nidetch, still trim (who calls herself an FFH, a formerly fat housewife) remains a compelling public voice. She still jets around the world, "pumping people up to lose weight."[2] Indeed, she is still proselytizing for Weight Watchers' program and philosophy. Moderation has always been at the heart of that philosophy.

Mutual Support

There are many keys to the success of Weight Watchers. However, what first distinguished it from all other programs and turned it into a quasi-evangelical movement was its combination of self-help and support, the support of people who had themselves been assailed by the overwhelming guilt and hopelessness often associated with being overweight.

Nidetch was the model from whom all others flowed, training group leaders, then called lecturers. However, when she began the Weight Watchers crusade—crisscrossing the Bronx, Brooklyn, Queens, and Long Island, helping others by going to people's homes, especially those too obese to negotiate their front door— she never thought of creating a business.

The other part of the Weight Watchers story, how her inspiring concept was transformed into a profitable business, is perhaps less well known, but equally dramatic.

---

2. *USA Today*, May 18, 1993.

A BUSINESS IS BORN

Soon after Jean Nidetch stumbled across her novel approach to losing weight, news of her successful "meetings" spread by word of mouth throughout the Greater New York area. Her services were in constant demand, and one evening, toward the end of 1962, Al and Felice Lippert invited a group of friends to their home in Baldwin Harbor to hear her talk about her diet and experience.

Today, pencil-thin Al Lippert recalls, "At first, we kind of did it for fun. Then, lo and behold, following some of Jean's suggestions, I lost seven pounds and Felice lost four pounds the first week. I could hardly believe it. So we hastily invited her back for the second week . . . and I became more and more interested in it as I lost more and more weight."

They met every week for over four months. Al eventually lost 40 pounds and Felice lost 50. The couples also became friends.

By this time, Nidetch was struggling to keep up with her busy schedule and losing money due to her mounting travel expenses and generosity. She refused to accept compensation for her services, and insisted on giving each person who lost 10 pounds in 16 weeks a gold pin.

Lippert, a merchandise manager for a chain of women's apparel stores, suggested that she form a business and "let people come to you." He told her he would help.

"I gave her a number of instructions on how to find a location," Lippert recalled, "such as how to set it up, and how to go about inviting people to come." Lippert was a born entrepreneur.

A four-way partnership was formed among Al and Felice, who had studied home economics and knew a great deal about food and nutrition, and Jean and her husband, Marty.

"By May 15, 1963, Nidetch was in a business called Weight Watchers."[3] Lippert found a location one flight up over a movie theater in Little Neck, New York, and, as he recalled, "negotiated with the landlord for a rent of $75, which I took out of my pocket.

---

3. *USA Today, op. cit.*

For another $10, I had somebody paint the place, and then we decided to charge what the movie house below was charging— $2—since I felt these meetings were just as entertaining and you got more out of it."

The day they opened, 60 people were lined up waiting to get in. Lippert says $85 is the total sum he personally invested in the business. After that, it grew like wildfire, all by word of mouth.

A FAMILY BUSINESS

The partners put in extremely long hours, and it was very much a family business. Manny Mark, Al's brother-in-law, looked after the books and eventually became the company's first chief financial officer. Elaine Robin, Felice's sister, who lived in Rhode Island and commuted to Long Island for 16 weeks to lose weight, opened the first franchise in Providence. Marty Nidetch helped with the meetings.

At first, Jean did all the lecturing, holding meetings three times a day, seven days a week. Although she loves to talk ("I talk the way I used to eat—compulsively"), it was becoming an impossible task for one person, especially with calls coming in from as far away as Pennsylvania and New Jersey.

Al had a brilliant idea. "I started looking for key people in the class who were losing weight and showed an aptitude and ability to communicate." These leaders would become the first generation of missionaries, thrilled to share their personal stories and help others gain control over eating.

In New York, a cadre of perhaps 100 leaders ran meetings every day of the week in every borough. Most were women and most, like Eileen Pregosin, who became a member in 1968, lost 93 pounds, and remained a leader for the next 10 years, basically led meetings "for love."

"There was a very evangelical spirit," said Pregosin, who eventually switched to the management side of the business, "and a warm family feeling prevailed. We didn't get paid for coming to a staff meeting. We didn't get mileage. Leaders would get offended thinking it was a business. The feeling was, can I do that and get paid for this, too?"

Albert and Felice Lippert, cofounders of Weight Watchers, at New York City opening to celebrate a new line of Weight Watchers brand food products.

FRANCHISING WEIGHT WATCHERS MEETINGS

Over the next four years, Lippert set up a regular training program, found new locations, registered the Weight Watchers International trademark in the United States and 26 other countries, and came up with another brilliant idea—franchising the meeting-room service.

Chuck Berger, brought over by O'Reilly from Italy to become president of Weight Watchers in 1978, credits Lippert's strategy and intuition. "It was brilliant because it got the company coast to coast very quickly . . . in four years, which would have been impossible if they'd tried to open up territory by territory themselves."

By 1968, there were 102 franchises in 24 states, the District of Columbia, three provinces of Canada, Puerto Rico, the United Kingdom, and Israel.

Lippert made it easy to get a franchise. His approach was to sell each territory for a small amount, and take a 10 percent royalty on the gross. Wall Street later called this strategy "giving away the razor and charging for the blades."

Again, sticking to his inspired formula for success, franchisees had to be graduates of the Weight Watchers program who had lost weight and kept it off. A majority of them were women (and their families) from the New York area, willing to pick up stakes and start a business in unknown territory from scratch.

There are a million rags to riches franchise stories. Hayden Davis, who joined the company as an attorney in 1970, just as the last bit of U.S. territory was being sold off, knows most of them, including one told to him by Sid Rifkin on a flight between California and New York.

"This guy had his own business," said Rifkin, "and his wife had gotten a Weight Watchers franchise for next to nothing, maybe $2,000. It was something for his wife to play with. He paid no attention to it. Meanwhile, the husband's business went from bad to worse, and he was waiting for the consequences of his failed business to come crashing down on him when his accountant said, 'Let me show you a financial statement of a client of mine. I can't show you the name, but what do you think of this business?' He showed him the financial statement, and the husband said what a wonderful business, why couldn't I have a business like that? The accountant said, 'You damn fool, it's your wife's Weight Watchers business.'" Sid was telling his own story, because the wife was Selma Rifkin, who owned a gold mine—the Los Angeles franchise.

Disbelievers and skeptics abounded, including brother-in-law Manny Mark, who, as Davis tells the story, told Lippert he'd do him a favor and "buy a pad of accounting paper," predicting that "by the time I'm done with that pad, this thing will be over."

But, of course, "this thing," or, as Nidetch called it, "my little project," kept growing, spurred on by impassioned, committed franchisees.

The franchisees were a special breed. According to Davis, not only were they real believers in the system, but they were "very emotional about it."

For example, the first time the company attempted to change its basic food program, in the early 1970s, and presented the changes at a franchise meeting in Scottsdale, Arizona, "I'm here to tell you," said Davis, "there were a lot of franchisees who went absolutely off the wall."

By then, Dr. W. H. Sebrell, nationally renowned ex-director of the National Institutes of Health and professor of nutrition at Columbia University, had accepted Al Lippert's offer to become the first medical director of Weight Watchers. He held the post from 1971 to 1979, and, together with Felice Lippert, head of the food and research department, was responsible for revising the original diet, "due to changes in foods available, better analytical data on the nutrients in foods, and changes in the Food and Nutrition Board's recommended daily allowances."[4]

To many franchisees, however, Nidetch's original diet was like a sacred text, inviolable. Davis recalled that one franchisee kept screaming, "They've taken away my unlimited vegetables." Others were going wild.

"Sebrell was just scratching his head and couldn't believe the emotional reaction to what he'd looked at as a significant improvement in the eating regimen. He didn't understand that unlimited carrots to some people meant they turned carrot color, they ate so many of them. They had lost weight on the original program, and they didn't want anything changed. That will just give you a feeling for how missionary it really was in those days."

---

4. W. Henry Sebrell, "Recollections of a Career in Nutrition." In *Founders of Nutrition Science: Biographical Articles from the Journal of Nutrition*, vols. 5–120, 1932–1990, American Institute of Nutrition, 1992.

Today, a whole range of foods, from chocolate to pizza, is on the program. Portion control and moderation remain the key.

However, given the emotion and provider mentality (as opposed to consumer marketing mentality) within the founding group, it's a miracle that the enterprise outlived its entrepreneurial origins. That it did is due largely to Lippert. His skill, vision, and judgment were instrumental in balancing evangelical passion with business prudence.

"He ran the business with absolute integrity," said Davis. In an industry generally noted for quick-buck artists peddling miracle cures, the ethical approach of Weight Watchers was fairly unique, giving it enormous credibility.

As the years went by and the field became more sophisticated, the company added to its staff top nutritionists, dietitians, physicians, psychologists, exercise physiologists, chefs, and home economists to introduce more scientifically advanced and varied diet menus and programs.

"That's why this program is considered a gold standard," said Moore. A successful Weight Watchers member herself, she became inspired through her experience to study nutrition and went on to earn doctoral and postdoctoral degrees at Columbia, the University of California at Davis, and Rutgers before joining the company in 1989. "No one has as many experts focused on a weight-reduction program as Weight Watchers International."

In 1967, Lippert, still juggling two jobs, almost collapsed, and finally committed himself full-time to Weight Watchers International. He never looked back. By then, the basic concept and foundation of this completely new business were mostly in place. It had many parts.

Expanding the Business

In 1967, Lippert spun off *Weight Watchers Magazine* as a joint venture with the publishers of *National Lampoon*. "Within six months, unlike most magazines," said Kent Kreh, executive vice president and publisher of the magazine today, "it was profitable. We were turning down advertising that we felt was inconsistent with our philosophy."

In addition, Lippert had come up with the idea of purchasing and selling useful items in the classrooms, such as scales for weighing food. Before long, according to Lippert, Weight Watchers was the largest user of postal scales in the country. By 1970, it was ordering half a million at a time.

He also developed a unique billfold to hold products, such as packets of skimmed-milk powder, bouillon, and sugar substitutes, that were difficult to find at the time.

Best of all, in 1965, Lippert began to engage food companies to produce lines of Weight Watchers brand foods for supermarkets. The most successful licensee, Foodways National, manufactured low-calorie frozen entrées. Lippert quickly recognized the potential for future growth in the food business, especially "proportioned food," like TV dinners, which would help members control portion size.

Lippert was exceedingly careful when choosing food companies eager to manufacture frozen, dry, and dairy low-calorie foods under the Weight Watchers brand label. Sounding much like Henry John Heinz, the Founder, he sought out, he said, "experts over whom I would have some quality control, and who, working with us, would come up with the types of foods that would fill the needs of Weight Watchers members."

In many ways, he ran the company as though it were a branch of the U.S. Public Health Service. Lippert even "invited the American Medical Association to participate in our seminars."

The company opened a camp for overweight children; it published its first cookbook, under the supervision of Felice Lippert, in charge of food research, nutrition, and recipe development at Weight Watchers International. Like almost everything else the company touched, the cookbook venture turned to gold. It sold one and a half million copies and was the first of over 20 bestselling Weight Watchers cookbooks that have sold over 12 million copies in North America to date. Additionally, the company publishes cookbooks in the United Kingdom, Australia, New Zealand, Germany, France, Holland, Italy, Austria, Sweden, and Finland.

In 1968, the company went public. Again, while many Wall Street experts were dubious at first, the public was not. The stock came out at $11¼ and closed on the first day of trading at $30. Eventually, it went as high as $60 a share and split several times.

Eileen Pregosin remembers another highlight of 1968, the fifth anniversary celebration of Weight Watchers held in the Forest Hills High School auditorium. "Jean said, when we are 10 years old, we'll take over Madison Square Garden. It was like a dream, a vision. Everybody applauded. And when our 10th anniversary came, we really did take over Madison Square Garden."

TENTH ANNIVERSARY CELEBRATION

For those who were there, like Pregosin, the 1973 Madison Square Garden celebration was a once-in-a-lifetime event.

"We brought in members from all over the world, and there was this incredible star-studded show." Bob Hope was there, and various other actors and performers, such as Pearl Bailey. But everyone was waiting to see Jean. She was the real star, and she finally appeared at around 10:30. She presented pins to members who had lost 100 pounds; she presented plaques and awards to people from the four corners of the earth.

"Then Jean started to speak," said Pregosin, "and they wouldn't let her off the stage. I think we stayed in the Garden until 1:30 in the morning. People were crying. It was just the most incredible experience. It was like being at Woodstock. It's the only feeling I can compare it to. A natural high. Everybody was exchanging stories and it was just a very beautiful and unique affair."

To the outside world, Nidetch was (and remains) the spiritual founder of the company. She traveled nationally and internationally, cheerfully giving endless magazine and newspaper interviews, appearing on coast-to-coast TV and radio talk shows, promoting the Weight Watchers program, and addressing enormous audiences wherever she went. Nidetch was born for the spokesperson

A once-in-a-lifetime event, the 1973 10th-anniversary celebration for Weight Watchers filled New York City's Madison Square Garden with members from around the world and featured Hollywood stars, such as Bob Hope and Pearl Bailey (above).

role, and in 1973 resigned as president of the company to pursue it further.

The Lipperts operated out of the limelight, bringing in new ideas and adding experts, like Dr. Richard Stuart, a behavioral psychologist, to enrich the program. They built a training department and developed the company's first manuals and guides. Russ Verano oversaw European operations. Carol Morton, a high-school German teacher and the youngest Weight Watchers lecturer in the New York area, helped launch operations in France, Holland, Italy, Germany, and other European countries. She spent three and a half years in Europe before returning to corporate headquarters.

In a further effort to professionalize management, Lippert hired Kent Kreh, then at General Mills, to become director of marketing. He joined the company in 1973 and oversaw the product businesses, including food licensees, working with them to expand their Weight Watchers brand line more aggressively. Kreh also signed up new sublicensees and became corporate liaison with the publishing operations, still managed by outsiders.

Between 1974 and 1976, as the core meeting business expanded overseas, Kreh quickly followed, signing up ancillary food and publishing licensees, replicating Lippert's original strategy.

"His strategy was to get members going to meetings, then to add things like foods, magazines, cookbooks, camps, a spa, restaurants, cooking utensils . . . developing these satellite products around the nucleus." Some succeeded, some failed. Kreh remembers how Lippert kept a little slip of paper by his phone and would add projects and ideas to that list. As he achieved one, he would scratch it off, and continue to add new ones.

By the early 1970s, however, Lippert realized that he had brought the business about as far as he and his management group could bring it. By the late 1970s, with revenues at about $50 million, he began to think about finding a food-company partner to take the Weight Watchers brand to higher levels of success.

"Along the way," Lippert said, "I had two heart attacks." He knew it was time to slow down.

Over the next few years, almost all of the major people in the food business, said Lippert, "made some sort of approach to me." As Lawrence J. McCabe, senior vice president and general counsel of Heinz, is fond of saying, "For every marriage, there are a hundred courtships in the acquisition area." Lippert was holding out for a special company with just the right chemistry. "I felt it had to be with people who were devoted to high principles and ethics, and who I was convinced would try to further the business, not exploit it."

ENTER THE H. J. HEINZ COMPANY

In 1976, Lippert was close to signing a deal with Pillsbury, but at the last minute, it fell through. Enter the H. J. Heinz Company.

Initially, Heinz wanted to buy a food licensee of Weight Watchers, Foodways National, a public company then up for sale, to integrate its low-calorie frozen dinners and portion-controlled entrées with the frozen-food facilities of Ore-Ida. It also manufactured bouillon cubes and sugar substitutes under the Weight Watchers brand label.

Though Foodways technically was free to make its own arrangement, O'Reilly discovered that Weight Watchers owned the license. To complete a deal with Foodways, Heinz concluded that it needed Lippert's blessing.

During the winter of 1977, a meeting was arranged in Palm Beach between Al Lippert and Tony O'Reilly, then president and COO of Heinz. The two men got along right from the start. They still do. Listening to each describe the other is like hearing mothers extol their favorite sons. The two men swapped jokes and stories for two hours while everybody held their breath, waiting for someone to raise the issue of the acquisition.

From the moment O'Reilly became involved in negotiations with Foodways, he understood that the more important prize was Weight Watchers International. For the acquisition to work, Heinz had to own the brand name, not just the food part. As Berger later put it, "The afterthought became a forethought."

Once the jokes and stories were over, and Lippert had given his blessing to the Foodways deal, O'Reilly casually said to Lippert, "I'd like to buy your business, too." To which Lippert replied, "If you're really interested, call me." Which he did.

The two men met four more times in New York at the Plaza Hotel, alone, without lawyers, accountants, or investment bankers, and, as Lippert recalled, "based on a mutual agreement and understanding" basically concluded the sale of the company. McCabe, then one of the Heinz attorneys involved in the deal, remembered sitting in the Oyster Bar at the Plaza while the two men "went head to head." Eventually, he was called upstairs. What still stands out in his mind is that "the entire transaction, which was about $70 million for that piece of it, was in Tony's handwriting on one sheet of paper. And it didn't take up the whole sheet of paper, either." In fact, the acquisition remained remarkably problem-free.

In 1978, for about $100 million, Heinz acquired Weight Watchers International and Foodways National. Lippert would remain CEO and chairman of Weight Watchers and go on the Heinz board. He is still there, and remains as enthusiastic about the corporate marriage as he was the day it took place.

A year later, Heinz acquired Camargo Foods from Bristol-Myers, a license holder for most of Weight Watchers brand dry grocery products.

Transition Years

Nevertheless, it was not a smooth, untroubled ride to success. In particular, the transition years, from 1978 to 1981, were difficult for a complex set of reasons. Not only did Weight Watchers move from family company to professionally managed company, but it moved from being a meeting service business with licensees to a more complex structure.

In fact, Heinz acquired two sides of one business, and, for reasons that made sense at the time, divided Weight Watchers three ways.

Foodways' frozen-entrée business, as originally planned, became a division of Ore-Ida. In fact, shortly after the acquisition, Foodways' president, Gerry Herrick, who reported to Paul Corddry, president of Ore-Ida, moved his headquarters from the suburbs of New York to Boise, Idaho. Foodways' research and development group, led by Joe Bradley, an experienced food technologist who had been with Heinz U.S.A. since 1970, remained in Connecticut, near its manufacturing plant.

Camargo Foods' so-called dry business, which included dry snacks, condiments, dairy and ice cream products, went to Heinz U.S.A. Both food businesses, then, became parts of much larger non–Weight Watchers operations.

The meeting service business remained Weight Watchers International with headquarters on Long Island. Each arm of Weight Watchers had a separate board of directors, and each reported to a different senior vice president.

Just as the ink dried on the acquisitions, the economy went into a late-Carter, early-Reagan recession. Instead of taking off, as expected, the Weight Watchers business remained flat and O'Reilly was gravely disappointed.

Each business faced different challenges, overcame initial transition problems, flourished, hit a wall, then regained momentum. Each business proved, yet again, that crisis is an opportunity.

CHALLENGES FACING WEIGHT WATCHERS

The challenges facing Weight Watchers International seemed more daunting, perhaps because the company was unlike any other Heinz business and uniquely complex. A service company and not a product company, "high touch instead of high tech," it also had four sets of customers, as its new president, Chuck Berger, quickly found out. These customers were (1) franchise owners, (2) meeting room leaders, (3) members, and (4) managers of company-owned territories.

Moreover, Weight Watchers International delivered its meeting service through a retail network of "stores" built by, as Berger characterized it, "homey and enterprising people who'd pulled themselves up by their bootstraps." The challenge was to professionalize the company and expand the meeting service, "while keeping its soul."

During this period, Berger immersed himself in the business, figuring out what made it tick and what would make it grow. He traveled around the country meeting franchisees. He looked at how other first-class service company models worked. He discovered, among other things, that in a transaction-based service business it's not just what you deliver, but how you deliver it, that makes for "service quality." (This was a lot more complex than measuring and maintaining quality in food on an assembly line.)

Berger also figured out that franchise and territorial expansion had masked the company's apparent unbroken record of membership growth.

Berger said to O'Reilly, "I can tell you about this business in four words. The bad news is that it's recession sensitive; the good news is that it's innovation responsive." He outlined a three-pronged strategy for the growth: first, develop an innovative weight-loss program; second, improve service delivery, that is, the entire meeting experience, as well as the weight-loss product; and third, begin to buy back franchise territories. This last part of the strategy would lead to greater uniformity of meeting-room quality and approach, increase national advertising weight, and deliver more profit directly to the parent company.

In 1981, Berger moved up to CEO and ran Weight Watchers International for the rest of the 1980s. At the same time, a World Headquarters strategic team, led by Andrew Barrett (and including Dr. Les Parducci, current president and CEO of Weight Watchers International), developed a structure to unify all three pieces of the business, which were not fully delivering on their promise. It included establishing a permanent interaffiliate steering committee composed of top people from each Weight Watchers business unit—Berger, Herrick, etc.—to meet monthly, think broadly about the Weight Watchers brand, and coordinate food and service strategies. This added management group would ensure that the arms and legs of the overall business moved in unison, the frozen and dry food products complementing the services, and the meeting-room business driving product growth.

Various studies confirmed that members, current and former, drove both sides of the business. Not only did they generate fees by attending meetings, but they were major purchasers of Weight Watchers brand supermarket products.

In January 1983, Barrett joined the service business, Weight Watchers International, as executive vice president, North

America. His first mission was to develop an innovative program for the January 1984 diet season.

Pulling together a team of key managers, Barrett bluntly conveyed the urgency of their task.

"We don't have time to study any further data," he said. "Come up with new ways to make it easier for customers to lose weight, and to make prospective dieters feel more excited about the program."

A week later, they started to assemble a customer-driven plan that would offer faster weight loss during the first two weeks. Ultimately they called it "Quick Start," and it took off like a rocket.

DOUBLE-DIGIT GROWTH

Launched to franchisees with, as Barrett put it, "more hoopla and excitement than we'd ever had before," and announced to the public via television, within 24 months, Weight Watchers International had doubled the size of its business. "There was no looking back throughout the eighties," he said. "After Quick Start, there was Improved Quick Start, then Quick Start Plus, and so on."

A yearly cycle of innovation, just as Berger had predicted, ignited double-digit growth from 1984 to 1989.

Barrett engendered new enthusiasm and ideas. He moved the company from its provider orientation to a marketing-consumer orientation. Without violating dietary or nutrition guidelines, the company upgraded program content, upgraded promotion, enhanced menu formats, added new foods, and placed greater emphasis on meeting people's lifestyle needs by providing more flexibility and choice. (Food in the program has always been based on an "exchange" system or range of choices within the same category, as well as other substitutions, hence the private Weight Watchers language, such as 'floaters,' 'optional calories,' etc., that is instantly recognizable to other members and a mystery to outsiders.)

For example, Weight Watchers International developed strategies for eating at restaurants, for enjoying parties, for giving parties, for following a vegetarian weight-loss program, and so on. It started an "At Work Program," which brought meetings to where more and more women were to be found, in the workplace. Today, there are 4,000 such meetings in operation. It also invested in training leaders in the field, to professionalize the system.

To Barrett, "Getting the organization focused against a faster and more frequent cycle of change and innovation was perhaps the most exciting management experience I'd ever had. I'd never seen businesses respond so quickly. I'd never seen volumes double." From 1985 on, he essentially operated as COO, adding Europe to his responsibilities.

Weight Watchers International not only was delivering double the corporate growth rate, but, as Barrett noted, "our sister affiliates on the food side of the business were also delivering incredible results as well."

WEIGHT WATCHERS BRAND FOOD

These results were attributable to massive product reformulation of the Foodways line and a host of new-product introductions.

As Bradley and others confirm, the Heinz Company's great strength is applied product development, that is, taking existing technologies and knowledge from industry and suppliers and quickly coming up with innovative products.

By 1981, working closely with suppliers, copackers, and factory managers, Bradley's research and development group reformulated 24 products, mostly tomato-based entrées, such as lasagna, veal parmigiana, and some fish entrées, and delivered them to supermarkets with new packaging, plus promotional and advertising support.

"It was the most challenging thing I've ever done in my career," said Bradley. Not only did he and his team have to learn about developing low-calorie food and how to make it taste better than existing products ("We used full-calorie products as our gold standard"), but they had to work closely with Parducci's program development group to make sure products remained consistent with strict Weight Watchers nutrition and dietary guidelines. It was a steep learning curve.

In 1982, they had the foresight to switch from aluminum-tray packaging to fiberboard. "We were one of the first to come out with a full line of microwaveable frozen entrées," noted Bradley. However, in 1982, Stouffer's Lean Cuisine brought serious competition to the frozen entrée market and overtook Foodways. On the plus side, it legitimized and expanded the overall market.

Between 1982 and 1989, Foodways introduced about half a dozen new products a year and did a bang-up business. "We set the industry record," said Bradley, "for consecutive share growth increases, about 62 successive quarters in a row."

The products not only were getting tastier, but new categories were being offered. For example, working closely with Weight Watchers International nutritionists, and breaking all the old rules, they pioneered the low-calorie dessert category. Not an immediate success, it took several years to get things right. However, both Herrick and Stan Darger, then head of marketing, went to bat for the new product line. "We rapidly discovered," said Bradley, "that in the dessert segment, chocolate is what sells." Their first big hit was chocolate mousse. The research and development groups also developed a joint working relationship with marketing that, according to Tom Mueller, general manager, technical services, "is unique in the food industry."

A confluence of factors, including working women's need for increased convenience, drove the food business forward.

With Lynn Redgrave as spokesperson, with the aging of baby boomers, with meeting-room attendance reaching historic highs (in excess of 48 million worldwide), and with a booming economy, the product side of the business reached record highs.

In 1988, Foodways surpassed Lean Cuisine in market share. Even more amazing, Weight Watchers brand frozen desserts outsold Sara Lee.

At the same time, Weight Watchers International began to buy back franchise territories. In 1978, it owned 10 percent of the franchise business. Today, it owns over 40 percent. "The remaining 60 percent," said Berger, "is in the hands of about 40 families."

WEIGHT WATCHERS PUBLISHING

In 1982, Berger also decided to bring publishing operations in-house in order to spur business growth. Kreh became publisher of *Weight Watchers Magazine*. He seems to have been born for the role. When he took over, circulation was about 700,000. Four years later, circulation reached one million. Equally significant, he transformed the publication from a virtual house organ to a general-audience magazine. In fact, only 10 percent of its readers attend Weight Watchers meetings.

Today, a majority of readers are married working women with a median age of 42, and only about 30 percent of the magazine is devoted to recipes.

Lee Haiken, editor-in-chief, says there's a lot of communication between the magazine and its readers.

"They call, write, and love talking to us," she said. "The emphasis is on quick, healthy, come-home-from-work, get-it-together recipes. This is really a lifestyle magazine. You don't have to be on the Program to follow any of our recipes. People who get the magazine know it as a healthier way of living."

The magazine, like Weight Watchers itself, is involved in a continual process of renewal to meet the changing needs of its readers. But some things don't change. It still refuses to carry ads for products that, as Lee Haiken put it, "could be considered snake-oil kinds of products."

In some ways, it is even more health conscious than before. For example, according to Kathleen Parmenter, vice president of advertising, *Weight Watchers Magazine* was the first major magazine to "walk away from cigarette advertising."

The magazine's main editorial thrust, said Haiken, is to offer information to "women who have made a commitment to self-

February 1968 inaugural issue of Weight Watchers Magazine.

improvement." While its style and tone are similar to those of Weight Watchers meetings—friendly, supportive, lighthearted—its focus is broader and more entertaining.

Seventy percent of the magazine is devoted to "health issues, nutrition issues, fitness, grooming, self-image, and psychology." It is a magazine for the whole woman, not just her "time in the kitchen."

With the aging of the baby-boom generation, the magazine's self-improvement message, which is essentially about "remaining vital and preserving a youthful lifestyle," will become relevant to an even larger audience.

Parmenter, tall, slim, and elegant, who lost 27 pounds through Weight Watchers, agrees. Devoted to the Weight Watchers lifetime program and philosophy of "disciplining yourself and learning to make choices," she pointed out that the magazine's tag line, "smart choices for living," is what she calls a "wellness schematic."

"We have an overall readership of about five million people because they trust us. The brand is like Mom and apple pie. If it's from Weight Watchers, it's good for you." In fact, she said, a study done by the American Wheat Council discovered that when looking for information on nutrition, most people turn to Weight Watchers.

Kreh and his entrepreneurial group, who work out of New York City offices, have become something of a minipublishing empire, extending the Weight Watchers brand through strategic partnerships. Joint ventures with Time-Life video and books divisions have resulted in the development of a best-selling series of exercise videotapes for the fitness market and a successful *Weight Watchers Smart Choice Recipe Collection* continuity program. Their recently established new strategic alliance with Paramount Communications offers multimedia opportunities to take the brand into the future. Plans are in the works for a wide array of new books, videos, audios, and electronic products aimed at health-conscious consumers.

Left to right: Dick Patton, Jean Nidetch, and Chuck Berger at Weight Watchers' 25th-anniversary celebration at the Waldorf Astoria Hotel in New York City. That year, 1988, the affiliate was delivering record profits and, as Tony O'Reilly declared in his address to gathered franchisees, licensees, managers, trainers, leaders, and staff, "Two plus two equals five, a concept we all aspire to and rarely achieve."

TWENTY-FIFTH-ANNIVERSARY CELEBRATION

By 1988, each Weight Watchers business unit was delivering record profits. That September, under the banner "People Helping People," Weight Watchers International celebrated its 25th anniversary with a three-day series of meetings and events, culminating in a dinner at the Waldorf-Astoria attended by franchisees, licensees, managers of company-owned operations, trainers, leaders, and field and headquarters staff.

Berger and O'Reilly spoke. Jean Nidetch, in her 60s—thin, glamorous, an electric smile framed by her signature corona of bouffant blond hair—received an award.

There was much to celebrate. As O'Reilly said, the concept of "pasting together three companies" to match the "mood of America" had actually worked. Since it had been O'Reilly's concept, its success was a big feather in his cap.

To O'Reilly's great satisfaction, worldwide attendance was nearly 50 million, and Heinz had "built a Weight Watchers business of $1.2 billion in worldwide sales."

A year later, the entire business had changed.

UNPRECEDENTED COMPETITION AND RECESSION

The success of Weight Watchers had begun to attract unprecedented levels of competition on both the service and product side. The years 1989 and 1990 were the years that Jenny Craig, Nutri-System, Slim Fast, and Healthy Choice got their acts together and began to spend huge amounts of money on television advertising.

At the same time, the economy went into a tailspin. In January 1991, the Persian Gulf war, during which few people stirred from their television sets, "totally destroyed the major diet season," according to Parducci, who was appointed president in February 1991. It severely hurt not only the entire weight-loss industry, but the overall economy as well, including the retail and restaurant food business.

However, it had already become apparent by the summer of 1990, while putting together Weight Watchers annual and five-year business plans, that, as Parducci said, "the company hadn't reacted quickly enough to competitive threats in the late 1980s."

Success, inevitably and understandably, had bred complacency and a reluctance to take risks. So many diet fads had come and gone without making a dent in the Weight Watchers business that it took a while to realize these new competitors had deep pockets and were not going to disappear.

Also, consumer preferences concerning methods of weight loss had shifted, and Weight Watchers International had not adjusted its strategies quickly enough.

In 1991, the prime market for Weight Watchers remained 25-to 54-year-old women. (In June 1993, *Consumer Reports* estimated that "fifty million Americans are dieting at any given time.") However, as Craig Frischling, manager, core business services, observed, "What defines dieters is not their age or income, but their dieting behavior." Do they prefer a group solution? One-on-one attention? Or do they prefer to go it alone? Most men, for example, are do-it-yourself dieters. Weight Watchers had limited itself to dieters with a preference for group help. By doing so, as Parducci noted, its approach had remained, "One size fits all."

That was appropriate for the 1980s, when dieters had few choices. But it left the field open to competitors who offered different diet options, including one-on-one advice and the sale at meetings of prepackaged low-calorie foods, for those who didn't want to grapple with food shopping or decision making. Prepackaged food plans, often quite expensive, but which required less discipline and offered more convenience, had been ignored by Weight Watchers International, in part because members could buy Weight Watchers brand foods in supermarkets.

In 1991, however, as membership stopped growing and retail food volume declined, the entire Weight Watchers brand embarked on a series of new strategic directions for the 1990s.

With competitive pressures mounting in a variety of Heinz businesses, O'Reilly went on the attack and, through a combination of fresh capital, new strategies, and creative restructuring, laid the groundwork for what he would soon call the "new" Heinz.

WEIGHT WATCHERS FOOD COMPANY CREATED

For Brian Ruder, the "new" Heinz began with what he thought was a routine phone call in June 1991 from his boss, Bill Springer, then president of Heinz U.S.A. Springer asked him to come upstairs and talk for a few minutes. There was something he wanted to chat about.

"I went up to his office," Ruder recalls, "with both exhilaration and shock. They were going to form a new company out of our Weight Watchers brand food products. O'Reilly wanted me to become head of the new company and run it."

Ruder, then vice-president of consumer products marketing, enjoyed tackling new responsibilities and "living on the edge a little bit." It energized him. Earlier, in February 1990, he had been further challenged by the addition of Heinz U.S.A.'s line of Weight Watchers brand food (dry, dairy, and ice cream) to his other responsibilities.

By now, it was clear that, as Ruder observed, "after one helluva good run between 1978 and 1989," the food side of the business was in trouble. Growth had stopped. During 1990 and 1991, there had been 20 months of no growth after 84 consecutive months of rise in market share.

The new Weight Watchers Food Company would start from scratch with a new game plan, new everything for over 240 Weight Watchers brand products.

Specifically, the food company's functions would include sales, marketing, research and development, finance, some manufacturing, and only one human resource person. Other functions— purchasing, distribution, and perhaps 40 percent of manufacturing—would be handled by sister companies, mainly its expert frozen-food affiliate, Ore-Ida.

Weight Watchers Food Company worried less about traditional hierarchies and more about building a flatter organization with flexible, consumer-responsive teams.

Within a month, the young affiliate was testing new product concepts on focus groups. By Thanksgiving, the company was staffed and people relocated to Pittsburgh. By Christmas, the research and development team was working feverishly on new products. By February 1992, the company had come up with a new consumer message and ad campaign, which would broaden the company's image: "Total indulgence, zero guilt."

By the fall of 1992, only 15 months after being formed, Weight Watchers Food Company had reconceptualized, reformulated, and repackaged about 60 percent of its 240 existing products. What had once been a 22-month new-product introduction cycle had been reduced to as little as 14 weeks.

However, the brand wars continued in the low-calorie and low-fat categories. Weight Watchers successfully launched a nutritionally superior product, Smart Ones brand low-fat entrees, but the pressure on margins intensified with the emergence of new competitors.

In 1994, Ruder was promoted to global coordinator of baby food, Heinz's second largest business, with international sales nearly equal to that of Gerber.

Michael McGrath, who had been a vice president at Kraft's Budget Gourmet, became the new president of Weight Watchers Food Company. The focus on good taste and nutrition continued.

WEIGHT WATCHERS INTERNATIONAL REVAMPED

The "new" Heinz also arrived at Weight Watchers International. Led by Les Parducci, a fresh management team embarked on a series of new strategic directions, which included moving meetings from church basements to attractive retail locations; simplifying the program; injecting more humor and fun into meetings; developing more exciting formats through video and other member materials; adding a preplanned, convenience-food option, Personal Cuisine; and marketing these changes with an empowerment theme, "You've got it in you to get it off you."

In record time, Weight Watchers International developed and introduced 72 new Personal Cuisine brand food products. By mixing and matching components from the retail line, Bradley's R&D group came up with everything from frozen and refrigerated foods to dry snacks, desserts, and entrées.

In 1992, Weight Watchers International launched the Personal Cuisine food option. Though Personal Cuisine foods require a modest capital investment to handle, store, set up, and distribute, franchise owners are eager to offer the option, according to Parducci.

Basically, Weight Watchers International moved from "one size fits all" to "a menu of weight-loss options" in a short time.

In addition, there's a much closer relationship between the food and service sides of the business. Today, the two parts of Weight Watchers are moving aggressively forward on innovative products and services to meet consumers' needs and make the business grow. More than ever, America needs weight-loss programs because, according to Harvard Medical School's Dr. George Blackburn, "about 34 percent of Americans are overweight, up from 28 percent in 1976–80. This is an epidemic."[5]

Weight-Loss Philosophy Unchanged

The company has not changed its basic goal, which is helping people to be physically and psychologically healthier through a balanced weight-loss program. Nor has it altered its philosophy, which is that helping people to achieve a healthier body weight means educating them about food, teaching them how to change their lifestyle habits and make choices they can live with over the long run. It remains opposed to gimmicks, deprivation, and the notion of "good" and "bad" foods. In addition, there is a greater emphasis on physical activity, which increases metabolic rate.

Weight Watchers continues to advocate safe, sensible weight control, and in 1992 supported New York City's "truth in dieting" regulation, which calls for prominent posting of the "Weight Loss Consumer Bill of Rights" and full disclosure of program costs, contract requirements, and possible health risks linked with rapid weight loss. With the United States still the most overweight country in the world, and illness associated with obesity a national health priority, it continues to work with health organizations to inform and educate the public.

Recently, the entire weight-loss industry has been buffeted by an "anti-diet" movement. Nevertheless, even during this difficult time, new Weight Watchers strategies have paid off and customer satisfaction among members remains at a record high.

---

5. Nanci Hellmich, *USA Today*, September 23, 1993.

Today, Weight Watchers is still regarded as best of breed. In fact, a 1993 *Consumer Reports* article concluded: "Anyone who wants to play the commercial-diet game should choose a program on the basis of cost, comfort and common sense. By those criteria, Weight Watchers was our readers' clear favorite. It costs less than the others, emphasizes healthful dietary habits, encourages relatively slow weight loss, and generally appears to provide the most satisfying, supportive experience."[6]

WEIGHT WATCHERS AROUND THE WORLD

Heinz owns Weight Watchers International service operations in the United Kingdom, France, Germany (including a booming business in the former East Germany), Sweden, Finland, and Switzerland. It works with franchise operations in Canada, Australia, New Zealand, Belgium, Luxembourg, Holland, Italy, Greece, Israel, Austria, and Ireland, among others. Forty percent of the business is outside of the United States.

Each country has different food habits, palates, and requirements. Thus, in Italy, any weight-loss program must include a daily plate of pasta and glass of wine. In France, butter and chocolate are worked in. Northern countries feature more protein; southern countries, more carbohydrates.

Perhaps the two biggest successes in recent years have been Australia and the United Kingdom, which have maintained strong growth in difficult economies.

Australia was one of the first non-U.S. affiliates to go into the food side of the Weight Watchers operation, in 1978. Basically, it licensed out the food business until the early 1990s, when it decided to manufacture and copack some products to give the company "more control" and better margins.

---

6. "Losing Weight: What Works. What Doesn't," *Consumer Reports*, June 1993.

A unique aspect of Weight Watchers in Australia is the fact that the franchise is owned neither by an individual nor by Weight Watchers International, but by Heinz Australia itself. Managing director Terry Ward took this step in 1989, and has developed a very successful business ever since. Rick Penn is both managing director of the service operations and 10 percent owner, which may help explain why, according to Ward, "It's going from strength to strength."

The U.K. is perhaps the brightest star in the non-U.S. Weight Watchers firmament.

Today, according to Robert Bailey, general manager of the food side of the business since 1990, the "Weight Watchers from Heinz" brand is rapidly expanding its already substantial portfolio of about 100 products into a number of new markets and categories. Not only does it already represent over 10 percent of total U.K. business, but it's the fastest growing part of the Heinz U.K. line and Britain's best-selling brand of reduced-calorie products.

The U.K. adopted the "Weight Watchers from Heinz" branding in 1985. It took over market leadership in the healthy-meals sector during 1991.

A key to the brand's success, according to Bailey, is "linking the tremendous respect consumers have for Heinz in the U.K. as a reliable, trusted food company with the highest per-capita consumption of Heinz-labeled products in the world with a very strong brand in weight loss."

As *Brand Magazine* noted in 1992, "The partnership of two heavyweights has produced 'Weight Watchers from Heinz,' a brand which has grown to 70 million pounds over 10 years." By 1993, it had grown to 90 million pounds.

Much like Weight Watchers Food Company in the United States, Bailey and his team are closely knit, entrepreneurial, and, as he put it, they "move very fast to take advantage of windows of opportunity available to us." From product development to market shelf now takes only 16 weeks.

Positioned more as "a healthy alternative" than as a "weight-loss" product, and priced on a par with standard Heinz lines, "Weight Watchers from Heinz" also employs a gentle kind of British humor in its advertising, which reinforces its mainstream positioning. That may partly explain the fact that U.K. per-capita consumption is above that of any other Weight Watchers brand. The years 1992 and 1993 were outstanding for the "Weight Watchers from Heinz" brand, despite an economy wracked by recession. With 45 percent of the U.K. population overweight and 60 percent trying to eat more healthily, it's easy to see why Bailey remains optimistic about the future.

The food business is also supported by consumers from the service side. Weight Watchers meetings in the United Kingdom attract a loyal core market of over 600,000 annually. The brand dominates the weight-loss field with a close to 50 percent share of volume and value, attracting consumers who have a profile similar to their U.S. counterparts in terms of age, sex, desired weight loss, and lifestyle.

Overall, in an era when people are increasingly focused on preventive health care and taking responsibility for their physical fitness, Weight Watchers has more relevance than ever, around the world.

The Beans and Soup Story

—~—

Heinz beans and soups may be sold all over the world, but in the United Kingdom, they have almost become national icons: trusted, respected, regarded with nostalgia and affection by old and young alike. As the *New York Times* of June 15, 1992, observed, "British expatriates have longings for home no less urgent than those of Americans abroad. . . . For the British, the cravings are apt to be for room-temperature beer, Heinz baked beans on toast, the hottest scoop on royal scandal and cricket."

Today, beans (nine varieties) are the number-one product, in terms of volume, in the Heinz U.K. line, with close to a 50 percent share of market. Indeed, largely due to the pioneering efforts of Charles E. Hellen, who may have recognized the popular potential of beans during his branch years in Boston, Britain is the highest per-capita consumer of baked beans in the world. Heinz sells a staggering 1.5 million cans a day.

Soup, number two in volume (selling about 1.1 million cans a day), is the best profit performer. The Heinz brand, with over 40 varieties in more than 60 sizes, has a leading command of the U.K. soup business with a share of 58 percent. (The next biggest name-brand player is Campbell, which sells only condensed soup, with a meager 10 percent share. Private-label soup has close to 17 percent of the market.)

245

Beans and soup, separate products, separately introduced, the reigning stars of the canned-goods group, have marched together like Siamese twins since the earliest days of the company, joined at the hip by shared virtues: convenience; nutrition; exceptional value, quality, and purity; good taste.

Strong "core" products, their varieties patterned largely to the consuming palates of each country, they remain in many (though not all) affiliates, the essence of the classic Heinz line.

In view of their staggering success in the United Kingdom, we will touch upon their U.S. origins, then largely focus on how skillful U.K. management, aided by historical circumstance, succeeded (where U.S. management did not) in turning these humble products into lucrative number-one brand stars.

Both products were launched before the turn of the century by the U.S. company: Oven-Baked Beans with Pork & Tomato Sauce in 1895; Oven-Baked Beans Boston Style in 1897 (the year the Bean Building was erected in Pittsburgh). Also in 1897, the "First of a great soup line was introduced. Cream of Tomato, ready-to-serve."[1]

Two years later, with an eye to dietary and religious markets (vegetarians, Catholics, and Jews), the company added (and may have innovated) Oven-Baked Beans in Tomato Sauce Vegetarian Style. In 1907, the parent company rounded out its line with Oven-Baked Red Kidney Beans. Interestingly, its first double-page advertising spread, in the March 1908 *Saturday Evening Post*, featured Oven-Baked Beans.[2]

Hand-wrapped, hand-packed cans of baked beans directly from Pittsburgh first landed on British shores in 1901, followed by cream-of-tomato soup in 1910 (which remains the most popular variety in the U.K. line).

---

1. According to Heinz archives (a skeleton history and brief outline of the H. J. Heinz Company assembled from employee publications), the first commercial manufacturer of beans, Van Camp, preceded the H. J. Heinz Company by four years.

2. H. J. Heinz Company's first Annual Report, 1948.

HARLESDEN, A MODEL FACTORY

Shortly after arriving in England, Hellen bought the venerable pickle and sauce manufacturer, Batty and Co. Ltd., and gradually phased in the Heinz label. In 1917 the company first turned a profit and officially became a British company. Hellen kept expanding. He inaugurated a decentralized sales and warehousing network, and, in 1923, purchased a 20-acre manufacturing site, Harlesden, ideally serviced by both a canal and railroad. Production began in 1925.

In the spirit of Pittsburgh, it became a model factory for its day, with manicured flower borders (and manicurists for female food workers), playing fields, a canteen, first-aid facility, and, most important, advanced equipment and technology from the United States.

Guided by the exceedingly capable Angus G. Stott, head of manufacturing from 1910 to 1937, Harlesden first turned out bottled goods such as pickles, sauces, salad cream (the first U.K. recipe), lemon curd, dried horseradish, and six flavors of calf's-foot jelly.[3] The growing Heinz network also distributed high-priced, imported luxury items, such as baked beans and soup.

Despite their high price, Hellen, an inspired marketer and long-term thinker, laid the groundwork for the future by running "advertisements for baked beans in the cotton and woolen areas of the North."[4]

Hellen's message and marketing strategy for beans not only were brilliant in the 1920s, but, given today's emphasis on the health advantages of nutritious low-fat, high-fiber foods, ahead of their time.

One of the first print ads noted that beans "build up body, brain and muscle," are nature's "most nourishing food," and should be on one's plate "at breakfast or dinner."[5]

---

3. *100 Years of Progress, The History of Heinz U.K: 1886–1986.*

4. Stephen Potter, *The Magic Number.* U.K., Reinhardt, 1959, p. 118.

5. Potter, *op. cit.*, 1910 print ad, p. 146.

Hellen not only made beans on toast a national dish, but put Heinz on the map. During the 1920s and 1930s, he plastered the Heinz name on billboards and cut-out constructions along railroad lines, and launched the famous "Joy of Living—For a Few Pence" campaign in 1927. Heinz Oven-Baked Beans with Tomato Sauce were prominently featured in that campaign ("If you would know the joy of living, eat Heinz baked beans and see how much better, jollier you'll feel . . . Here's a dish to make breakfast, dinner or supper the cheeriest meal of the day"), along with the ongoing tag line: "No preservatives, no artificial coloring."

In 1931, young Jack Heinz (left) met with his father, Howard Heinz (second from left), and Charles E. Hellen (center) and other senior executives (unidentified) at the Harlesden factory. Hellen joined the U.S. company as a salesperson in Washington, D.C., in 1899; rose to become Boston branch manager; and, sent by the Founder to run the infant U.K. operation in 1905, transformed it into a hugely profitable affiliate, over which he presided until his death in 1944.

The famous Heinz U.K. "Joy of Living" advertising campaign began in 1927 and emphasized nourishment, no preservatives, and no artificial coloring, as well as good taste. The following year, British-made baked beans first rolled off production lines and, with lower prices, sales began to soar.

In 1928, Heinz beans gained enough popularity to justify local production. It was a momentous decision.

"The date of dates in British history," wrote U.K. historian Stephen Potter, "is 10th September, 1928. By this year the 1925 capacity of the Harlesden plant was doubled. This was the consummation of the planning of a quarter of a century. A small start was made with food ready to serve, and packed in cans made by Harlesden's own can making department. Spaghetti and the big family of soups were not to come till 1930. The first choice—and this makes the key date even more important—was Baked Beans."[6]

Local production meant lower prices. Now more people could afford this early convenience food. Sales took off. "Within 12 months, sales reached £443,000 [British pounds sterling]—more than double the value of soup sales, and 10 times those of spaghetti, though not much ahead of £403,000 chalked up by ketchup."

As the Great Depression overtook England, Hellen hammered away at the high nutrition of beans ("Every pound of Heinz Baked Beans is equal in food value to one pound of prime steak"[7]), low cost ("You can get four of these one-pound tins for the price of one pound of steak"), and unique taste ("Heinz Baked Beans are different, baked not just boiled, baked till they are golden-brown, mealy and digestible").

In 1934, Hellen sent W. B. "Willie" Cormack to Australia to help get the business going. The first product to roll off the production line, on October 1, 1935, was none other than Baked Beans in Tomato Sauce, followed by canned spaghetti and five types of soup.

The British canning and bottling industry was in its infancy. Heinz U.K., with its technology imported from the United States, was the clear leader. "There was no one," observed John Connell, retired managing director of Heinz U.K. (1972–1976), "who could produce an edible baked bean apart from Heinz." (Connell's father had briefly worked for Heinz as a salesman in Scotland,

---

6. Potter, *op. cit.*, p. 109.

7. 1930 U.K. advertisement.

Michael Belinsky, left, shares a light moment with Tony O'Reilly as he guides the chairman through the 350-acre farm where the Zimbabwe affiliate has conducted test plantings of navy pea beans. Heinz has been so involved with the Michigan pea bean that, in the late 1980s, a cadre of Heinz U.K. agronomists introduced the bean to the sub-Saharan climate of Zimbabwe, where it now thrives and where Heinz's Olivine Industries packs Heinz-brand baked beans.

and received an engraved silver spoon from Howard Heinz to commemorate the birth of son John, who, in turn, first joined Heinz before the war, then rejoined it in London a decade later.)

The type of bean used, smothered in tomato sauce with a bit of pork for flavor, was the Michigan navy bean. (Pork disappeared during World War II rationing, then later reappeared as one of many varieties.) According to Lee Harrow, "Heinz U.K. remains the biggest buyer of Michigan navy beans. They come over and contract for a major part of that crop."

Heinz U.K.'s baked beans do not taste like Heinz U.S.A.'s baked beans. Heinz U.K. not only produced a unique product, but it produced one that was far more successful than its humble U.S. parent.

"The ability of U.K. technologists to get those navy beans soft enough, very quickly, without their becoming mushy, was the whole secret to their success," said Harrow. The U.K. recipe is also sweeter.

"Prewar Heinz," said Connell, "was the clear leader in quality, but prices were high and per-capita sales low."

Three varieties of beans—pork, curried, and vegetarian—already added up to one third of Heinz U.K. sales. Soups were still under 10 percent, and the company kept adding new varieties, "hammering home quality to emphasize acknowledged product superiority and justify premium price."[8] British soups were thicker, heavier than soups in the United States.

Soup ads were targeted to an upscale market. The soup line now included bean, onion, consommé, pepper-pot noodle, beef broth, gumbo Creole, clam chowder, Scotch broth, mock turtle, vegetable, and cream-of-spinach, cream-of-mushroom, cream-of-oyster, cream of green pea, cream-of-celery, and cream-of-tomato.

In 1934, a new soup line was installed at Harlesden; by 1938 there were 20 varieties, including meat soups such as mulligatawny and genuine turtle with vegetables. Postwar Harlesden factory director of manufacturing Peter Dixon still remembers the unloading of beans from the canal barges and turtles being stacked and hauled up into the soup kitchen.

Many still recall the Dickensian atmosphere and routines of prewar office work. William Haxton, for example, who joined the Edinburgh sales branch in 1935 as a ledger clerk and retired as head of personnel 45 years later, would debit by hand a trade account on the left side of a ledger, and the cash clerk, sitting next to him, would credit it on the right side.

The incomparable English sales force drove the business forward. According to retired managing director Tony Beresford, who joined the company in 1931 as a junior clerk at the tender age of 16 and switched to the sales force five years later, Heinz

---

8. *100 Years of Progress*, p. 22.

"Her Guests Couldn't Believe It" trilled the copy headline on a full-page 1935 Heinz U.K. ad featuring a formal, white-tie dinner, butler and all. It proclaimed the virtues of ready-to-serve Heinz "homemade style" soups.

salesmen were far more advanced in their training and techniques than those in other companies, and absolutely relentless. "We were told we should cover every street on our territory," he recalled. "We should go into every public house, hotel, greengrocer, fishmonger, butcher, and so forth, and be talking about the Heinz Company, and even though we didn't sell anything at the time, we would be registering the name all the time. I mean, sometimes I used to go into insurance companies and say, 'Now, do you give any of your clients Christmas presents?' "

Beresford's mother played bridge with Mrs. Hellen, who asked her husband to take young Tony on. Beresford recalled the day he began work. "A chauffeur arrived at a quarter to nine and picked me up, then went on to pick up Mr. Hellen, and when we arrived at headquarters, he proceeded to walk around the factory with me, saying 'Do you see this? Do you see that?' It was a terrible handicap, because I mean everybody regarded me as a sort of spy, so it took a fair time to live that down."

The prewar sales force was 700 to 800 strong and a fairly disciplined organization, hence its "Red Army" nickname. All at least five feet, 10 inches tall (preferably six feet), carrying black bags and furled umbrellas, wearing stiff white collars, dark suits and black bowler hats; they were supposedly a cut above the rest and of impeccable disposition, courtesy and style as they descended upon the family grocer. (John Hinch heard that there was a marker on the door so that an interviewer knew at once whether a candidate reached the required height.) It also should be noted that many of the English retirees interviewed, such as Beresford, Haxton, Crabb, and King, remain long, lean, looming presences, remarkably fit.

According to Beresford, "All the trade used to say, we could always tell a Heinz man. We could see him coming down the street. He doesn't have to introduce himself when he enters the shop." It was the highest of compliments.

The equipment provided for the salesmen looked equally smart. "Chromium-plated, shining things," said Beresford, "so that they would stand out when you put them on the counter." In fact, with what appeared to be a silver chafing dish for beans, a polished thermos flask for hot soup, and highly colored glass bottles "conjured out of a protective green baize bag,"[9] the sampling ceremony was elegant and dramatic.

Salesmen carried out consumer samplings three Saturdays out of four—as did female demonstrators, whose appearance and personality were considered as important as their knowledge of the product. The fourth Saturday was dedicated to the all-important sales convention, which often lasted until midafternoon.

The operations side of the business also attracted first-rate people because, in the humane Heinz tradition, people were treated well and working conditions at Harlesden, recalled Beresford, "were absolutely remarkable for their day." They included a subsidized canteen, and holidays with pay. "Everybody looked out for each other." During the war, for example, "if an employee's house was hit by a fire bomb, the next morning, people from the factory would be there repairing the place."

Even better, unlike most companies in the seasonal food business, rather than rely on seasonal temporary help, Heinz offered employment 52 weeks a year. It encouraged a sense of family in a company still run by family.

By 1939, war was imminent. Beresford had worked his way up to head salesman. "In August, we had our great soup campaign. I was trying to sell a big account, 3,000 cases of soup—they'd never bought more than 100—when the phone rang." Beresford was informed that the War Office expected him to report for duty that night. His client suddenly realized that war shortages lay ahead and said, "Good heavens! Well, the last thing you do when you get home is to write out that order for 3,000 cases of soup and get it sent in tomorrow."

---

9. H. J. Heinz Company Annual report, 1986, p. 7.

*A 1930s U.K. branch team preparing to attend the annual sales confer-
ence. The incomparable British sales force, nicknamed the "Red Army,"
drove the business forward. Distinguished in appearance—five feet, 10
inches tall or taller, with black sample bag, furled umbrella, stiff white
collar, and black bowler hat—each salesman was thought to be a cut above
the rest and of impeccable disposition.*

THE WORLD WAR II YEARS

From then on, as Junius Allen recalled, "Many Heinz products
were under the counter and only given out to the best customers."

The war, of course, ushered in an era of short supplies and
allocation. Despite the fact that the soup building was bombed
twice, in 1940 and 1944, production tonnage rose during the war.

All processors were recruited to turn out nonbranded wartime foods for both civilian rations and the armed forces. According to Fred Crabb, in charge of government contracts during the war, Heinz headquarters staff was dispersed into three buildings, to protect both lives and documents.

The know-how of Frank Shires (later knighted Sir Frank Shires for his wartime work), director of manufacturing, working with the Ministry of Food, made Heinz a leader in food manufacturing and distribution during the war. Heinz U.K. manufactured dehydrated vegetables, and invented a self-heating can for soups and milk, which could be lit by a cigarette. Ten million self-heating cans landed with allied troops on D day.

Heinz emerged from the war with its products better known and its leaders more respected than ever. It joined the Food Manufacturers' Federation (FMF) in 1946, becoming more of an industry leader, and in 1949, Shires became FMF president, paving the way for other Heinz people, including Beresford.

Though there was little need for salesmen and selling during the war, soup and baked beans could be purchased with British rations, and advertising continued.

"Fuel economy in a can!" proclaimed an austere headline in an austere World War II ad, directed to civilians learning to cope with fuel and food rationing. "When you're tempted to overrun your fuel consumption," said the copy, "remember that Heinz can give you warmth of the healthiest kind—the kind that springs from within. For good nourishing foods like Heinz oven-baked beans and Heinz perfect soups are regular stores of bodily fuel defeating the stealthy chill and giving you new energy."[10]

After the war, owing to Shires, Heinz had substantial allocations of available food and packaging materials, which gave it a distinct market advantage. (Sugar, for example, was rationed through 1954 and tinplate through 1960.) When Heinz brands were reintroduced, they were avidly snapped up by consumers. The trade fought to get more food and bigger allocations.

Contemplating the unparalleled postwar success of Heinz U.K. products, it's fair to suggest that they were the right products at

---

10 *100 Years Of Progress.*

the right price at the right time. The economy was shattered. The English were starved for nourishing, quality food at a reasonable price. Those able to provide it were in a uniquely advantageous situation. At the same time, great credit must be given to Heinz U.K. management for grasping postwar opportunities and rapidly building and controlling its main markets before domestic and overseas competitors could establish beachheads.

Heinz had trouble keeping up with demand. In the late 1940s, it converted a wartime munitions factory at Standish, in Lancashire, into a processing plant. The site was chosen for its proximity to locally grown produce and a plentiful labor supply. Before Heinz came into the area, the only other employers were the coal mines and cotton mills. "Heinz was like heaven on earth by comparison," recalled one retiree. "A lot of families worked at Standish and a family atmosphere prevailed."

The Golden Years

The brand created in the 1930s and solidified in the 1940s boomed in the 1950s and 1960s. These fast-growth decades were Heinz U.K.'s golden years. By 1960, recalled Connell, "Heinz U.K. had a very profitable business, with 70 percent of the bean and soup markets, 75 percent of canned pasta, 70 percent of salad dressings, 90 percent of ketchup, and nearly 100 percent of baby food. They had 100,000 trade accounts and no effective competitors."

In 1963, the British affiliate supplied to the parent company a whopping 90 percent of consolidated world income. Without its cash flows, the H. J. Heinz Company might well have gone out of business or been taken over.

Roy King, who joined in the forties when Cormack reigned as managing director (1946–1956), recalled those peak performing years. "It was one of the top two or three brands in the country. The housewife, the mother, could feel absolute trust in the integrity of the product, that it was going to be flavorsome and nutritious. Good value for money. Trustworthy and reliable. It was the housewife's friend."

King fondly recalls his early days as a salesman. "When you joined—in the old days—you were told that the company wanted ambitious young men and that you could have any job you liked except Jack Heinz's job, because he had the right name, so you couldn't be that.

"The policies and principles of the House of Heinz—its fundamental ethics, high standards, and dignity—were almost like a religion, featured first on any sales meeting agenda. You would almost put your hand on your heart and swear," said King. "The sales conference was a key feature in the salesman's life. Very formal. The Japanese get laughed at for their company songs in the morning. We didn't have a company song, but it was a similar thing."

King summed up why the art of selling for the H. J. Heinz Company was so special. "It satisfied your ethical aspirations. People need these moral imperatives to satisfy their hunger."

King was an outstanding salesman, as the following recollection suggests. "Salesmanship. It was wonderful. You would carry a flask and you would have a can of soup in the flask, tomato soup, beef soup, and on a cold morning, you would sample little tiny cups of soup. Sampling food, giving people food, is one of the most sensual things you can do. They are immediately disarmed. Everyone loves food and loves a good taste, and Heinz always had a very good spicy taste, distinct taste. You would pour a bit of soup down somebody's throat and they would melt in your arms." Joining the company was, as King put it, "like joining a family rather than just having a job."

Mike Baldwin, who signed on after the war at age 20 and became factory manager at Harlesden at the age of 39, conveyed a similar emotional attachment. Born a few miles down the canal from Harlesden, he recalled, "While the managing directors were gods, they moved on the same plane as you did, had coffee in the same canteen as the workers. I said, 'That's the sort of company I want to work for.' "

Kitt Green, in Wigan, 200 miles north of Harlseden (near Standish), opened in 1959 as a £7 million showcase, and became known as "the baked beans centre of the world."

Today, the largest food-processing plant in Europe, with 19 highly automated production lines, including the world's fastest bean lines, Kitt Green turns out over one million cans of beans and soup a day, as well as ketchup, baby food, and puddings. It was officially opened by Britain's queen mother, accompanied by Jack Heinz, Frank Armour, and Junius Allen.

Kitt Green, known to locals as the "big place on the hill," was visible evidence of Heinz U.K.'s spectacular growth. During the 1950s, sales began doubling every four and a half years.

Nineteen sixty was a pivotal and highly dramatic year. The American soup giant, Campbell, with its line of condensed soups, decided to assault the ready-to-serve U.K. market. Despite the fact that Heinz dominated the business, according to Beresford, then head of U.K. sales and marketing, when Pittsburgh heard that Campbell was coming, they "went rapidly to panic stations," and wanted Heinz U.K. to switch from ready-to-serve to condensed soup. Of course, Campbell was clobbering Heinz in the United States, so it was reasonable for Pittsburgh to assume the worst.

In fact, Campbell made the classic mistake of trying to export American taste to England. While Heinz lost 10 percent of market share the year after Campbell landed, ultimately Campbell's condensed soups were rejected by the British public. To defend itself, Heinz U.K. mounted a two-pronged counterattack on Campbell, and got all 10 percent back and then some.

First, it agreed to offer a small line of "condensed recipe soups," later withdrawn from the market when it became obvious that U.K. consumers preferred ready-to-serve soups.

Second, and more significantly, in 1961, it launched the biggest promotion ever run by a food company, the 57 Mini-Minors soup competition. A £1 million promotion, it rewrote the marketing history books and became a classic of its kind.

Instead of one top prize, there were 57 deluxe Morris Mini-Minors. Announced in all the media, it created a firestorm of attention. Budgeted for 250,000 entries, it received three quarters of a million via Heinz soup labels. (Each contestant won, at the very least, a can of soup.)

"It caught the imagination of the grocery trade and the consumer," said Bruce Purgavie, who joined the company in 1959 and today is head of European business development.

In July 1959, England's queen mother officially opened Heinz U.K.'s enormous factory in Kitt Green. Located in Wigan, a mining town in the north of England whose dreadful living and working conditions became world renowned through George Orwell's Road to Wigan Pier, *the area welcomed the postwar arrival of Heinz and the employment it provided. Today, Kitt Green is the largest food-processing plant in Europe, with 19 highly automated production lines, including the world's fastest bean lines. And Wigan is known as "the baked beans center of the world."*

Mounting consumer events and promotions designed to build the business remain a particularly effective marketing tool in the United Kingdom, and one for which the company has developed a reputation. Fifty-seven vacations as prizes drew over a million entries in 1963, and in 1966, the company gave away 57 customized, convertible Wolseley Hornets (now classic collectibles). In 1986, as part of the Heinz U.K. centenary year, Heinz gave away—one day at a time—100 Austin Rover cars customized with the nameplate "H57." According to marketing manager Julian Todd, it was again the biggest consumer promotion ever run by Heinz. Supported "for only the second time in 31 years"[11] on television, it attracted a record 11 million entries. With close to 60 million people in the United Kingdom, and only about 19 million households, that is an incredible response.

Fred Crabb, managing director between 1956 and 1963, was a key architect of the company's postwar success. Crabb modestly calls himself a "one-dimensional organization man." He was far more than that. "Crabb was a breath of fresh air," said Connell. "He brought McKinsey into the U.K. in the 1960s. He saw the shortcomings in personnel and management techniques. He was a man of great brain power and did more for the U.K., in my opinion, than anybody."

During his reign, the company moved, in a manner of speaking, from the 19th to the 20th century, shifting from clerks and hand-inscribed ledgers to its first mainframe computer, from a totally sales-driven company to a more sophisticated mix of marketing, promotion, and sales. England, the nation of shopkeepers, was slowly giving way to the supermarket revolution.

Crabb joined Heinz two years after Harlesden was built, in 1927. During his 42 years with the company, respected for both his financial acumen and management skills, he enjoyed a close working relationship with both Jack Heinz and Burt Gookin. A member of the parent board, he was also the first of a new breed of affiliate executives who began to make regular trips across the Atlantic.

Also, Heinz U.K. under Crabb set up a postwar process to source tomato paste and tomato products from continental Europe. Con-

---

11. "One Hundred Years of Feeding the Family," *Marketing Review*, October 1986.

nell, then controller, visited every processor in Italy, and helped to pioneer tomato production in Italy, Portugal, and Morocco. Crabb worked closely with Pittsburgh to acquire companies in Europe, and took a more professional approach to nurturing up-and-coming managers.

"Right up until the 1950s," said Crabb, "we had a management team of functional specialists, because in the prewar days, managers, whether they were in the factory, accounting, or sales, were not encouraged to stray outside their departments."[12] Crabb began deliberately to cross-fertilize talented employees, like his successors, Beresford and Connell, moving them through sales, marketing, and manufacturing, to create more multidimensional executives. It had never been done before.

As much as Crabb modernized the management of the company, to a young man's eyes, it was still a fairly conservative place.

"The company," Andrew Barrett recalled, "was very staid, very British. Everybody called everybody above them Sir."

Barrett joined Heinz in September 1961 and returned three decades later to become managing director. He still remembers the smell of mulligatawny soup wafting down Waxlow Road on his first day of work. He also recalls "row upon row of ladies who tracked orders coming in and going out" on the vast, open, second floor at Harlesden, converted into a huge dining hall during ceremonial anniversary banquets.

Though Crabb rose much farther than most of his peers, he now shares with many Heinz employees of his generation a feeling of great good luck. "I joined a pickle company," he recalled, "dined with dukes and duchesses and had a fascinating life."

Compared with today's relentless pace of change, Cormack, Crabb, and Beresford presided over a more tranquil period. That would soon change. In the meantime, Harlesden was bursting at the seams. The company needed bigger and better research, quality, and administrative quarters, and so moved to Hayes Park in 1964.

Crabb envisioned the place as "headquarters for a European organization," as well as for Heinz U.K. Jack Heinz brought over

---

12. *The 57 News, U.K.*, October 1967, vol. 9, no. 10.

Harlesden's vast administrative second floor led a double life. By day, it was home to a battalion of desks, with "row upon row of ladies who tracked orders coming and going out." By night, as this 1938 photo illustrates, it easily converted into a grand dining hall for ceremonial banquets.

Gordon Bunshaft from Skidmore, Owings and Merrill, the man who had designed Pittsburgh's Research Building. Bunshaft erected two supermodern buildings overlooking more than 150 acres of rolling greenery dotted with grazing black-and-white holstein cows. Only eight miles from the brick and mortar of urban Harlesden, it was light years away in setting and spirit.

Inevitably, perhaps, the rate of growth was slowing down. However, huge volumes of soup and beans continued to keep seven filling lines going night and day at Harlesden (which closed its canned-goods lines in 1992). Trade unions came to Kitt Green in the late sixties, ending the one-big-happy-family atmosphere that had long prevailed.

As 1970 rolled around, more attention had to be paid to profit than volume, to efficiencies and unit costs. When O'Reilly became managing director in 1969, part of his mission was to improve margins. "The 1970s," O'Reilly accurately predicted, "would be much tougher than the 1960s." Perhaps the biggest postwar change in Heinz was the shift of power away from Heinz U.K. that had begun in the 1970s.

Roy King was marketing and sales director in what he called the "nonglory days of the seventies." It was a period marked by "tough competition in nongrowth markets," plus a difficult environment: labor unrest, strikes, price controls, the oil crisis, procurement problems, higher taxes, soaring interest rates, and a rapid shift of power from food manufacturers to large retail chains. All this, recalled King, added up to "rising costs, extremely high inflation, up to 25 percent, and very bad economic conditions." Volumes peaked around 1974. Connell saw inflation coming and astutely raised prices to protect the company's profitability.

ADVERTISING CLASSICS

Defending its markets, advertising and promotion went into high gear. The company's most famous ad campaign was born during these difficult times. Young and Rubicam came up with the classic copy line, "A million housewives every day open a can of beans and say, Beanz Meanz Heinz." It remains "a national catch phrase, with a thousand variations dreamt up by the public."[13] The campaign kept Heinz number one and lasted a decade.

The Thatcher 1980s, like the Reagan 1980s, were a booming

---

13. *100 Years of Progress*, p. 48.

Heinz U.K.'s most famous ad slogan, "Beanz Meanz Heinz," is now a national catch phrase with thousands of unofficial variations. The product of Young and Rubicam, it kept Heinz number one and ran for a decade.

decade, which also spawned more sophisticated consumer eating patterns and taste. With a new emphasis on choice and convenience, Heinz started to roll out more varieties of beans and soups. In the mid-1980s, beans enjoyed a big upturn in popularity when the F-Plan Diet (low-fat, high-fiber) became the rage, supported by similar government recommendations about healthy, high-fiber foods. As Mike Sargent, head of U.K. public relations put it, "Beans became trendy. They went from being seen as cheap, filling, good-tasting fast food to health food."

At the same time, cheaper supermarket competition revived. Heinz launched a new ad campaign, "Millions of Little Britons": humorous TV commercials showing famous British characters growing up with Heinz Beanz. The English generally bring more of a sense of humor to advertising than do their U.S. brethren. Roy King insists, for example, "The 57 Varieties absolutely tickled the British eccentric sense of humor, as did the notion that it was an English company with an American subsidiary."

Soup advertising, according to category manager Bob Morrison, continued to press emotional buttons. A much-loved campaign of the 1970s, "Heinz soup will always make things better," not only won awards, but pushed Heinz soup to its highest share in a decade. Other memorable print campaigns have been built around the copy line and notion of "Heinz Souper Day," with such variations as "Heinz Souperman," "Souperyear," and "Souper Savings."

It is estimated that 70 percent of soup is consumed at lunchtime, largely by families with children, and thus soup is increasingly positioned as a light meal in itself. With 80 percent household penetration, growth has been achieved through increased segmentation.

During the past 20 years, competition on this Texas-sized island has become intense, especially as the grocery trade has increasingly concentrated into large chains, such as Tesco, Safeway, and Sainsbury. Three or four huge customers dominate the business.

"In fact," said Purgavie, "the retail grocery business in the United Kingdom is generally reckoned to be probably the most concentrated and sophisticated in the world." Competition has driven extraordinary efficiencies in retailing. (Profit margins are also higher, which is beginning to attract European retailers into the United Kingdom.) The level of computer technology at the retail level, for example, is more advanced than in the United States. Software programs are capable of ordering products; allocating shelf space; regulating energy output in stores, including the intensity of refrigeration; and minimizing inventory. Great emphasis is now placed on just-in-time management.

Heinz U.K. Centennial

In 1986, Heinz U.K. took advantage of its centenary year to build on the warmth felt by most consumers for Heinz with a blitz of trade and consumer promotions, exhibitions, galas, and a touch of nostalgia that boosted sales and goodwill. The year was kicked off by a white-tie-and-tails dinner. Jack Heinz and Tony O'Reilly invited nearly 300 guests to the Mansion House, official residence of the lord mayor of London, during which Henry J. Heinz II reminisced with eloquence about "the remarkable man who was my grandfather," recalling "quick flashes of white side whiskers, laughter, some sternness—and Sunday prayers."[14]

There were giveaways, children's parties, a treasure hunt, the car-a-day "blockbuster" promotion, a £1 million donation to the World Wildlife Fund (now called the World Wide Fund for Nature), a National Fun Day that attracted over a million children and adults, and a nostalgic two-and-a-half-minute reel of 30 years of memorable and well-loved television ads.

Also, at a ceremony at 10 Downing Street, O'Reilly handed over the deed to Cape Cornwall to Prime Minister Margaret Thatcher. This, the only cape in England, was bought by the U.K. company as a centenary birthday gift to the nation.

---

14. *Heinz News, U.K.*, March 1986.

MANAGING CHANGE

During the late 1980s, Heinz remained market leader, but began to lose some market share to lower-priced competition. In 1985, managing director John Hinch announced a £150 million investment program, Most Productive Operator (MPO), to streamline operations and improve plant efficiencies through training and technology, including the installation of high-speed lines (up to 1,200 cans a minute) at Kitt Green and Harlesden.

"In the past," said Hinch, "managing was managing the status quo. Today, it's managing change. Constantly looking for improvements and looking to do things better."

The MPO program was enhanced by Total Quality Management (TQM) in 1989, which, as Mike Baldwin, Kitt Green's general manager–sous-chef, pointed out, is really an updated version of the Founder's business philosophy and premise, "to do a common thing uncommonly well brings success."

TQM has provided the worldwide company with a common language and way of looking at work. Phrases such as price of nonperformance or PONP, meeting customers' requirements, benchmarking, and doing it right the first time are now part of the Heinz lingua franca around the world, from Pago Pago, Elst, Latina, and Zimbabwe to Burley, Pittsburgh, Cincinnati, and Kitt Green.

In 1992, prompted, in part, by the worst U.K. recession in years, as well as further concentration in the retail trade and a sudden influx of cheap European budget brands (cheaper even than private label), Heinz again needed to lower prices to retain market share and stay competitive.

In fact, in 1991, Heinz turned in its first drop in U.K. pretax profits for years as the recession bared its teeth and the company faced the toughest trading conditions in its history.

The company implemented a more targeted version of TQM, called Manufacturing Excellence, as a way of working smarter and drawing ideas from those who actually deal with factory, production, and operations issues. Process evaluation teams (PETs), composed of workers and managers from the shop floor to senior management, focused on different aspects of production, procurement, etc., in order to find ways to cut costs and improve efficiencies.

These programs have succeeded in keeping Heinz U.K. competitive, increasing its volumes and thus freeing up funds for new marketing programs supported by national television.

In 1993, for example, with a £5 million advertising budget, Heinz again went on the attack, unveiling its newest campaign, "Heinz Buildz Britz." According to category manager Margaret Burke, "It focuses on the folklore in Britain of Heinz baked beans," as well as the "full of beans" notion of family fun. The main consumers of Heinz beans are mothers with children.

During 1991–1992, Heinz also ran a graphically bold, corporate branding umbrella campaign with a strong product focus. Large pastel drawings showed Heinz products in close-up without actually showing the Heinz name. The campaign swept 20 international awards.

Overall, Heinz has successfully fought back competitive assaults. Heinz beans and soups remain among the best-selling products in the country, and Heinz remains one of the top four brands in the United Kingdom.[15]

AUSTRALIA AND NEW ZEALAND

Australia is a miniversion of the United Kingdom. It leads the baked-bean and soup markets (producing a range of 53 soups), with shares of around 50 percent in both markets. Heinz Australia has pioneered extensive research into the health benefits of baked beans through the department of human nutrition of the Commonwealth Scientific Industrial Research Organization. The results have underscored the unique health properties (low fat, no cholesterol, high protein) of the product to a new generation of consumers, which has done much to strengthen the market.

---

15. "Top 100 Brands," as compiled by Nielsen, December 1992.

Jack Heinz (far right) and Australian Prime Minister Sir Robert Menzies (to his right) happily ladling soup from a huge vat at the official opening of the H.J. Heinz Company plant in Dandenong, Australia, in 1955.

Looking ahead, Australia and its newest regional companion, Wattie's in New Zealand, anticipate significant opportunities for export to Asian countries. Their comparative advantage includes advanced technology; efficient, low-cost manufacturing; and the area's "clean green" image. Together, these strengths should help to access a variety of new markets. Eventually, Australia and New Zealand will develop indigenous products that are tailor-made to the special and widely different cultures in the Asian economic community. At the same time, they look forward to leveraging their assets through the development of significant manufacturing and marketing synergies.

SOUP AND BEANS IN THE UNITED STATES

On the other side of the Atlantic, the fortunes of soup and beans have been almost the reverse of their history in the United Kingdom. That is particularly true with respect to Campbell and the H. J. Heinz Company.

Just when Heinz U.K. handily beat back Campbell in the early 1960s, Heinz U.S.A. was at its lowest ebb. For example, in "57 Varieties of Trouble," in its April 1, 1964, issue, *Forbes* wrote about the soup business, "Slow, slow, slow. This has been the Heinz story. Not until 1941 did it start making condensed soups. Campbell had already been doing so for a good 44 years and Campbell had the market cornered. Today, Campbell makes around 80 percent of the canned soups in the U.S.; Heinz probably makes about 8 percent."

After the war, Heinz was producing 15 kinds of condensed soup and four varieties of beans. However, in both the United States and Canada, it never regained a respectable market share in Heinz branded soup—though not for lack of trying. Gookin, Townsend, Corddry, Jack Heinz and his son John all participated in valiant attempts.

In 1963, for example, Jack Heinz became the company spokesperson on television and in print for Heinz soup (probably the first corporate leader in the country to do so, decades before Chrysler's Lee Iacocca and Remington's Victor Kiam made it so chic).

Then came the reorganization at Heinz U.S.A., and strategy shifted. Both Burt Gookin and Paul Townsend, vice president of marketing, knew that they were losing money every time they sold a can of retail soup. In fact, at the top of Gookin's to-do list was, "Fix the soup business." So they spearheaded the move into private-label soup.

"We pushed the heck out of the institutional soups," said Townsend. He also stopped retail advertising.

The last hurrah began in 1965. That was the year Corddry launched the Happy Soup line for children, with the late Senator John Heinz as his product manager. According to Corddry the product "that was the most interesting and fun, and perfectly

"Skinny chickens make thin soup," says Henry Heinz. "We don't use them."

Heinz
Souperman

Over the years, soup, with all its warm, homey, satisfying connotations, has produced some of the company's best print ad campaigns. They include, in the United Kingdom, Heinz Souperday and variations, such as Souperman and Souper Savings. In the United States, the Skinny Chicken ad campaign, signed by H.J. Heinz II, was equally memorable.

executed, turned out to be a disaster . . . Happy Soup." It was followed, in 1967, by another launch of a premium, ready-to-serve retail line of chunky Great American Soups, with a red, white, and blue label. It was another failure with consumers, a puzzling one since it was an excellent product, backed by a lavish advertising campaign featuring dancer Ann Miller. But for a variety of reasons, including a cutback in marketing dollars for Great American Soups, both products ultimately failed.

Heinz U.S.A. quietly exited the retail soup business. It was a bitter blow for Jack Heinz and the entire company, but a wise business decision.

Today, the private-label soup business is both huge and, with no advertising costs, immensely profitable. Overall, canned soup is the fourth largest dry-grocery category in the supermarket. According to Bob Roussey, general business manager, Heinz leads the private-label category with a massive 87 percent share. It's the second largest Heinz U.S.A. business after ketchup. Heinz manufactures over 50 varieties of soup under 140 different labels.

The big story of the past 10 years has been the delivery of higher quality at lower cost. That has involved, among other things, a $116 million investment in Pittsburgh's state-of-the-art, highly computerized Pittsburgh factory, dedicated to soup and baby food. (Soup is also manufactured in Muscatine, Iowa, and Tracy, California.) It has also involved what Roussey calls "a total quality management approach to the business, understanding our customers' requirements and designing a program to meet those requirements."

Business is also growing on the institutional side of Heinz U.S.A.'s business where, incidentally, the Great American Soup brand name was reintroduced in 1979. In 1991, Heinz also bought the number-one brand in food-service soup, Chef Francisco, a premium frozen soup.

One of the keys to Chef Francisco's success has been packaging innovation. This proprietary soup's 13-sided tub thaws quickly, can be used as a measuring device to add milk or water, and interlocks for shipment in small, efficient cases. Chef Francisco has also jump-started a substantial frozen-soup food-service business for Heinz Canada, which now enjoys about a 45 share of market.

On the beans side, Heinz U.S.A. manufactures only vegetarian beans. It has always been the leader in this category, and still remains the number-one share brand, with about 55 percent of the market. Its greatest claim to fame, said former product manager Diane Roberts, is that it was the first kosher-approved national brand, endorsed by the Union of Orthodox Jewish Congregations of America in 1927. Today, many nonmeat Heinz products, such as ketchup, enjoy the kosher seal of approval. Two full-time rabbis inspect Pittsburgh factory procedures—strict start-up and cleanup rules must be followed—every day. Heinz vegetarian beans dominate the New York City and Los Angeles kosher markets, and are also shipped to Israel. Overall, however, they are but a small piece of the Heinz U.S.A. product pie.

The Ore-Ida Story

—⁓—

Frozen potatoes are to Americans what canned beans are to the British—a favorite family food, often a comfort food, a staple, nutritious product, and huge business. Potatoes are also the fourth biggest crop in the world, after wheat, rice, and corn, and play a major role in the American diet, almost twice the size (46 percent) of rice (22 percent) and pasta (24 percent).

Specifically, retail and food-service frozen potatoes are a $2.3 billion business, and, according to the National Potato Board, the average American devours 131 pounds of potatoes per year in every form, preferably baked and fried. In fact, only ice cream outsells potatoes in the frozen-food category.

Ore-Ida commandingly leads its category in U.S. retail super-markets (close to a 50-brand share), the way Heinz commandingly leads canned beans on U.K. grocery shelves. It's the quality brand generations of Americans feel good about serving to their families.

Consumer commitment to Ore-Ida is off the charts. "With the possible exception of the Heinz ketchup franchise," said market-ing guru Larry Lubin, "I have never seen loyalty to a brand like this." And, according to regional sales manager Henry vonSalzen, "It's still at an all-time high." In fact, Ore-Ida is one of the strongest consumer franchises in America and within the Heinz company.

Ore-Ida has gone from a one-plant company to one of North

America's largest diversified frozen-food processors. Its factories still produce many of Weight Watchers brand frozen-food products. Also, in addition to frozen potatoes, through a series of acquisitions, it has become a leading supplier of coated vegetables, stuffed pasta, and frozen appetizers to the retail and food-service business.

Ore-Ida is one of the largest producers of processed potatoes in the nation. In a single day, one plant produces enough french fries that, if placed end to end, would reach from Canada to Mexico. The company's potato volume is about one billion pounds, 50 percent retail and 50 percent food service. However, as O'Reilly has pointed out to security analysts, "We make 85 percent of our operating income on retail and only 15 percent on food service." Gross margins are far higher on the retail side.

To senior vice president David Sculley, "Ore-Ida has the capability of being the most important growth engine to the entire worldwide company in the 1990s . . . a barn burner of a company."[1]

John Heil, former general manager of Ore-Ida marketing, calls Ore-Ida "one of the Heinz Company's true treasures."

Heinz management created that treasure. It gradually transformed a small business and poorly managed regional player into a national powerhouse brand. How the "fearsome fivesome"—one of many names, including the A team, for the five senior managers, Paul Corddry, J Connolly, Gerry Herrick, Ed Osborne, and Bob Pedersen, who turned the company around—created the brand is one of the great turnaround success stories of the company.

1965 ACQUISITION

Ore-Ida Foods, Inc., with headquarters in Ontario, Oregon, was acquired in 1965, just at that pivotal moment in Heinz history

---

1. Remarks to senior operating managers in Plover, Wisconsin, in 1992.

when the U.S. side of the business was scrambling for profits. Jack Heinz was CEO, Frank Armour president, and Burt Gookin had moved up to executive vice president of Heinz U.S.A.

"Ore-Ida was spearheaded by Frank Armour and Bill Mewhort, vice-president, finance," said Don Wiley, then the Heinz Company's general counsel. Mewhort had been vice president, finance, at StarKist, and was the only StarKist executive to come to Pittsburgh.

Ore-Ida appeared to be a profitable frozen-potato business. Its sales in 1965 were about $30 million. But as one of the fearsome fivesome, Ed Osborne, recalled, "The money made in the first year of the acquisition was due to the price of potatoes, which went sky high because of a crop shortage. The company sold several cellars of fresh potatoes and diverted them from processing into the fresh market." In other words, the money wasn't made from the frozen-potato business, but from market factors.

Osborne and his wife lived through the entire drama. He had joined the Heinz Company in 1948, straight out of the Wharton School, after being interviewed by CFO Frank Cliffe, controller Burt Gookin, and treasurer Carl Brinkman. Gookin and Cliffe had convinced Osborne that "Heinz was a sleeping giant" with enormous potential for a young man. "He was absolutely right," said Osborne, "although it took about 15 years for that prophecy to come true."

Osborne helped Gookin set up the standard cost system in 1949, followed Brettholle into the job of insurance manager, and participated in the late-1950s changeover in the U.S. company from direct selling to distributors, which shrank a sales force of 1,500 to 500, cut back 78 warehouses to 30, and eliminated a fleet of 500 little white trucks, "washed every night," making store deliveries of as small as half a case. In 1965, as assistant to Armour, Osborne became part of the Ore-Ida acquisition team, then virtually commuted between Pittsburgh and Oregon for several years, and eventually became part of its top management.

At first, altogether in the hands-off Heinz tradition of acquisitions, Gookin and Armour left the Ore-Ida people and policies in place, fully expecting the company's profitable history to continue. They were in for a series of sad surprises.

The Grigg Brothers

Ore-Ida was a young company with a remarkable 14-year history. In 1951, two Mormon brothers, Nephi and Golden Grigg, bought at auction an old World War II frozen-food factory owned by the Bridgeford Company. In the midst of the auction, according to Don Masterson, retired vice president, industrial relations, who grew up in the area and joined the company in 1960, the brothers recessed the bidding, which had gone higher than anticipated, mortgaged their homes, found other investors, including Ross Butler, to put up funds. They then bought the plant and immediately shipped fresh corn to California markets in large, ice-refrigerated vans.

William Penn, retired manager of production scheduling, started working in the Ontario plant in 1952 during the corn season. "Nephi was a gutsy man who took a lot of chances," he recalled. "A big, agile guy who weighed around 300 pounds and stood about five feet, nine inches tall," Nephi was the driving force behind the business.

Much like the Founder 100 years before him, Nephi launched his business career "as a teenager by raising fresh corn and selling it door to door, using a horse and wagon."[2] One of 13 children, Nephi attended school through the 10th grade and later wrote in *Breefs by Neef*, "Sometimes I felt guilty for not going back to school, but everything I ever did was part of my education. I guess I always felt that education could come in a lot of ways."

The brothers processed their first french-fried potato in 1952, and a year later developed one of the company's most famous products, Tater Tots. It's still one of the company's top sellers. Not only was it a delicious morsel, but it transformed a heretofore wasted by-product of the potato (slivers shorn from the square section used to form French fries, normally sold for pennies as livestock feed) into a profitable product. Ground, mixed with

---

2. *ORE-IDA Profile* of F. Nephi Grigg. (An in-house publication.)

spices, extruded, and cooked in hot oil, it was considered a revolutionary innovation, which Nephi test-marketed in his own unique way. Here is how Ore-Ida officially recounted the story.

"After accumulating about 15 pounds of Tater Tots, Nephi Grigg packed them in dry ice and flew to a National Potato Convention held at the Fontainebleau Hotel in Miami, Florida. Just prior to the convention breakfast, Nephi bribed his way to the head cook on the lower floor and arranged to have the Tater Tots cooked, placed in small saucers and distributed on the breakfast tables for sample treats. These were all gobbled up quicker than a dead cat could wag its tail . . . the decision was made to proceed full speed ahead."[3]

Nephi, president of Ore-Ida and a member of the Heinz board for over three years, said Tater Tots exemplified one of his favorite mottoes: "You'll Never Go Broke by Taking a Profit." He used to enjoy sharing his homespun maxims for success with business audiences, such as, "Bite off more than you can chew, then chew on it."

"The Grigg brothers," said Masterson, "tried to get people interested in frozen foods . . . called on their first accounts themselves, briefcases filled with samples on dry ice. Nephi Grigg was the classic self-made man and entrepreneur. He had the franchise for the Tucker automobile in several counties; he owned packing houses; he'd been in the furniture and insurance business. He was a fast mover, a good fund raiser, folksy guy, and very good salesman."

Ore-Ida's main business was the processing and selling of frozen-potato products. It also produced frozen corn on the cob, mixed vegetables, onion rings, chopped onions, and dehydrated instant mashed potato flakes.

The company lacked professional management. The Griggs largely surrounded themselves with family and friends. For example, Nephi's brother-in-law, Otis Williams, was vice president of operations, and his son-in-law was head of public relations.

---

3. Nephi Grigg, "The Tater Tot Story," p. 4. (A corporate brochure.)

F. Nephi Grigg, founder of Ore-Ida, published Breefs by Neef, *which described, among other things, how Grigg developed Tater Tots, the product that launched Heinz into the frozen-food business when it acquired Ore-Ida in 1965.*

Tater Tots took a previously wasted by-product of the potato and turned it into a delicious and profitable product. Ground, mixed with spices, extruded, and cooked in hot oil, it was considered a revolutionary innovation.

More unusual was the fact that principals in the company, such as the Griggs, Williams, and Vanessa Anderson, also grew and supplied potatoes to the company. According to Osborne, it wasn't unusual to find four people at one potato contract negotiation who could have represented either side. Osborne sat in on one Burley, Idaho, meeting with Nephi and Williams representing management and Golden and Anderson representing the growers. "It was a very honest, open discussion in which both sides were representing their interests, but then they had to keep in mind that they'd have switched sides of the table just as easily as not and argued the other guy's point of view." At best, it was a complex and unorthodox situation.

Nevertheless, between 1951 and 1960, said Penn, "it was all growth. We got to the point where we couldn't manufacture enough potatoes to meet the market." Technological innovation spurred growth. For example, the storage of potatoes was still quite primitive. "You could only run the plants from August through April," recalled Penn. "Then they developed long-haul storage in the 1960s." California potatoes could now keep a factory running 12 months a year.

"The first frozen potatoes," said Penn, "were packaged in a nine-ounce box." That was because the Griggs had inherited the retail packaging machine from its corn operations. "Then they went to one-pound cartons," said Penn, "which was a big innovation, and in 1959, polyurethane packaging came into the business and changed the whole world of frozen food."

Between 1953 and 1960, the Ontario plant turned out about 300,000 pounds of potatoes a day. (To make 300,000 pounds of finished product requires using 600,000 pounds of raw potatoes a day.) In 1960, to meet demand, a second factory was built in Burley, Idaho. It produced another 500,000 pounds. Then, in 1961, the company went public, which gave it more funds to buy more factories, including an additional facility in Burley, known as Burley 2, and a plant in Greenville, Michigan. A fellow Mormon, Governor George Romney, wooed Ore-Ida to Michigan by not charging for the land on which the factory was to be built, thus putting jobs into a depressed area of his state.

During 1964–1965, Ore-Ida doubled its capacity and discovered that it had overbuilt, which is why the Grigg brothers suddenly decided to sell the company.

The Ore-Ida–Heinz stock transaction was equal to about $27 million of Heinz stock. It provided a source of fresh capital to Ore-Ida, and, in 1966, helped Heinz (with Star-Kist Foods, Inc.) to increase consolidated net income from the company's U.S. operations from 22 percent in 1965 and 15 percent in 1964 to 35 percent. It also boosted consolidated sales.

In 1965, the sales and marketing arm of Ore-Ida was handled by a national broker organization, D.B. Berelson, based in San Francisco. Dave and Bill Berelson brought added capital, including their own, into the business. Osborne considers Dave Berelson one of Ore-Ida's early heroes, "the master broker for the company in the 1960s, and a major investor who helped keep it going when it was struggling, which eventually made him a fairly sizable Heinz shareholder." Bill Moseley, who worked for Berelson, became the head of Ore-Ida's sales organization through the early 1970s.

Ore-Ida lacked marketing expertise, which was one of the reasons why, after the acquisition, Paul Corddry asked Gookin for the Ore-Ida marketing job. He and his wife had a yen to live on the West Coast and moved to San Francisco in May 1967.

"Everyone was real high on this acquisition when it happened," recalled Corddry, "and then as they started digging into it, they saw there were some problems."

When Corddry landed in San Francisco, he realized that the product was "basically being pushed through the system. There was no advertising or consumer marketing. The Berelsons had done a very good job, and Ore-Ida had a 20 share market, but brand recall was about 6 percent. Nobody really knew the brand. We were essentially just a commodity."

Corddry and an outside consultant, Joel Smilow, put together the company's first marketing plan, which allocated a modest $300,000 for the media budget. (Corddry managed to persuade the western division of Doyle Dane Bernbach to take on the account, although it normally didn't touch anything under $1 million.) After an intense eight-until-midnight week, pulling facts and figures together, Smilow said to Corddry, "Well, I gave you a lot of advice this week, but I'm going to give you your best advice right now. . . . Get your resumé out on the street immediately. This thing is a disaster."

Short term, Smilow was right.

BLACK MONDAY

Shortly after the Ore-Ida acquisition, the company suddenly started losing money, and no one knew why. In 1967, Gookin asked Armour to head a team to study Ore-Ida, then located in Ontario, Oregon. Connolly was also on the team that discovered mismanagement. Managers were contracting with themselves as potato growers on terms advantageous to themselves.

On August 19, 1967, known forever after as "Black Monday," Gookin flew to Oregon and virtually fired Ore-Ida's entire senior management team. "In fact," recalled Connolly, a member of the investigative group that led to the dismissals, "the rumor going around Ore-Ida was that the Federal Trade Commission [FTC] was investigating Heinz's acquisition, and Burt was rooting for the FTC." The jokes and war stories about those early days are legion.

Frank Armour, described by both Osborne and Connolly as "an unsung hero" of this difficult time, was temporarily put in charge of the company by Gookin. Nearing retirement, with nothing to gain from venturing to remote Ontario, Oregon, with his wife, but totally devoted to Heinz, he moved from Pittsburgh to the top floor of the four-story Moore Hotel (the tallest building in town). He brought, among others, Connolly and engineer Bob Rolfe, who later became head of technical services and a member of the management board.

Connolly, until then a lawyer, had gotten a "battlefield promotion," as he described it, moved his family to Idaho, and suddenly became responsible for procurement, logistics, operations, agriculture, and research and development.

Armour flew down to see Berelson and Corddry. "The good news," said Corddry, "was that I was promoted to vice president

In 1968, Ore-Ida moved its headquarters from Ontario, Oregon, to Boise, Idaho, and drew from other Heinz operations to assemble a young, top management team ranging in age from 32 to 49. Above, four of the "Fearsome Fivesome" at the January 21, 1968, ribbon-cutting ceremony at new Ore-Ida offices in Owyhee Plaza, Boise. Ed Osborne (rear left); Bob Pedersen (front left); Paul Corddry (center, without glasses); next to him and partly hidden, J. Wray Connolly (right); and, cutting the ribbon, Governor Samuelson (front right). Gerry Herrick, then vice president of operations, was not in attendance.

of marketing. The bad news was that I was asked to move to Boise, along with other members of the new A team."

Eventually, Bob Pedersen became president and chief executive officer; Ed Osborne, vice president of administration; J Connolly, vice president of planning and distribution; Gerry Herrick, vice president of operations; and Corddry, vice president of marketing. Don Masterson, from Ore-Ida's middle management, moved up to general manager of industrial relations.

"Second-level management," recalled Osborne, "turned out to be like finding gold. Among them were people like Masterson, Pete Helming, Gerry Herrick, Jack Dunsmore, head of quality control, Sam Haddad in research and development, and Glen Green, a kind of genius with machinery."

In 1968, right after Christmas, corporate headquarters—about 75 families—moved to Boise. The Ontario newspaper blamed the move on unhappy wives who had come from Pittsburgh and couldn't take small-town life. In fact, it was because, as Bob Pedersen told Penn, "We were spending more time concerned about the manufacture of the potato and how the potato was cut instead of being out there trying to get a cut of the market." Headquarters needed to distance itself from the day-to-day concerns of operations.

To those like Connolly and Osborne who had put in their time in Ontario, "Boise was spectacular." To Corddry in San Francisco, Boise looked like nowhere. Armour persuaded Corddry to try it. "Do it for me for six months," said Armour, "then if you don't like it, you can go back to Pittsburgh." Corddry and his family fell in love with Boise and stayed for 18 years.

"Boise is the worst place in the world to recruit somebody into," said Corddry, "because it just sounds like the end of the world. The only thing tougher is to try and transfer someone out." Indeed, with its friendly people, lovely climate, and individualistic spirit, it strikes many as an unspoiled paradise. That was particularly true in 1968.

Armour retired in 1968. When he retired, according to Connolly, the young Ore-Ida team, mostly in their 30s, whom Armour used to refer to as "his kids," gave him a bronze potato with a little plaque that said, "To Frank Armour, whose greatest fault was caring too much."

THE TURNAROUND CHALLENGE

Corddry had not taken Smilow's advice in 1967 because he was intrigued and challenged by the idea of turning Ore-Ida around, and decided it was doable.

"While we didn't have very good brand awareness, there wasn't anybody out there in the competitive arena." General Foods and

Birdseye were not supporting their brands and ultimately would get out of the frozen-potato business. "We had one of those competitive situations where if you did something, you could really make great gains."

Long term, Corddry was right. The turnaround just took a bit longer than anyone thought it would, from 1968 to 1972—four tough years.

"I think there were stages there that our careers, all of our collective careers, were very close to being ended," admitted Corddry. Osborne recalled that at one point, in the early 1970s, senior vice president Connell "kind of folded up his book and said, 'Fellows, I just hate to tell you this, but you're bloody well bankrupt.' "

The group even considered the possibility of a leveraged buyout by management (unheard of in those days) if Heinz decided to pull the plug. "We were dedicated and committed to a man," said Osborne. "Each one of the five of us believed in the thing." And, he added, "Burt Gookin had the patience to tolerate our lean years," despite the fact that, in the beginning, almost everything that could go wrong did go wrong.

In July 1969, a major fire destroyed most of the Ontario plant. "Rolfe and the people he hired got the factory back by the end of January, so we didn't lose the corn and onion seasons," recalled Osborne. "And we had a far better factory when we started up again."

Far more serious was a dreadful piece of real estate called Skyline Farms, incorporated as an Ore-Ida subsidiary in 1966. "They called it the world's biggest potato patch," said Masterson. Another venture, purported to be a semiprivate venture of Nephi and Golden, who both developed the property as entrepreneurs and principals of Ore-Ida, it ostensibly was bought to assure adequate potato supplies.

As the 1967 Heinz Annual Report optimistically proclaimed under a gorgeous photograph, "From barren wasteland to world's largest potato acreage in less than a year." Further on, it reported that "more than 240 million pounds of potatoes" were being cultivated. The first planting year produced the best results. After that, the yields were terrible.

As John Connell recalled, "It was an absolute disaster." Skyline

Farms was located on a plateau about 2,500 feet up. A salt layer two feet underneath the surface made it impossible to grow anything. "They brought in great machinery and chopped and churned the whole place up. Plus, water had to be pumped up 2,500 feet from the Snake River." Irrigated with sprinkler pipes that needed to be moved by hand, "it was squirted all over 25 square miles to no good effect at all," said Connell.

Worst of all, moving those sprinklers was back-breaking work. "We used everybody, from the local football team to Navajo Indians from New Mexico and Arizona," said Masterson.

They grew wheat, sugar beets, and alfalfa, and never made a penny. As one wag put it, "Every potato cost a million dollars." In 1973, prodded by O'Reilly, who had taken over from Connell in September 1971 as area vice president, the money-sucking venture was finally sold.

Skyline Farms, looking like a successful operation in this July 1968 photograph, proved to be, in John Connell's words, "an absolute disaster." Acquired in 1966 to assure adequate potato supplies, it supplied more headaches than potatoes and ultimately was sold.

During the 1970s, as capital became more expensive, Heinz began to look at its businesses as investment centers rather than as just profit centers. Bill Agnew, who replaced Mewhort as CFO in July 1971, recalled the first planning meeting at Ore-Ida just after O'Reilly had taken over as senior vice president. "I can remember going through an exercise with the management group that showed that, basically, they would about break even in five years." They were seeking major funding for future marketing.

Ore-Ida's A team caught on to more sophisticated financial and strategic planning approaches real fast. As Agnew pointed out, "Ore-Ida did everything we asked them to do, and is one of the great stories of Heinz because they just turned that company around."

But not before they resolved an ongoing difference of opinion between sales and marketing over how to move the business forward. Do you push the products through as had been done in the past? Or take the higher risk and costlier marketing route— investing in packaging, consumer testing, advertising—to establish a brand franchise?

The young management team fought it out. Weldon Moffat, an industrial psychologist brought into a management retreat at the Scottsdale, Arizona, Camelback Inn, later told Corddry, "It was the wildest looking group of people I'd ever seen." Corddry had a huge bushy head of hair in those days; Connolly, a brush cut.

It was one of their better management board meetings. "We thought we were communicating reasonably well," said Corddry. Moffat was supposed to take the group through team building exercises that afternoon. "Well, Weldon," said Pedersen, how would you rate us on a scale of zero to 100?" Moffat replied, "About four."

By the early 1970s, the company was beginning to turn its first profit when it had another unforeseen setback. President Richard M. Nixon and Secretary of the Treasury John Connolly announced the imposition of wage and price controls. Ore-Ida had just increased its price for the first time in three years, and was forced to rescind it. Osborne, working with the law department and government, managed to get price relief after about eight months.

Corddry took charge of sales and marketing in 1971 and the

A team, under Pedersen, roared forward. Years of planning suddenly began to pay off, including investments in quality, new products, improved technical services, new facilities, packaging and logo redesign. Costs came down, price premiums rose, and with more money to spend on marketing, business boomed.

The process of turning the company around had taught Connolly, among other things, that he loved the management side of the business. In 1973, just as all the hard work was paying off, Connolly got a phone call from Gookin. He wanted Connolly to come back to Pittsburgh to become corporate treasurer. "If you can imagine being unqualified for anything," recalled Connolly, "I was really unqualified for that." He told Gookin, "No thanks."

"Then one day—I'll never forget that day—Burt called me and said, 'There is a nonstop flight from Boise to Pittsburgh that leaves at 11:45 and you have a seat on tomorrow's plane. I would like you to be in it.' So that's when I became treasurer." After which his career took off. He became president of the Hubinger Company, the head of Heinz U.S.A., and served as senior vice president in Europe and World Headquarters, retiring from the company and board in 1993. Paul Renne is now corporate treasurer.

The 1970s were the Pedersen years. Between 1971 and 1982, the company moved from about a 20 share to a 50 share of the frozen-potato business.

O'Reilly saw that things had turned around. According to Corddry, "He recognized that Ore-Ida might be one of the company's growth stars and brought support in the form of marketing and capital investment money." Ore-Ida became O'Reilly's first big success. "His support was unlimited," said Osborne, "once he was convinced that Ore-Ida was right and we were right."

THE GLORY DAYS

"When we started to turn the thing up, it just flew," said Corddry. By 1976, Ore-Ida accounted for "virtually half of all frozen-potato products sold in retail stores."[4] It was the beginning of what Mick Tyler, today's vice president of retail marketing, calls "the glory days."

Corddry became executive vice president in 1975 and, when Pedersen retired, president of Ore-Ida from 1977 to 1986. These were the Corddry years of growth, acquisitions, and immense profitability. In 1986, Corddry was promoted to senior vice president and moved back to Pittsburgh. In 1989, he transferred to England as senior vice president of Europe, where he remained until his decision to take early retirement in 1992 at the age of 55.

According to John Heil, who joined the company as regional sales manager in 1978 and rose to general manager, marketing, in 1987, Corddry was a "charismatic and visionary executive who attracted a very motivated and loyal cadre of managers. He also stayed ahead of the curve with the consumer."

A vigorous believer in strong, brand-franchise building, he invested in consumer research, consumer advertising, and a Doyle Dane Bernbach family-oriented television campaign. Its signature phrase, "When it says Ore-Ida, it's all righta!," solidified the brand name. In 1978 alone, for example, the company spent more than $15 million on network TV and women's-magazine advertising, "making it one of the biggest spenders in the frozen-food business."[5]

Corddry also emphasized broker communications as a key to increasing space on the freezer shelf. As with soups and baby food, more varieties helped Ore-Ida to by far lead the frozen-potato category.

By 1978, guided by Corddry and Dick Blott, vice president, sales and marketing, Ore-Ida's market share had surpassed 50 percent and become the number-one frozen-food item in the United States in terms of retail tonnage.

The A team built both the underdeveloped frozen-potato category, which grew about 2 to 3 percent a year, and Ore-Ida's share of the category, which grew about twice as fast, at about 8 percent a year.

---

4. H. J. Heinz Company Annual Report, 1976.

5. *Sales and Marketing Management*, December 12, 1977.

"When It Says It's Ore-Ida, It's All-Righta." Doyle Dane Bernbach television campaign that solidified the Ore-Ida brand name.

In 1975, the company added a second factory in Ontario, and in 1979, built a new facility in Plover, Wisconsin, which proved to be such an outstanding and efficient facility with such high-quality potatoes that Ore-Ida doubled Plover's size in 1983.

ORE-IDA'S RUSSET BURBANK

Potatoes, like tomatoes, are mostly water. Frying a potato basically eliminates water and concentrates taste. The solid content of a potato is about 18 to 20 percent. Ninety percent of all potatoes processed by Ore-Ida are the russet Burbank, which have a larger proportion of solids to water than other varieties, and thus, in addition to good taste, deliver higher returns.

Ore-Ida was the first company to make a consistent, high-quality retail french fry in a business where—contrary to most businesses—the gold standard has always been the food-service fast-food product. Consistent consumer advertising drove home the message of Ore-Ida's superior russet Burbank potatoes. CEO Pedersen stood in a potato field and talked about how the quality of the french fry depended on good-quality potatoes ("Ore-Ida doesn't make any french fries from damp, soggy potatoes"), thus educating the public and capturing premier brand leadership. The company has retained that role to this day.

Its top varieties were, and remain, crinkle cuts and Tater Tots. Also introduced during those years were valued-added products, such as hash browns, home styles, and Crispers!, also made from ground-up scraps and extruded into a new form of french fry.

Corddry initiated strategic moves that are still paying off, including the introduction of Ore-Ida potatoes into Japan, where, with a 20 percent national share, it remains market leader. He expanded the food-service area, as well.

Until 1976 or so, said Pat Kinney, vice president of sales, food service was "the stepchild of retail and less than 25 percent of the company's volume." Between 1976 and 1979, under general manager Wayne Durfey and national sales manager Mike Frelleson, the food-service sales force was upgraded, as were its brokers, and the company "got serious" about developing food-service products and acquiring major fast-food accounts. (Shoestrings for these accounts remain Ore-Ida's biggest food-service item.) This rise in food-service volume meant that the plants could run at full capacity, thus reducing costs and optimizing profitability.

By the mid-1980s, when the retail french-fried-potato category began to slow down, food service continued to grow. In fact, it moved from mid-1980s' volumes of 340 million to late 1980s' volumes of 450 million to today's volumes of over 500 million pounds.

ACQUISITIONS

It was Corddry whose frozen-food diversification strategy prompted the acquisition of Foodways National. Indeed, 1977–1979 were years of nonpotato growth.

"The potato business was still moving very nicely when we bought Foodways in 1978," said Corddry. As it turned out, "Foodways was Ore-Ida revisited."

Foodways National, the frozen-entrée part of the Weight Watchers business, moved to Boise and, run by Herrick, reported to Corddry.

In 1979, the two companies moved to new joint headquarters— a handsome, custom-designed, cedar-and-glass building perched a few yards from the tree-lined Boise River.

Its magnificent, parklike setting overlooks a public green belt, with paths constantly used by joggers and bikers, that runs along both sides of the river. Whenever Ore-Ida's managers are accused by Pittsburgh of being too laid back, Boise management suspects it's largely due to the idyllic look of their work environment, a far cry from the modest, gritty 19th-century brick home of Heinz U.S.A.

Nevertheless, it's true that the organizational culture, according to Masterson, who retired after 31 years, was consciously set up to be "informal but professional and to promote openness." This was hardly surprising for a young group of senior managers in a young, western company unencumbered by the past and flush with success. (In 1979, for example, *Sales and Marketing Management Magazine* bestowed its "Most Distinguished Award" on the Ore-Ida marketing group for its skillful marketing of frozen-food products.)[6]

"Also," said Masterson, "we made a conscious decision not to have an executive wing, but to have all the vice presidents in their own area with their people." They also encouraged younger managers to make presentations to the board, giving them an opportunity to "strut their stuff."

---

6. H. J. Heinz Company Annual Report, 1979.

In 1979, Foodways National and Ore-Ida moved to new joint headquarters, a handsome, custom-designed cedar-and-glass building perched along the tree-lined Boise River.

In 1980, Ore-Ida bought Gagliardi Brothers—Blott took over as president and CEO, moving to West Chester, Pennsylvania—with its regional Steak-umm line of products.

Ore-Ida continued to test new products, but, as Linda Tiffany, who joined the 10-person research and development facility in Boise in 1969, recalled, "It took us a long time to get new products out." In 1982, the research and development group restructured and inaugurated an improved product development system, the Project Review Committee (PRC). An innovative, team approach, it met four times a year, and helped to focus and prioritize new-product development. After the 1978 Foodways National acquisition, it also worked on Weight Watchers brand products.

Jim Matthews, now head of research and development at Ore-Ida, joined Foodways National's Connecticut research and development team in 1980. His first assignment was to reformulate the entire line. "We worked fast and hard," recalled Matthews. While the formulations were done in Connecticut, much of the testing was done in Ontario.

"Foodways was the Listerine of frozen dinners," said Corddry. "Lousy food, medicinal-looking packaging."

Foodways National spent about a year and a half fixing old products, and then turned its attention to launching new ones. Just as Foodways National had finished repositioning the original Weight Watchers brand line, "Lean Cuisine came in and just whipped by us so fast," said Corddry, "we thought we'd been totally outmaneuvered."

In the end, Corddry and Herrick convinced O'Reilly to "take them on." Both brands did extremely well, building the category. Foodways National eventually overtook Lean Cuisine. It also added a major profit stream to Ore-Ida, which carried it through the 1980s.

THE ENVIRONMENT CHANGES

As baby boomers aged, households with children under 15—Ore-Ida's key consumers—began to shrink. The frozen-potato category flattened out.

Between 1982 and 1987, however, Ore-Ida's lack of volume growth was masked by increased profit margins derived from a combination of lower costs and constant price increases, as well as by, as David Sculley put it, "the electrifying performance of Foodways." Between 1981 and 1987, Ore-Ida's profits doubled. But in 1987, the Ore-Ida bubble burst for three reasons: falling sales volumes, a huge potato crop, and Foodways National's loss of growth momentum.

Potatoes, like tomatoes, are a cyclical business. Large crops drive down the marketplace price, which means that the price differential between private-label and brand products widens. In 1987, according to Mick Tyler, "Ore-Ida's price premium was about 50 percent." Also, of course, when supermarkets are giving away free bags of potatoes, which is what they did in 1987, consumers buy fewer frozen products. The reverse is equally true. When potatoes are expensive, the consumer tends to buy more frozen potatoes at home, as do restaurants. So expensive potatoes are positive on both the retail and food-service side, good on demand and price.

Yet Ore-Ida strongly rebounded between 1988 and 1991, increasing the frozen-potato category 28 percent, and with it, Ore-Ida volume. Market share went back up from 44 to 50.

Herrick Years

Gerry Herrick took over as Ore-Ida CEO in 1986. (John Glerum followed Herrick as CEO of both Foodways and Ore-Ida, and retired in 1991.) According to Tyler and Heil he was a hands-on manager and facilitator who got marketing, operations, and research and development to march together; launched a "back-to-basics" program, dedicated to product quality; and increased marketing support.

Even more important, according to Lubin, Herrick understood that the company wasn't just in the "quality french-fry business," but as various consumer studies underscored, "Ore-Ida was in the business of making Mom feel like a better Mom."

"This product not only had incredible equity, but 'unique' equity with the consumer," said Lubin. "Every time Mom served the product, she had a happy meal, because the kids loved it and she felt good about it, too. Ore-Ida potatoes made for a home-run meal."

In other words, Ore-Ida began to tap into the magic of the brand by building on what Lubin termed "the mother love strategy." Doyle Dane turned out commercials that emotionally linked good parenting to rewarding kids with a home-run meal.

At the same time, the company launched new lines of value-added products, which expanded the business. They included twice-baked potatoes, microwave potatoes, and battered fries.

"Sales are built on new items," said vonSalzen, "just like automobiles are built on new styles. Ore-Ida is doing more with the potato than was probably ever imaginable years ago."

Sales are also built by motivated and well-rewarded brokers. Ore-Ida's regional managers spend a great deal of their time training and educating their brokers and coming up with new incentives for them. Since 1980, Ore-Ida has provided what many brokers consider "the best and classiest incentive program in the business"—Super Shuffle—for brokers who attain or surpass volume goals in potatoes, corn, and onions.

Today, there are about 50 product varieties at retail alone (a constant pruning process removes the lowest performers), with every conceivable taste, ranging from baked potatoes topped with salsa and cheese, onion Tater Tots, Texas Crispers, and western-style toaster hash browns to various types of twice-baked potatoes.

Ore-Ida's expanded product line came to be known as John Heil's "own-the-potato" vision. Heil had realized, while listening to focus groups, that one of the reasons french fries couldn't grow as a category was that homemakers would only serve them with a few main dishes. So Ore-Ida moved from a limited french-fry product range to a limitless frozen-potato range. "It was my first big aha!" His second quickly followed, giving birth to the battered-fry line, which, like flavored potato chips, opened up a wide range of new flavor possibilities.

Ore-Ida became a major force in every segment of the frozen-potato category. Not only did these moves reignite category growth, but they helped to sustain price levels. In 1990, the company generated its largest profit and again began taking price increases.

It also entered the 1990s with a new wave of nonpotato acquisitions focusing on the specialty retail frozen market. These included Bavarian Specialty Foods, Inc., Celestial Farms, Inc., and Continental Delights. The company also added a new factory in Pocatello, Idaho, and bought a vending machine company for french fries.

A Watershed Year

Nineteen ninety-one turned out to be another watershed year. In July, Foodways National became part of the new Weight Watchers Food Company. In September, Ore-Ida integrated units of the JLFoods acquisition, a major supplier of frozen foods to the food-service industry (among them, Bagel Bites, primarily sold in warehouse and club stores), and Delicious Foods, producer of coated vegetables and cheeses. At the same time, it was hit by another one–two punch: the recession and largest potato crop in the history of the company. It was 1987 all over again.

Price differentials between private label and Ore-Ida were once more too great. Recession-battered consumers sought lower-priced brands. Category volume slumped; Ore-Ida lost three to four share points and profits were down. Ore-Ida recognized it was time for a change. To recharge itself and grow, it would have to become a leaner and more focused entrepreneurial culture.

Like its sister, Weight Watchers Food Company, a recommitted "new" Ore-Ida began to fight back under the leadership of CEO Bob White and the enthusiastic, down-in-the-trenches oversight-style of senior vice president Sculley.

Just before Christmas 1991, Sculley flew to Boise to assess the situation, and after "two days of seeing people in action, seeing a commitment to reducing cost and an array of new products that absolutely knocked my socks off . . . I called Tony O'Reilly and said I couldn't be more excited . . . Ore-Ida is a diamond in the rough. 'And by the way,' I added, 'we need $6 million between January and April to get our share back, and $30 million for products we haven't tested yet but seem like a pretty good idea.' "[7]

Sculley, a man who truly loves products and still involves himself in focus groups, packaging, and key media decisions, was most excited by two innovative products that had the potential to give the entire frozen-potato business a sizable volume boost: micro-waveable mashed potatoes from a special Swedish process, for

---

7. Remarks to Ore-Ida brokers, May 1992.

which Ore-Ida owns the patent rights through the year 2002; and Fast Fries, the first retail oven-baked product to duplicate the taste and crunch of fast-food restaurants' french fries, at half the price. The shoestring fry is coated with a superthin batter to achieve the oven-crisp effect.

Ore-Ida's array of new products, after a fairly long new-product drought, had the potential to deliver 150 million pounds of incremental business, hence Sculley's optimism about the company's future.

According to Meg Carlson, vice president, specialty products, the company launched a record 42 new products in retail, food-service, and club stores.

Success required risk taking, flexible managers, breaking old paradigms, doing more with less, moving aggressively and swiftly. It meant redesigning processes, becoming more customer and consumer oriented, being more profit and cost driven.

Ore-Ida stemmed and turned the tide. It reduced prices, and aggressively promoted existing products, while also introducing new ones. The combined strategy energized Ore-Ida's troops.

Indeed, fueled by its new products and strategies, Ore-Ida has revved up for another growth spurt. To help get it there, the company has reorganized under president and CEO Dick Wamhoff, who moved from StarKist to Ore-Ida in May 1993 after Bob White retired.

"Wamhoff," said Kinney, "is a take-charge kind of guy. He hit the ground running."

Two days after his official arrival and taking a leaf from the Heinz U.S.A. mid-1970s reorganization, he divided the company into three focused strategic business units: retail marketing for the Ore-Ida product line; food-service marketing for potatoes, coated products, baked goods, and specialty products; and new-business development.

In a sense, each business unit is a minicompany. Each vice president has been given clear accountability, clear cost-reduction and growth goals, as well as dedicated resources, including factories. The name of the game is to respond ever more quickly to shifting customer and consumer needs. Ore-Ida is particularly proud of the fact that Fast Fries moved from concept to supermarket freezer in only six months.

Ore-Ida's growth strategies are definitely working. By mid-1993, the retail frozen-potato category was growing again, up 6 percent, and Ore-Ida's core line had grown from 43 percent to over 50 percent. Growth was spurred, in part, by the successful introduction of Fast Fries and mashed potatoes.

"Fast Fries are already one of the top 10 in our line," said Tyler. "Consumers love them, and there is still plenty of upside growth potential."

Ore-Ida introduced the product with a bang. "It spent a whopping $5 million for a single week's worth of TV ads to ballyhoo the product," reported the May 3 issue of *Food Business* magazine. Within the first year, it expects to spend an unprecedented $30 million for extensive media and trade support, as well as on direct mail and couponing.

Mashed potatoes, while a slower volume build, said Tyler, "are not only a strong addition to our product line, but, from what we can see, all incremental business."

Nothing on the market resembles this product, which consists of tiny frozen pellets of riced potatoes, to which milk is added. As one reviewer enthused, "This new product is so good and innovative, I predict it will be the beginning of a whole new frozen-mashed-potato section in supermarket freezers."[8] It, too, has been backed by significant marketing dollars.

On the food-service side of the business, Ore-Ida enjoys about 10 percent of the market.

Food service is more an operator-driven business where leverage resides in offering advantages to the restaurateur, such as consistent quality, value, and custom-tailored products.

Forty-five percent of the food-service pie is potatoes, 45 percent is coated vegetables, and 10 percent other products, such as baked goods, Italian pasta, and sandwiches.

In 1993, Ore-Ida made a key $90 million food-service acquisition of Moore's frozen onion rings and Domani frozen pasta, both from Clorox. In a single move, it has transformed Ore-Ida into the leading supplier to the nation's $856 million frozen-appetizers category. It's a category of the food-service business that grew 42

---

8. Bonnie Tandy Leblang and Carolyn Wyman, "Frozen Mashed Potatoes a Tasty Innovation," *The Pittsburgh Post Gazette,* July 7, 1993.

percent between 1986 and 1991. Clearly, it will solidify Ore-Ida as a major player in food service.

Ore-Ida specialty products are already 15 to 20 percent of sales, and have the potential eventually to equal the retail potato business. Led by Meg Carlson, a well-seasoned executive who has moved steadily forward since joining the Weight Watchers marketing team in 1982, the company is solidifying national distribution of Bagel Bites and increasing that of Igor's Piroshkis (pocket sandwiches). Another key goal is to become the number-one national stuffed-pasta brand, which is another reason Ore-Ida acquired Domani. It will complement the company's existing Rosetto brand stuffed-pasta line.

It's been said that one of the best-kept secrets about Heinz is its major role as processor and supplier of frozen foods. With the latest Moore's and Domani acquisitions, the secret may be out. In any case, reenergized, reorganized, and well focused to support its expanding product mix, Wamhoff fully expects Ore-Ida is on its way toward becoming a "barn burner" of a Heinz company.

The StarKist Story:
Tuna and Heinz Pet Products

The acquisition of StarKist in April 1963 marked a key turning point in the H. J. Heinz Company's fortunes. The stock transaction between two family-run food companies (the Heinz Company traded 286,279 shares of cumulative preferred stock for StarKist's outstanding stock) was a bold and critical move that advanced the interests of both parties.

With a single stroke, the acquisition added StarKist sales of $70 million to the parent company's U.S. sales and earnings, which were at an all-time low. It brought to the Heinz board a man Fred Crabb called "a born entrepreneur," StarKist's president, the inimitable Joseph J. Bogdanovich, known to everyone as Joe B. And it catapulted Heinz into a new and growing sector of the U.S. food business with its first major non-Heinz brand.

Joe B was prompted to sell the privately held family business, in which he held a majority share, because his five sisters, Lucretia, Dorothy, Mary, Katherine, and Geraldine, were seeking financial independence, and because the tuna industry was changing.

Bigger companies were taking over family businesses. In fact, the week before Heinz announced its intention to acquire StarKist, Ralston Purina announced its plan to buy Van Camp, which marketed tuna under the Chicken of the Sea and White Star brands.

Van Camp then dominated the business with about 80 percent of the tuna market. StarKist "needed some strength," said former president and CEO John Real. A lawyer, he joined StarKist in 1955 as assistant to the president, Joe B.

Interestingly, the Ralston–Van Camp marriage worked poorly, while the Heinz–StarKist union became a model of success.

Gookin, it turned out, was exactly the right executive for StarKist. "He assisted in the financing," said J. G. "Jerry" Scharer, then head of marketing, "and didn't interfere with our methods of procuring, selling, or marketing tuna." "Van Camp wasn't smart enough to leave management alone," added Scharer, who would later follow Joe B as StarKist president.

Gookin was pressured to change StarKist's independent ways. John Real recalled that in the 1960s, "there was a strong push by some to have StarKist products handled like Heinz products, through direct salesmen instead of brokers. We fought that tooth and nail. Gookin finally put his foot down and let us continue as we were. Van Camp did the opposite. They went from brokers to direct sales. It hurt them, and we took advantage of that fact."

Ultimately, the two canned-tuna giants reversed their fortunes. Chicken of the Sea lost market share (the original owner, Van Camp, eventually quit), and StarKist ascended to the number-one spot, where it remains to this day, almost three times as big as Chicken of the Sea in terms of market share.

The marriage got off to a rocky start due to a non-StarKist botulism incident. Two Detroit-area women died of botulism in March 1963 after eating Great Atlantic & Pacific Tea Company brand tuna. It briefly devastated tuna sales moments after the acquisition papers were signed. However, "Scharer led the recovery," said Real, both by convincing grocers of the importance of tuna to their profits, and by keeping advertising and marketing budgets up.

Sales recovered within the year, and the Heinz Company's first major acquisition turned out to be a master stroke.

Thanks to StarKist's explosive growth, Heinz domestic sales and earnings steadily rose. In fact, a decade later, over 70 percent of U.S. profits emanated from StarKist!

StarKist's performance may well explain why, as Tony O'Reilly genially noted at Joe B's 80th birthday party in May 1992, "Joe never felt that Heinz bought StarKist. He always felt StarKist bought Heinz." It also explains why Bogdanovich and his hot-shot management team (particularly Scharer and Real) were regarded with such respect and affection by those who vividly recall those years.

"StarKist," said Don Wiley, was "loaded with a lot of strong-willed managers who were very good at their jobs, who ran autonomously for years and generated the earnings the company needed for years . . . they were smart guys. They really knew how to run the tuna business. I liked them."

Wiley, now on the Heinz board of directors and vice chairman of the company foundation, was the lawyer on the deal. "When we acquired them," said Wiley, "all of the guys at StarKist thought they were better than their counterparts at Heinz, and—except for the finance side—they were right."

Indeed, by 1963, Joe B—with a lean management team—had expanded his father's California cannery into a global organization, and transformed tuna into America's most popular fish product, thus creating today's $2 billion industry. Over the next 20 years, StarKist would become the number-one brand and launch the enormously successful 9-Lives cat food, again helping to create and expand a new, multibillion-dollar pet-food industry.

MARTIN BOGDANOVICH LAUNCHES COMPANY

The tuna business first started in the United States because of a natural disaster. Sardine canneries had been operating out of San Pedro, California (south of Los Angeles), since 1896. By 1903, it was a giant industry. Sardines were first canned in Maine in 1877. They were a different type of fish, packed in a flat 3½- or four-ounce can, while California sardines were packed in tall 15-ounce cans. Hundreds of thousands of cases were packed and sold around the United States. Suddenly, sardines disappeared from California waters.

Tuna, regarded only as a game fish by Americans around the turn of the century, was rediscovered as a food product by Alfred

P. Halfhill. In 1903, he steamed an albacore in a redwood box, sold 700 cases for $3,500, and launched a new industry.

Historically, tuna was considered a great delicacy by both the ancient Greeks, who called it *thynnos*, and the Incas, who called it *xatunkama*. A member of the same family as the mackerel, streamlined and built for speed, tuna are perpetual-motion machines. Because tuna must move to breathe, they even swim when asleep. Tuna travel in compact schools and have been clocked at speeds of up to 45 miles per hour.

In 1908, Martin J. Bogdanovich (1882–1944) emigrated to San Pedro from a fishing village on the Dalmatian coast of the Adriatic Sea. He and his bride, Antoinette Simich, arrived in this flourishing community of Yugoslav fishermen overlooking Terminal Island while on their honeymoon. In classic, rags-to-riches, only-in-America fashion, they built an industry and family fortune.

Bogdanovich worked for other fishermen, saved his money, and in 1910 bought *The Ripper* for less than $2,000, which launched him ("one man, one boat" as the company profiles are fond of pointing out) on his independent business path. At a 1984 50th-anniversary "This Is Your Life" party for Joe B, where he was given a replica of *The Ripper* by employees, he said it was actually his father's second boat.

During one of Martin's longer fishing trips, he ventured to Santa Barbara, visited a friend with an ice plant, and got the revolutionary idea of storing crushed ice on his boat to freeze his catch. This enabled his boats to travel greater distances and still return with fish in a "fresh state."

Martin kept adding boats and, according to Joe B, bringing more cousins over from Yugoslavia to run the plants. (Most of StarKist's plants and operations, well into the 1960s, were run by relatives of the Bogdanovich and Simich families.) After he began to use ice instead of kelp to keep fish cool, his boats caught three times as much fish as everyone else's, and made three times as much money. With 20 family boats running, in 1914, he opened the California Fish Company, a retail market.

By 1913, nine plants on Terminal Island were canning albacore and selling 115,000 cases a year. Sardines had come back and, along with mackerel, still were a major part of the canned-fish business. They were deep fried in oil and then packed.

Martin J. Bogdanovich, born in Dalmatian, Yugoslavia in 1882, took his new bride to San Pedro, California, in 1908. Two years later, he bought his own fishing boat, and in 1917, invested in the French Sardine Company, which his son Joe B would later expand and build into StarKist.

In 1917, sardines again disappeared. At the same time, World War I meat shortages provided the tuna industry with a major boost. The U.S. government, seeking new, economical sources of protein, turned to tuna and bought as much fish as could be harvested. Martin appreciated the profit to be made. He and five partners invested their life savings in a small cannery, the French Sardine Company (capitalization: $10,000). Martin became its first president. Incorporated on November 10, 1917, its first office was located at 183 Fish Harbor Wharf, San Pedro. At the company's April 1, 1918, board of directors meeting, the other elected officers included Nick Vilicich, vice president; Joseph M. Mardesich, secretary; James Mirkovich, treasurer; and Ivo Mirkovich, foreman.

The next 20 years—with the depression, fluctuating fish prices, and increasing competition—were a struggle. Many canneries went under, and three of Martin's four partners sold him their interests. But the French Sardine Company continued to grow.

Tuna came and went as mysteriously as sardines. In 1925, the California fishing industry was turning out about one million cases of tuna, but again faced disaster when, in 1926, albacore tuna disappeared from local waters, prompting a whole series of industry changes. These included adding yellowfin and skipjack to the

StarKist's Plant 1 production line on Terminal Island. "When the sardines came in," recalled John Zelovich, "it might be two in the morning. They would blow the whistle and that was everyone's call to go to work. People stayed on the job until the fish were all packed, even if it took two days." Zelovich's father was a plant foreman, who retired after 48 years. His mother worked in the first-aid department. "My grandparents worked there, my aunts, uncles, sister. It was just what you did. It was like a family. Everybody fought like a family, too, but after the fish were packed, everybody sat down and had coffee together."

Chartered tender of the French Sardine Company, S.S. Golden Star, circa 1937. Martin Bogdanovich kept adding boats to his fleet, and came up with the idea of using ice instead of kelp to keep fish cool, which enabled his boats to travel farther, catch more fish, and make more money than competitors.

BLUEFIN
(THUNNUS THYNNUS)

SKIPJACK
(KATSUWONUS PELAMIS)

ALBACORE
(THUNNUS GERMO OR THUNNUS ALALUNGA)

YELLOWFIN
(NEOTHUNNUS MACROPTERUS)

Premier-priced albacore, or white-meat tuna, is considered the finest tuna because of its mild taste and firm texture, and runs between nine and 70 pounds. Fishing is limited to the warm months of the year. Yellowfin, skipjack, and bluefin are known as light-meat tunas. Yellowfin can be found in tropical climates and, at between 30 and 70 pounds, is ideal for canning. Skipjack, the most abundant tuna, swims in equatorial waters. Bluefin is primarily a Mediterranean 15- to 18-pound fish. To this day, no one knows much about tuna, where they spawn, where they can be found, or where they are headed, all of which adds to the romance and mystery of the hunt, and the constant uncertainty of procurement.

product line. This prompted longer trips to find tuna, which, in turn, brought larger boats and, ultimately, refrigerated boats.

With local tuna no longer a certainty and fishermen forced to venture down the coast of South America as far as Peru—3,500 miles away—to track and catch their nomadic prey, the fleet changed in the 1930s from family-run small-boat operations to tuna clippers. Fewer, but far more expensive, vessels were now able to travel 10,000 miles from home port, stay at sea up to four months, carry a crew of 10 to 18, and hold from 150 to 350 tons of refrigerated fish.

From the beginning, Martin marketed his products—mainly sardines, mackerel, squid, and anchovies—through a broker, the Van Landingham Company in Los Angeles. According to Joe B, "The French Sardine Company got into the tuna business in a very small way, mainly packing private-label *tonno* (Italian for tuna). We had a big Italian trade in New York, Chicago, and San Francisco."

In 1926, the company also marketed tuna under two brand names, Belle Isle and Robidoux. Martin's first attempt at advertising, dropping 2,000 coupons over the city of Buffalo, New York, was a distinct failure. In 1932, sales had reached $600,000.[1]

Joe B grew up in the business, working in the cannery, spending summers fishing with the fleet, listening to and watching his father operate. Canneries not only bought fish, but advanced money to fishermen (in San Pedro and San Diego), underwriting their increasingly expensive voyages.

Joe B officially joined the company in 1934, after he graduated from the University of Southern California (USC) with a major in business administration. By then he knew everyone in the closely knit business, from hook-and-line Yugoslav fishermen and Portuguese skippers to competitive canners up and down the coast.

Father and son "clashed and agreed, clashed and agreed," said Scharer, who met Joe B when both were freshmen at USC. Scharer joined the company in 1935, during the depth of the Great Depression. "Martin ran the company," said Scharer "with an iron fist."

---

1. From Jerry Scharer's personal history of the company, an album of photos and text compiled by his secretary, Shirley Lynn, in December 1958.

The French Sardine Company took to the air in August 1928. It dropped 2,000 coupons for Belle Isle tuna over the city of Buffalo, New York. The dramatic move made good newspaper copy, but was a financial failure.

JOE B TAKES OVER

In 1937, Martin turned over active management to Joe B. He and Scharer created the strategies that would ignite explosive postwar growth.

During World War II, tuna clippers were commandeered by the U.S. Navy for surveillance and to carry supplies and troops, so tuna available for canning declined. But by 1942, the French Sardine Company was prospering. Joe B had convinced his father to buy up everyone's sardine supplies, in addition to their own, and sales had already grown to $4 million.[2]

---

2. "A Thumbnail Sketch," Star-Kist Foods, Inc., slide-show presentation to brokers, 1979.

By 1944, the company had become the number-one sardine–mackerel producer in the country, boasting a 75 percent share of market and sales of $6,500,000. And all this was achieved, as Martin pointed out, without spending a nickel on advertising.

Martin and Joe Bogdanovich were idolized in San Pedro. "The whole community respected that family," said Matt Mattich, retired StarKist office manager, "because they created so many jobs and helped so many fishermen." Mattich, a tall boy, had lied about his age, and started working, at the age of 13, in the sardine packing room of Plant 1, where the original StarKist began. His wages were 90 cents an hour, and he still has his first W-2 form from the French Sardine Company. Practically one of the family, he retired in 1992 after 47 years with the company. He had the unique distinction of holding two full-time jobs for 25 years. He put in 100-hour work weeks, juggling a variety of increasingly responsible jobs at StarKist, plus holding a full-time job with the Los Angeles City Fire Department.

Scharer worked for "Doc" Williams, head of sales, and between 1937 and 1948 traveled the 48 states twice a year as the company's only salesperson, calling on the trade with brokers. By the time he retired in 1983, he had expanded the broker force from 30 to about 100. Scharer became vice president of sales in 1947 when Williams died, vice president of marketing in 1957, president in 1976, and vice chairman in 1978.

Scharer and Joe B were eager to brand their tuna and begin national advertising. Martin believed they were doing fine without the added effort and expense. Then, at a 1941 brokers' convention in Chicago, fate stepped in.

Joe B and Jerry were approached in their hotel room by Barney Tast, a former White Star broker from Salt Lake City, who wanted to help them build tuna sales, and suggested the StarKist brand name, as well as a kissing couple on the label. Scharer immediately told Joe B, "This is the brand we want." Joe negotiated and closed the deal with Tast. The company got the brand and Tast got the StarKist account in his territory for life. In 1942, the StarKist label first appeared on tuna cans, minus the kissing couple.

The war again brought opportunities and challenges. Rationing created an increased demand for inexpensive sources of protein. A new generation of Americans—in the trenches via K rations

In 1953, the French Sardine Company officially changed its name to Star-Kist Foods, Inc., headed by president and CEO Joe Bogdanovich, seated at his deak in the early 1950s.

and at home—discovered tuna and clamored to buy the product. There was little around. Sixty percent of the company's output went to the U.S. government, which procured tuna for lend lease and military use. It later awarded the French Sardine Company its highest honor for outstanding achievement as a war food processor. However, said Scharer, whatever went out, did so under the StarKist label, initiating a national distribution effort.

In 1944, Martin died of a heart attack suffered during a bond rally, and Joe B officially became president and CEO. In addition to Joe B and Jerry Scharer, the postwar management group included Nick Trutanich, a brother-in-law; Don Loker, another brother-in-law; Julie Bescos, sales manager; Tom Virgil, marketing manager; and Bob Pedersen, who eventually shifted to Ore-Ida.

Although sardines were still the company's major business, Joe B had the vision to see that the future was tuna.

The French Sardine Company began investing in StarKist tuna advertising and marketing, which was fortuitous because, in 1952, sardines again disappeared—this time for good. It almost put the company out of business. Joe B sent Scharer to Cape Town, South Africa, in search of sardines. Nevertheless, it was a propitious moment for the tuna industry.

Postwar Appetite for Tuna Grows

Postwar Americans became very mobile, and took their tastes with them, including tuna, which until then had largely been favored by ethnic populations on the East and West Coast. Now, families in the Midwest also began to discover its advantages. Volumes surged as families with growing numbers of children (the baby-boom generation) turned to this versatile, nutritious, convenient, and inexpensive source of protein that had been largely unknown to the average American consumer only a few years earlier. Tuna is richer in protein than beef. Also a source of amino acids, riboflavin, and niacin; high in vitamin B_{12}, as well as vitamins A, D, and E; low in calories and without cholesterol, it has been called a perfect food.

Guided by Scharer and outside ad man Bob Davis, who Scharer called "one of the best all-time advertising men I've ever met," and who had Hollywood connections, the company launched its first "Tuna of the Stars" promotion and a national advertising campaign in newspapers, magazines (including a full-color page ad in *Life*), and on the radio. It put StarKist on the national map.

Consistent advertising and marketing sold the health and nutrition story to homemakers, as well as the many ways in which tuna could be prepared. Suddenly, in the late 1940s and 1950s, tuna sandwiches, tuna-salad molds, tuna delight, peppers stuffed with tuna, and tuna casseroles became staples of the American diet. Within a decade, and with expanded advertising on the Arthur Godfrey Show, plus more than 200 radio and 30 television stations, StarKist sales had exploded to $46 million.[3]

---

3. 1979 presentation to brokers.

In 1950, the company became the first major tuna canner to emphasize research, building a new lab for R&D, quality, and product development in Long Beach, across the bay from Terminal Island. Then, with demand straining its old facilities, the company invested $2 million in constructing the world's largest and finest tuna cannery. The 200,000-square-foot Plant 4 opened on Terminal Island in 1952.[4] And, in a move that confirmed the supremacy of tuna, in 1953, the French Sardine Company officially changed its name to Star-Kist Foods, Inc.

The first Tuna of the Stars promotion, guided by Jerry Scharer, then sales manager (above), included publicity stunts with comics Abbott and Costello (leaning on tuna can), as well as Arthur Godfrey and Bob Hope. The Tuna of the Stars campaign was put together on a shoestring budget. Hollywood actors sought publicity and, unlike today, were obtainable for a modest fee.

---

4. Mayor Fletcher Bowron of Los Angeles proclaimed the opening day, November 12, "Martin J. Bogdanovich Day." The ceremony was attended by 3,000 people. Speakers included Senator William F. Knowland of California. Later, there were guided tours of the plant for the public.

StarKist Roams the World for Tuna

Joe B and Scharer were basically running the corporate show. They were soon joined by John Real. Together, the three J's traveled the world in search of tuna. "Is there such a thing as a short trip with Joe B?" Scharer joked at his 50th birthday party. "If he invites me to lunch, I pack a suitcase." Three-week trips often stretched to three months, moving from Seoul to Dakar, and points in between. Joined by Bob Hetzler in 1960, who became executive vice president of procurement and operations, they ushered in StarKist's international expansion, first fueled by its quest for new sources of tuna, and then by its search for canneries.

"When Joe B and management started making trips to Japan to buy tuna," said Hetzler, who joined StarKist from the Inter-American Tropical Tuna Commission as assistant to the foreign fish procurement manager, "the fish were sold through trading companies represented by brokers." They made two to three trips a year to Japan, cultivating business relationships. Today, Joe B continues to oversee Heinz Japan.

"Joe spoke what we called bar Japanese," said Hetzler. (Joe also speaks Italian, French, German, Spanish, and Croatian.) Having grown up around Asians, including Japanese fishermen, he understood and appreciated their culture.

"Joe B has a very oriental mind. He thinks long-term, not quarter to quarter," said Masahira Ogawa, president of Heinz Japan. His relationships in Japan now extend back 40 years.

In 1960, with labor costs rising in the United States, StarKist opened an enormous new plant in Mayagüez, Puerto Rico, which allowed the company to market its products more aggressively in big eastern markets and to take full advantage of emerging tuna fishery off the coast of Africa. In 1963, it established a third major cannery, in Pago Pago, American Samoa, to pack both white and light tuna and to utilize supplies of raw fish available in the South Pacific. Pago Pago would also become the major base for StarKist's South Pacific fishing fleet.

In the early 1970s, Ben Thomas, now corporate secretary and assistant general counsel, then a member of the corporate law department still operating out of Pittsburgh's North Side, became

StarKist's legal counsel. It meant virtually commuting to California every other week and traveling the world negotiating fishing rights. As he recalled, "I slept in grass huts in the South Pacific . . . wrote a brief by lantern light . . . and went through a coup in Ghana in 1972." StarKist and adventure seem to have gone hand in hand.

StarKist led the industry in developing new fishing areas, and, as Hetzler noted, "in setting up fishing bases—contracting a fleet to operate on that base, collecting the fish there and shipping it to one of our canneries."

It was a global company decades before the term came into fashion. "StarKist launched local fishing operations and industries in the Philippines, New Guinea, the Indian Ocean, and at three locations in Africa, Korea, and China," said Hetzler. Joe B developed alliances on every continent, procuring fish for StarKist from fleets in every ocean.

Demand was outstripping supply and, when fish supplies were very tight, said Hetzler, "the company that had the fish supply had the business."

The tuna business is unique for a variety of reasons, the chief one being that it is a procurement-driven business. "Sales plans are tied to procurement plans," said John Heil, former vice president of marketing. Chris Lischewski, vice president, business development and procurement, agreed. "You make or break your cost based on procurement."

That's because, unlike almost any other food business, roughly 70 to 75 percent of product cost derives from the price of fish, or about 20 to 30 times the cost of the tomato-industry ingredient.

Hetzler, after 32 years with the company, never forgot street-smart Joe B's negotiation strategy, "Don't pay the price, but don't lose the fish!"[5] On the other hand, Joe B never second-guessed him on any decision.

Also unique is the fact that the business still depends on personal relationships. Whether with fishermen, trading companies, brokers, or canners, everything comes down to who you know and

---

5. *Stars*, vol. 1, no. 2, 1991.

how far back you know him. "Joe B was a tremendous ambassador," Hetzler recalled. "Everybody in the world loved Joe B. Agreements were basically handshakes followed up by one-page agreements. . . . We still have contractual arrangements that were initially made 20–25 years ago."

"Joe was very popular with fishermen," said John Real. Those who performed extra well were rewarded with cars and trips and parties. In 1954, the annual Fishermen's Fiesta gained national prominence under StarKist's direction.

"Thousands attended the gala affair. Vice President Richard Nixon delivered the keynote speech. James Francis Cardinal McIntyre, archbishop of Los Angeles, officiated at the Blessing of the Fleet. Don Loker, vice president of public relations, StarKist, was general chairman."[6]

In a business where even fish quality is a function of who is out on the boat, these personal ties paid off. As Ralph Ward, formerly vice president of operations, said, "You can't talk about fish quality without talking about a specific fisherman, comparing one guy against the other, the way he manages his boat, the way his crew works, what kind of an engineer he has, and that kind of thing."

Moreover, "fish prices and fish availability are so volatile," said Ward, "that unless you understand the psychology of fishermen and world conditions, you can lose a lot of money very quickly."

With Scharer driving sales forward, creating an ever-growing procurement need, "Joe B used to worry that we were going to run out of tuna," said Scharer, "but we never did. We ran short, but we never ran out."

That's because Joe B understood that information is power. He and his energetic managers built a worldwide network of people who fed him information about who was fishing, where they were fishing, what they were catching, what the competition was doing, at what price and in what ocean.

Joe B has always lived and breathed the business. "They should transplant a phone in his hand," said Mattich. "He is always on the phone. Now that there are cellular phones, he's always on two phones. He just has to talk."

---

6. Scharer's personal album.

According to Real, "When Joe B was with the company, he was probably the most informed person in the whole world on what was happening at sea with tuna fishing." Dave Williams, who joined StarKist in 1983 (and now is senior vice president and chief financial officer (CFO) of the Heinz Company), called Joe's "fantastic communications network . . . a little like a CIA operation. Joe B had a shortwave radio and was constantly in touch with his overseas contacts. He would talk to the chauffeur, the mail clerk, the secretary, anyone to find out what was going on in the business."

Even today, it's a hands-on, 24-hours-a-day, seven-days-a-week industry. And everybody knows everybody.

"I've only been here five years," said Ward, "but the more you're involved, the more you spend all your time on the phone talking to some foreign country trying to figure out what's going on. It's almost like a futures market mentality."

In fact, though Heinz and StarKist superficially were similar (family-run food companies with high-quality products), no two cultures could have been less alike.

Where Heinz in the 1960s was bureaucratic and run along fairly conventional management lines, StarKist was free-wheeling and entrepreneurial (Fred Crabb, head of Heinz U.K., said Joe B's favorite question was, "Well, Fred, what do you read between the lines?"). Those qualities precisely suited the high-risk, high-stakes international tuna business.

Joe B is equally famous for his bantering, just-one-of-the-boys ways. John Murray, general manager of technical services and head of Samoan operations for a number of years, recalled introducing Joe B to the governor of Samoa. "I'm Joe Bogdanovich and work on the night shift in the warehouse," he said. "Who are you?" Joe B still revels in his offbeat role. At his birthday fete, he managed to deliver a hilarious string of one-liners with impeccable timing. "Now that I'm 80," he quipped, "I've decided to change my personality and become a lovable eccentric."

Joe B shared with Gookin—and every outstanding executive— an ability to choose and nurture talented, first-rate people to whom he was loyal and who returned that loyalty, and a nose for where the business was headed. StarKist, said Scharer, "had a better vision of its future."

By 1955, with an emphasis on Hollywood star endorsements, national advertising, and marketing, StarKist had become the largest tuna packer in the world, taking over from Van Camp.

CHARLIE THE TUNA IS BORN

Yet, it was the advertising of Leo Burnett that made StarKist, with both Charlie the Tuna and Morris the Cat, a household name and doubled volume growth.

Scharer shopped for a national agency when Davis became ill and sold his agency. After interviewing the top eight in the country, Scharer "insisted flat out that we go with Burnett." He was particularly impressed by Leo Burnett himself and George Hamm. The agency was already known for its "comical critters," such as the Jolly Green Giant, the Pillsbury Doughboy, and Tony the Tiger.

When StarKist first turned to the Chicago agency in 1958 (with a $1 million budget), it had about 14 percent of the tuna market. That year the StarKist fisherman first appeared as the company's trademark symbol on its label.

In 1961, StarKist decided to go for more distinctive, television-targeted advertising, and Burnett came up with a character to embody the company's high-quality product.

Tom Rogers, who joined Burnett in 1960, invented "Charlie the Tuna." Rogers had spent some years in New York hanging out at Hanson's drug store, which he called "Schwab's East" because it was filled with showbiz types. Given the assignment, he instantly thought of one of the street characters he'd met there, "a song writer and con man, even when it wasn't necessary." He became his model for Charlie the Tuna, and Rogers immediately wrote the first commercial. Charlie looked like a 1960s hipster, reclining on a deck chair with cap and sunglasses, talking about how it's a "status thing" to be picked by StarKist. Rogers created seven other concepts in case Charlie didn't fly. (Also involved in Charlie's embryonic days was Geraldine Bogdanovich, sister of Joe B.)

At the creative review, Leo Burnett himself stood up and said about Charlie, "That's the one." Charlie's authentic New York voice was that of the great actor Herschel Bernardi.

Rogers also recalled his first meeting with StarKist's brass, especially handsome Scharer, "a wonderful man, suntanned, marvelous looking, straight out of central casting." When he saw Scharer begin to grin, he knew Charlie was working.

Though the public loved Charlie when he first came on the air in 1962, with a quality theme built around the line, "Only the best tuna get to be StarKist," sales went nowhere.

Scharer felt Charlie had become a symbol for tuna as opposed to StarKist, and, upset with Burnett, cut Charlie out for a year. Burnett sent senior executive Jack Kopp to a presentation. "He heard me talking about the problems we were facing, and asked me if we could go for a walk," said Scharer. "We walked four times around the old Lafayette Hotel in Long Beach, and I extracted from him the promise that he kept until he retired as chairman . . . I would get the top people in each of the departments that worked on the account."

That's when the campaign changed, or, as Burnett describes it, "the campaign went into its second phase," emphasizing taste. Heinz had just bought StarKist, and eagerly supported Charlie's reentry into television.

By 1963, tuna was becoming a favorite food of Americans. "Industry sales were at the 15 million case level, about half of what they would be by 1979."[7]

A new round of advertising more closely tied Charlie to StarKist with a series of memorable commercials in which Charlie becomes highbrow in his tastes, but still is rejected because "StarKist doesn't want tuna with good taste, StarKist wants tuna that taste good." That's when the campaign took off.

In 1966, StarKist became the top media spender and moved up to a 32 percent share, with Chicken of the Sea at 39 and Bumble Bee at 15. A whole series of commercials, showing Charlie getting involved with poetry, Shakespeare, and ballet, ran from 1968 to 1979, heavily emphasizing StarKist quality.

---

7. Scharer presentation to brokers.

By 1979, StarKist and Chicken of the Sea were neck and neck, each with 36 percent of the market.[8]

Tuna in Natural Spring Water

Suddenly, during the late 1970s, consumers became concerned about weight and health issues. In 1980, StarKist capitalized on the health trend and pioneered "Tuna packed in natural spring water." Using Charlie to reinforce the message of "great taste and great for your waist," StarKist finally became the number-one brand of tuna in 1984.

Hardly an overnight success, StarKist's long-term advertising investment paid off handsomely. Not only was it the number-one brand, but tuna was now the fifth largest dry-food category on supermarket shelves. Even better, it was the number-one dry grocery profit producer per square foot in the business.[9] In fact, by 1989, StarKist's flagship pack in water was the number-one canned-food dollar producer.

A $1.5 billion worldwide business, the United States alone consumed well over 40 million cases, with 89 percent of U.S. families purchasing tuna. And by now, there was a style, and a size, for every consumer's taste and need: solid white albacore or light chunk in spring water or vegetable oil; giant size, regular size, family size, individual servings; dietetic packs, low-salt packs, old-style tonno, etc.

StarKist now needed to procure over a quarter of a million tons of tuna. Fortunately, just about the time the company moved to the Burnett agency and dramatically expanded business, new fishing techniques and more sophisticated quality control and canning technology allowed the company to keep up with demand.

---

8. *StarKist Advertising History*, courtesy of Leo Burnett.

9. "Adventure on the High Seas," StarKist video, 1989.

Fishing methods in some parts of the world still include the hard labor of pole-and-line live-bait fishing. Men throw bait (sardines and anchovies) overboard, and then dip short bamboo fishing poles into the resulting fishing frenzy, whipping the tuna back onto the deck. The slightly less strenuous jigging method uses several lures trolled behind the boat. When tuna bite the line, they are pulled aboard, the fish removed, and the line returned to the water. Long-line fishing floats a continuous line, sometimes 40 miles long, on the water, from which shorter, baited lines are suspended. Each day, the line is brought in and removed by hand.

CATCHING AND PROCESSING TUNA

Perhaps the single most revolutionary change was the 1959 conversion by fishing fleets to purse seining. In this method of catching fish, a school of fish is encircled with an enormous nylon net—three quarters of a mile long and hundreds of feet deep—attached to a steel cable running through large metal rings, which, as in a drawstring purse, draws the net shut. A hydraulic lift pulls the huge net filled with fish back toward the boat. Smaller nets scoop out the tuna, which are immediately sent down a wet chute into refrigerated compartments, where they are frozen in brine.

What once took four months for a clipper ship to catch could now be caught in 10 to 45 days. But there were other, less salutary side effects—as would become apparent years later.

After the boat docks, a labor-intensive cooking and canning process begins, with seven quality-control checks. Up to 2,000 tons of tuna are separated by size and type, loaded into bins, and samples taken to a lab for U.S. Department of Agriculture (USDA) tests that measure levels of mercury, salt, nitrate, water, oil, fat, etc. The bins move into freezers where whole fish remain until ready to be thawed in fresh water, hand butchered, washed, separated by size, steamed whole on racks, tested for temperature and aroma, cooled by a computerized mist system for three to five hours, and hand filleted (or loined).

The remaining parts of the fish are separated for use as either pet food, animal feed, or other products, such as fish meal, fish solubles, fish oil, and fertilizer. No part of the fish is wasted.

The fillets and chunks of tuna are then canned and vacuum packed. The sealed cans are given a final sterilization, cooled, labeled, and sent off to grocery shelves with an eight-digit code that can pinpoint who caught the fish and where, when it was processed and packed, and the date the can was sealed.

During the 1970s and up to the mid-1980s, StarKist moved from strength to strength. "We were flying," said Scharer, "everybody was a team. It was a successful culture . . . and we also had cat food."

9-LIVES AND MORRIS THE CAT

The cat-food business had first caught the imagination of Joe B and Scharer in the mid-1940s. Like Tater Tots, it turned a byproduct of tuna into a profitable business.

The French Sardine Company introduced Staywell cat food, a product that failed due to the company's lack of experience. Then StarKist quietly reentered the business in the mid-1950s with 9-Lives, a brand name dreamt up by the company's copyright lawyer, according to Scharer.

It began with the basic, red-meat tuna product, an operation led by Virgil and Bescos. Jerry Scharer's son Roy, who joined the company in 1957, eventually headed up the marketing of pet food. In the 1950s, most people fed cats table scraps, but pet food quickly turned into a high-growth and highly competitive business. By the mid-1960s, "Puss 'N Boots, Purina, and Friskies were all aggressively marketing their products, putting great pressure on the 9-Lives brand. As the market expanded, 9-Lives case volume grew, but the brand was losing share of market."[10]

StarKist again turned to the Burnett agency.

Pet food is unlike any other food category because the consumer never tastes the product. At the time, most ads emphasized warm and fuzzy feelings about cats, so when the agency came up with the idea of creating a feisty, finicky "spokescat," it was a fresh approach.

"Morris the 9-Lives Cat" first hit the airwaves in 1969. A big, orange-striped tabby, he had been found in a New England animal shelter by his handler, Bob Martwick. With his trademark "independent attitude" and finicky ways, cat lovers took to him instantly. The message that 9-Lives would please even the most finicky cat built the business. In three years, the brand rebounded and captured 21.5 percent of national sales, which added up to about eight million cases a year. By 1974, 9-Lives exceeded $81 million in sales and was being produced at all three canneries—Terminal Island, Puerto Rico, and Samoa.

Morris introduced a series of new products: in 1970, the first formed cat food, burgers, and dry cat food; in 1972, morsels; in 1975, the soft-moist category; in 1984, Unique recipes; in 1986, crunchy meals; in 1988, cat treats, and so on.

Indeed, Charlie the Tuna and Morris the 9-Lives Cat are a lesson in the value of equity-building advertising. Regardless of dollars invested year to year, they are forever linked to their products. Charlie will never be good enough for StarKist, and Morris will never settle for anything but 9-Lives. In fact, consumer awareness of Morris remained at 94 percent in 1991, behind only Mickey Mouse, Bugs Bunny, Kermit the Frog, and the Pillsbury Doughboy, even though Morris had been off the air since 1988.

---

10. 1979 presentation to brokers.

PET-FOOD BUSINESS SKYROCKETS

During the 1970s and 1980s, StarKist expanded into the dog-food arena. In 1971, it bought Tuffy's Dog Food and began marketing both dry dog food and dry cat food. In 1979, it acquired Jerky Treat, a meat-based dog treat, building a new category whose sales, within two years, went from $7 million to $20 million. Then the company introduced a second treat, Meaty Bone, a biscuit with a meat coating. As Mike Milone, vice president of Heinz Pet Products marketing, put it, "The company created the indulgent dog treat category." It continues to be a high-profit area.

Pet foods had become "the second largest tonnage category in the supermarket . . . sales were skyrocketing."[11]

In the early 1980s, StarKist Foods appeared to be on top of the world. Sales were close to $1 billion. It accounted for over 40 percent of U.S. tuna consumption, including a 55 share of private-label brands. It maintained an international chain of bases and fish sources. In 1984, StarKist tuna share reached its all-time high—greater than the next two competitors combined. On the pet-food side, 9-Lives sales reached record volumes; Meaty Bone and Amoré, a gourmet cat food, were rolling out. Morris the Cat had become the most popular animal celebrity in America.

Yet, having pioneered two new food categories, the StarKist affiliate began to slow down. In 1983, O'Reilly named Dick Beattie, who had moved from Heinz U.S.A. to Hubinger to Heinz U.K. and ultimately to StarKist, "the Heinz company's Mr. Fix-It with my manager's toolbox," as CEO. "The profits at StarKist were declining dramatically over the last few years prior to my arrival," said Beattie. The first non-StarKist person to lead the company, he stayed through 1988.

The fundamentals of the tuna business had changed. Basically, the western Pacific had opened up as a fishing area and suddenly there was too much tuna. Prices and profits nose-dived and StarKist found itself with excess manufacturing capacity and high

---

11. Scharer 1979 broker presentation.

overhead. Labor costs were about $7.50 an hour at Terminal Island, $4.50 in Puerto Rico, and $2.75 in Samoa. "It didn't take a rocket scientist to see what was wrong and what had to be done," said Beattie. Impressed with the Puerto Rican operation, he introduced a third shift and had the unpleasant job of closing Terminal Island in 1985. It was the end of the tuna business in San Pedro.

BEATTIE'S VISION: TWO SEPARATE BUSINESSES

StarKist also cut back its investments in fishing vessels, reduced fish prices, and, under Beattie, further developed the pet-food business, which he saw as the company's future growth vehicle. It was Beattie's recommendation to divide the company into two distinct parts—procurement-driven seafood and marketing-driven pet food—to better focus on each part.

"Dick had the vision," said Bill Johnson, who joined Heinz U.S.A. in 1982 as general manager, new business, and became group vice president of pet food in 1987. "He saw that pet food could play a much larger role in the Heinz family."

"Beattie brought a broader perspective to StarKist," said Ralph Ward, "including the reality that we had to be the low-cost operator."

Dave Williams, who joined Heinz U.K. in 1967, became Beattie's vice president of finance in April 1983. He imposed more rigorous financial control and reporting systems.

In 1988, one of Beattie's last major accomplishments before retiring was to vault Heinz into second place in the pet-food business with three acquisitions: Champion Valley Farms from Campbell's, which brought the Recipe brand dog food distributed along the East Coast and produced in Bloomsburg, Pennsylvania; the Mavar Shrimp and Oyster Company, which added a major presence in the value-priced cat-food category with the Kozy Kitten brand; and the pet products division of California Home Brands (CHB), which brought a large private-label canned-pet-food business plus Skippy Dog Food.

HEINZ PET PRODUCTS

Heinz Pet Products now manufactures a dizzying array of pet foods. 9-Lives in every form and texture still dominates the canned-cat-food category. Other brands include Amoré, Kozy Kitten, Jerky Treats, Meaty Bone, Skippy Premium, Reward, Recipe, and Tuffy's. The company is also America's largest producer of private-label canned dog and cat food.

But expanding the business so quickly brought its share of problems.

Bill Johnson raided every other Heinz affiliate to staff Heinz Pet Products, which, with three acquisitions in nine months, about doubled in size, but lacked the infrastructure and experience to handle new people, products, and factories. "I think we all underestimated the compounding effects of separating from StarKist and assembling these acquisitions at the time."

When the two companies officially split in mid-1988, with Johnson becoming Heinz Pet Products president, 9-Lives profits and market shares were eroding, costs were too high, factories were poorly managed and underutilized. Johnson first focused on the cost side of the business.

Dick Wamhoff arrived in November 1989 as executive vice president of operations and logistics to institute an aggressive cost-reduction program and consolidate operations within the pet-food business. Heinz Pet Products went from 55 warehouses to four and reduced 11 factories to six.

The factory in Bloomsburg, Pennsylvania, is now the largest and most efficient pet-food plant in the world. With 500,000 square feet on a 98-acre site, Heinz Pet Products invested $60 million in the plant and now has seven high-speed lines that handle 60 percent of its total canned sales. Also, since the container accounts for over 50 percent of the raw materials used in the finished product of canned dog and cat food, its in-house can-making facility represents a significant cost advantage. In 1992, Heinz's newest and biggest high-tech distribution center, which holds more than five million cases, was built next door.

In four years, Bloomsburg dropped its cost per case by one third and quadrupled productivity. At the same time, total volume

Heinz Pet Products' Bloomsburg, Pennsylvania, plant is now the largest and most efficient pet-food operation in the world. In four years, its cost per case dropped one third and employees almost quadrupled productivity.

grew four times. Bloomsburg's successes were replicated in Pascagoula, Mississippi, and Terminal Island, California. This eventually allowed Heinz Pet Products to lower prices, handle volume growth, and regain acceptable profit margins.

In 1989, Johnson decided to move Heinz Pet Products out of California to Newport, Kentucky, part of the greater Cincinnati area, to further reduce costs and alter the culture.

"We no longer could afford to be overshadowed by the seafood business," said Johnson. That had been its historic role and mindset, and it was no longer appropriate.

"It was a tough thing to do, because a lot of people had just moved to California . . . but the process created by far the closest management group in the company, because at the time no other company had been through what we'd been through." That is, they were not just picking up their families and moving, but also were turning a company around.

Johnson, whose father was a National Football League football coach for 42 years, is fond of comparing the job of CEO to that of head coach. "People are your number-one asset. You run the plays with people. . . . In my view, the job of a CEO is to convince people they can do things they didn't think they could do."

Fierce Competition

Johnson had a difficult task ahead of him because of the mounting competition. In fact, with the exception of the Weight Watchers Food business, no business in the company turned as fiercely competitive in the 1990s as the $6 to $8 billion pet-food category.

To begin with, there were nine major players in the United States, among them heavy hitters such as Mars, Nestlé, Grand Met, Quaker, Colgate-Palmolive, Ralston Purina, and Nabisco.

On top of that, with pet food the number-three dry grocery category in the United States with annual sales about $6.5 billion, a war for the consumer dollar was raging at the retail level. Supermarket chains with traditional products, which had dominated the market, were losing volume share to nonfood mass merchandisers, such as Kmart, Wal-Mart, and club stores, as well as specialty outlets such as pet stores, pet supermarkets, and veterinaries' offices. The specialty channels were promoting premium-price products, such as Science Diet, which, as Mike Milone, vice president of marketing, asserted, totally changed the rules of the game.

Finally, due to this intense competition, traditional pet-food prices had declined over a 10-year period.

In 1991, in an effort to greatly accelerate margins, Heinz Pet Products tried to take its prices up, got hit hard by the recession, lost market share, and quickly changed its entire strategy.

Customer-Focused Strategy

Recognizing that the pet-food business is trade driven, once it had gotten costs down and margins right, Heinz Pet Products switched its focus from consumer to customer marketing. It did so in a variety of ways. First, it reorganized from product management to category management, so as to better focus on dealing with the trade. Then it emphasized tactical, in-store activities over media advertising and promotion.

Heinz Pet Products also developed niche products very carefully. "We have not introduced a plethora of new products supported by aggressive spending or advertising," said Johnson. "In fact, I don't think we've run a commercial in this company in three years."

Heinz Pet Products has focused on its high-margin products, especially its gourmet dog food, Reward, and its snack business, bringing out new varieties such as Grill Bits and Hot Doggies. Heinz Pet Products is the number-two player in pet snacks and, with new products driving the category, will continue to increase the business.

The company is pursuing private-label with many grocery and nongrocery retailers, such as Wal-Mart, Kmart, and PETsMART. Today, it has about 65 percent of the canned cat food and 40 percent of the canned dog food private-label market. Also, in January 1993, it entered into a joint venture with Veterinary Centers of America to develop, manufacture, and market new specialty pet products and services.

These strategies have already paid off. Between 1988 and 1993, Heinz Pet Products' market share has grown from 8 percent to about 14 percent of total U.S. pet food, and profits have about doubled. Indeed, Heinz Pet Products has completed its transformation from stepchild to star. Today, pet food makes about twice as much as seafood.

Pet food remains a growth business. The single population is increasing, especially among urban working people, who are driving the explosion of cat ownership. People are having fewer children, and acquiring pets as surrogates. And an aging population is also seeking companionship or dealing with the "empty-nest" syndrome by adding pets to their home.

"People treat their pets better than their children," said Johnson. They do not hesitate to pay for expensive food, clothes, treats, and toys, or to take pets to the vet. "You sit in a focus group and listen to people talk about their animal," said Johnson, "and you'd think they were talking about a spouse or child." The emotional attachment is intense. Pets provide unconditional love, and Americans treat them as one of the family.

Global Markets

Pet food is an $18 billion global market, underdeveloped in other parts of the world, including Europe and Asia. Heinz Pet Products is spearheading increased international growth. Heinz U.K. introduced 9-Lives cat food and Award dog food in January 1993 under the umbrella title "Heinz Petfood Products."

StarKist is also aggressively building its tuna businesses in non-U.S. affiliates, including Japan, Canada, and Europe. In the United States, it helped to introduce four varieties of tuna under the Heinz label, filling one of the few remaining gaps in its canned-food market. Chris Lischewski is spearheading global tuna opportunities. "Europe will be a 45-million-case market," he said. "Our goal is to get 30 percent of the market, sourcing tuna out of Ecuador and Africa."

Both the tuna and pet-food sides of StarKist Foods are among the first businesses actively to pursue interaffiliate, joint-venture opportunities. They are another good example of the "new" Heinz in action, bringing together manufacturing, procurement, and marketing expertise across borders to grow the business when and where opportunities beckon.

Tuna Business Changes

Back on the tuna side of the business, beginning in 1989, as Keith Hauge became CEO, tumultuous changes shook and forever changed the industry.

Asian investors bought StarKist's two major competitors, Bumble Bee and Chicken of the Sea, both of which had the advantage of 20- to 50-cents-an-hour labor costs. More interested in cash flow than in margins, the Asian strategy apparently was to hold the line on prices and increase market share. A price war ensued and StarKist was faced with the same challenge as pet food, to sharply reduce operating costs.

HEINZ FIRST TO ADOPT DOLPHIN-SAFE POLICY

A year later, on April 12, 1990, in a dramatic move that further transformed the procurement side of the industry, StarKist—the largest purchaser of light-meat tuna (about 12 percent of the world's harvest) and the largest tuna processor in the world—became the first tuna company to adopt a "dolphin-safe" policy. It would not purchase any tuna caught in association with dolphins, and asked U.S. government observers to monitor boats in relevant areas to certify that no dolphins are harmed. It also continued to refuse to purchase, process, or sell tuna caught with gill or drift nets, which are dangerous to many forms of marine life, not just dolphins.

The issue had been building since purse seining began to dominate tuna fishing. Why? Because for reasons no one yet understands, in the eastern tropical Pacific Ocean, a coastal zone extending from Chile to southern California, dolphins swim above schools of yellowfin tuna. Thus, when the drawstring is closed and encircles the tuna, the dolphins are also trapped.

As O'Reilly stated at a packed Washington press conference, the initiative, hailed by environmentalists around the world, was "a recognition of increased consumer concern for the environment." Competitors were forced to follow StarKist's initiative. Since then, Europe has also adopted dolphin-safe practices, and the deaths of dolphins have dropped. But from the business point of view, the decision was very disruptive. One competitor continued to use tuna caught in drift nets and enjoyed a significant price advantage for nine months. Also, there were shortages of tuna.

TUNA AND PET FOOD RECOMBINE

Andrew Barrett took over from Hauge between 1990 and 1992. He and his team, including John Heil, who moved from Ore-Ida to StarKist to become head of marketing in 1990, developed a set

Senator Joseph Biden

Dr. A.J.F. O'Reilly
Chairman, President, and CEO
H.J. Heinz Co.

Tony O'Reilly, Heinz chairman, president, and CEO, announced on April 12, 1990, that StarKist would become the first tuna company in the world to adopt a "dolphin-safe" policy. This move was applauded by environmentalists and permanently transformed the procurement side of the industry.

of marketing strategies to make the business more profitable again. These included initiating micromarketing tactics with the top 25 national customers to leverage brand strength and increase market share, and developing a stable of new retail, value-added products to help the business grow, including Charlie's Lunch Kit, a convenient, shelf-stable lunch product.

At the same time, the team attacked the cost structure. In August 1992, Wamhoff, now the company's low-cost-operations expert, moved over to StarKist to again wring efficiencies out of the factories. Tuna on the shelf was cheaper than it had been in 10 years.

Barrett also recommended combining and consolidating backroom and administrative portions of the tuna and pet-food businesses to reduce costs further. Wamhoff became president of

StarKist Seafood and helped to manage this transition, which ultimately led to recombining a slimmed-down StarKist Seafood with Heinz Pet Products and, in 1993, to StarKist's leaving Long Beach, California, to rejoin its sister operation in Newport, Kentucky.

Star-Kist Foods, Inc., is now headquartered in a sleek glass building, Riverfront Place, overlooking the Ohio River and the downtown Cincinnati skyline.

Johnson became president and CEO of Star-Kist Foods, Inc., and then senior vice president and board member. Barrett became managing director of the affiliate where he began his career, Heinz U.K., and Wamhoff took over Ore-Ida.

The strategies have paid off. The profits of Heinz Pet Products and StarKist Seafood are each up about 30 percent. In fact, in 1993, StarKist moved its share from the mid-30s to the mid-40s, an all-time high.

Now that dolphin-safe practices are becoming implemented worldwide, StarKist has expanded and better focused its worldwide procurement to ensure steady sources of high-quality, low-cost tuna for its global tuna business. And the TQM process continues to identify new opportunities for cost savings. As Pete Bowen, head of StarKist marketing, expressed it, "We think tuna could be a real big growth vehicle for Heinz over the next five years."

LOOKING BACKWARD INTO THE FUTURE

"The successful companies of the 1990s," said Dick Wamhoff, "will be those that are low-cost producers and value-added sellers of products in the marketplace. And it can never stop. You can never stop challenging yourself, trying to find new tools to improve quality and reduce costs."

They will also be companies that understand the vast, dynamic, and changing international business environment. "It is an environment that demands management without borders," said O'Reilly at a September 10, 1993, Carnegie Mellon University conference. In this "new post-Cold War economic order . . . barriers are being dismantled and. . . . We are witnessing a great awakening through much of the world. It is the awakening of consumer consciousness. Much of this awakening is inspired by a revolution in communications technology."

Consumer aspirations now exceed national boundaries, and, as O'Reilly pointed out, "Some of these aspirations are for specific brands." These include, of course, the venerable Heinz brand, which began so modestly 125 years ago.

The global economy beckons. It would not have surprised the Founder. It will not surprise the present generation of Heinz leaders.

O'Reilly, his cadre of affiliate presidents, and the Heinz family of employees are an increasingly focused team of competitors, trained to win on every continent and in every part of the world.

Fred Crabb said that Joe B used to run up to him in the 1960s, when Heinz U.K. was doubling its profits year after year, and ask, "What's your secret? What's your secret? How do you get those numbers?" And Crabb would answer, "It's a team effort."

In 1994, after 125 years, it still is

AFTERWORD

The Heinz to Come

~~

Anthony J. F. O'Reilly
Chairman, President, and Chief Executive Officer
H. J. Heinz Company

The history of the H. J. Heinz Company is more than a chronology; it is a challenge. For a century and a quarter, Heinz has been a leader in practically every aspect of food processing. Concurrently, we have sustained a solid financial footing, a strong balance sheet, and a clear sense of identity and direction. Heinz remains independently owned and one of the three most profitable major food companies in the world.

Inspired, though not bound, by our tradition, we have embarked on a future course for even greater growth. We base our strategies on the strength of our leading brands, and the exceptional global opportunities that await in such markets as food service, sauces and tomato products, baby food, frozen potatoes, weight-loss, pet food, and tuna.

The full potential of our brands and markets is far from known. We expand it constantly by internal improvement and external expansion. The present Heinz generation, like the first, is animated by an appetite for discovery and a confidence in the power of change.

Over the years, Heinz has continually refashioned itself through restructuring. Most recently, we have reconfigured our manufacturing operations between the United States and Canada, becoming a truly North American company. We have invested in training and technology to further raise efficiency and productivity throughout the world. We have implemented transformative labor agreements, streamlined administration, and created a new service company to take full advantage of computerized order processing. We have divested ourselves of companies in markets where we had no comparative advantage. In sum, we have sharpened our focus, improved our efficiency, and channeled our resources to their most productive ends.

Fortified by restructuring, Heinz provides its brands strong but flexible marketing support. Since the early days of the clear bottle and the pickle pin, Heinz has been noted as an innovative marketer. The marketing of the 21st century will be more targeted and strategic than ever before.

We have a wide range of marketing approaches, including mass media, trade, data base marketing, and consumer promotions. Heinz's strategy in the information age is to employ the best blend of marketing methods to speak directly to the consumer and to nurture the brand loyalty that we have cultivated so successfully.

Since the Founder's legendary journey to London, Heinz has ventured out to make its brands citizens of the world. Our acquisitions bring us ever closer to that goal.

Overseas acquisitions in Europe, the Middle East, Asia, Africa, and the Indian subcontinent have given Heinz an exceptional strategic presence in the fastest-growing markets of the world. For example, the 1993 purchase of Wattie's Limited in New Zealand complements Heinz's operations in Australia and Japan, positioning us at each point of a great Pacific triangle that contains a rapidly growing and increasingly wealthy population.

The impact of our overseas markets is magnified by our global leverage. We now have the opportunity to realize the full potential of Heinz by deploying resources and constructing strategies on a truly global scale.

The liberalization of trade is a major factor shaping our industry in the 1990s. We regard this as an opportunity for Heinz to optimize its manufacturing capability to an unprecedented degree. We have invested in highly advanced facilities in the United States and Europe, boosting their capacity and enabling us to supply consumers across entire continents, instead of mere countries.

Our Global Procurement Task Force is a true 21st century concept, finding the most efficient suppliers around the world and consolidating purchasing of key raw materials across all Heinz affiliates. Such value-engineering of packaging and raw materials will yield a constant flow of savings in future years.

Another example is our inter-affiliate sales throughout Europe and our expanding exports to fast-growing markets.

At the same time, we are leveraging our strengths in both food service and baby food, two businesses poised for global expansion.

Heinz's growth strategies are at once revolutionary and traditional. New tastes, exceptional quality, and unmatched value—Heinz has striven to provide these from the days of the Founder. The world has changed much in 125 years. It has changed much in my 20 years with the company. But the fundamental virtues of the Heinz brand remain as highly prized as ever.

As Newton said, we can see so far because we stand on the shoulders of giants. Great men and women who came before us built a great company. We have kept faith with our corporate ancestors and made Heinz an even more prodigious global enterprise, with exceptional strength, stamina, and performance. We now resolve to ensure that the brands of Heinz will remain the first choice of consumers around the world, today and for generations to come.

Appendix

~~

HEINZ WORLD MANAGEMENT

THE AMERICAS

HEINZ U.S.A.
Pittsburgh, Pennsylvania
Established 1869

1989–present	William C. Springer, President and Chief Executive Officer, Heinz North America
1986	David W. Sculley, President and Chief Executive Officer
1980	J. Wray Connolly, President and Chief Executive Officer
1977	Richard B. Patton, President
1973	Raymond F. Good, President
1971	J. Richard Grieb, President
1966	Norman E. Daniels, President
1964	R. Burt Gookin, Executive Vice President
1963	Frank T. Sherk, Executive Vice President
1959	B. Dent Graham, Executive Vice President
1954	Frank Armour, Jr., Executive Vice President

ORE-IDA FOODS, INC.
Boise, Idaho
Acquired 1965

1993–present	Richard H. Wamhoff, President and Chief Executive Officer
1992	Robert N. White, President and Chief Executive Officer
1991	Gerald D. Herrick, Interim President and Chief Executive Officer
1990	John C. Glerum, President and Chief Executive Officer
1986	Gerald D. Herrick, President and Chief Executive Officer
1977	Paul I. Corddry, President and Chief Executive Officer

342

| 1968 | Robert K. Pedersen, President and Chief Executive Officer |
| 1965 | F. Nephi Grigg, President |

STAR-KIST FOODS, INC.
Newport, Kentucky
Acquired 1963

1992–present	William R. Johnson, President and Chief Executive Officer, Heinz Pet Products and Star-Kist Foods, Inc.
1991	Andrew L. Barrett, President StarKist Seafood Company
1988	Keith A. Hauge, President StarKist Seafood Company
1983	Richard L. Beattie, President and Chief Executive Officer
1978	John J. Real, President and Chief Executive Officer
1975	Jerry G. Scharer, President
1944	Joseph J. Bogdanovich, President

WEIGHT WATCHERS INTERNATIONAL, INC.
Jericho, New York
Acquired 1978

1991–present	Lelio G. Parducci, President and Chief Executive Officer
1981	Charles M. Berger, President and Chief Executive Officer
1978	Albert Lippert, Chief Executive Officer

WEIGHT WATCHERS FOOD COMPANY
Pittsburgh, Pennsylvania
Established 1991

| 1994–present | Michael R. McGrath, President and Chief Executive Officer |
| 1991–1994 | Brian Ruder, President and Chief Executive Officer |

CRESTAR FOOD PRODUCTS, INC.
Brentwood, Tennessee
Acquired 1991

| 1993–present | Donald J. Kerr, President and Chief Executive Officer |
| 1991 | Thane A. Pressman, President and Chief Executive Officer |

H. J. HEINZ COMPANY OF CANADA LTD.
North York, Ontario, Canada
Established 1909

1991–present	John Crawshaw, President and Chief Executive Officer
1989	Andrew L. Barrett, President and Chief Executive Officer
1988	William C. Springer, President and Chief Executive Officer
1977	Thomas D. Smyth, President
1968	Albert Forsyth, President

1967	John A. Connell, President
1962	Edward V. Anderson, President
1958	Frank T. Sherk, President

ALIMENTOS HEINZ C.A.
Caracas, Venezuela
Established 1959

1980–present	John M. Werner, President and Chief Executive Officer
1975	Louis J. Pacini, President
1970	John G. Johnson, President
1968	Emil Hoigne, President
1965	George O. Myers, President
1959	Gerald K. Warner, President

HEINZ BAKERY PRODUCTS
Mississauga, Ontario, Canada
Established 1992

1991–present	Paul W. Sneddon, President and Chief Executive Officer
1989	Nick J. Iacovelli, President and Chief Executive Officer
1986	Edward Krucker, President

HEINZ SERVICE COMPANY
Pittsburgh, Pennsylvania
Established 1993

| 1993–present | Jack L. Burley, President |

EUROPE AND AFRICA

H. J. HEINZ COMPANY, LIMITED
Hayes, Middlesex, England
Established 1905

1991–present	Andrew L. Barrett, Managing Director
1982	John Hinch, Managing Director
1981	Richard L. Beattie, Managing Director
1979	R. Derek Finlay, Managing Director
1974	Charles F. Lowe, Managing Director
1971	John A. Connell, Managing Director
1969	Anthony J. F. O'Reilly, Managing Director
1964	Anthony Beresford, Managing Director
1963	Joseph E. Hutchinson, Managing Director
1956	Frederick G. Crabb, Managing Director

1950	W. B. "Willie" Cormack, U.K. Chief
1941	Henry J. Heinz, II, President
1919	Howard Heinz, President
1905	Charles Hellen, Director

H. J. HEINZ CENTRAL EUROPE
Brussels, Belgium
Established 1984

1989–present	Jean-Claude Jamar, Managing Director—Central Europe
1977	Robert M. Kuijpers, Managing Director—Central Europe
1973	John H. Newhall, Director—Central Europe
1970	Nicolo Pellizzari, Area Manager—Benelux, France, Germany

HEINZ ITALIA S.P.A.
Milan, Italy
Acquired 1963

1992–present	Lino Ghirardato, Chief Executive Officer
1978	Luigi Ribolla, President
1975	Charles M. Berger, President
1973	Nicolo Pellizzari, President
1968	Aldo Tartarelli, President
1964	Oscar A. Pio, President

HEINZ IBERICA, S.A.
Madrid, Spain
Established 1987

1992–present	Luigi Ribolla, President
1991	Jose A. Arnaldo, Managing Director
1987	Paul I. Corddry, President

INDUSTRIAS DE ALIMENTAÇÃO, LDA.
Lisbon, Portugal
Acquired 1965

| 1991–present | Leonardo A. P. Caeiro, Managing Director |
| 1965 | Jorge R. Giralt, Managing Director |

COPAIS CANNING INDUSTRY, S.A.
Athens, Greece
Acquired 1990

| 1990–present | Emmanuel A. Kaldellis, Chairman, President and Chief Executive Officer |

MAGYAR FOODS LIMITED
Kecskemeti, Hungary
Established 1992

1992–present   Michael J.B. Smither, Managing Director

CUSTOM FOODS LIMITED
Dundalk, Ireland
Established 1992

1992–present   John F. Hinch, Chairman

H. J. HEINZ (BOTSWANA) (PROPRIETARY) LTD.
Gaborone, Botswana
Formed 1988

1992–present   John W. Rudd, Managing Director
1988   I. Laurie W. Bagshaw, Managing Director

OLIVINE INDUSTRIES (PRIVATE) LIMITED
Harare, Zimbabwe
Acquired 1982

1988–present   Rory W. Beattie, Chairman and Managing Director
1982   Douglas N. Dibb, Managing Director

CAIRO FOOD INDUSTRIES SAE
Cairo, Egypt
Established 1992

1992–present   Moataz Al Alfi, Chairman and Chief Executive Officer

ASIA/PACIFIC RIM

H. J. HEINZ AUSTRALIA LTD.
Doveton, Victoria, Australia
Established 1935

1988–present   Terry Ward, Managing Director and Chief Executive Officer
1981   Edward S. Churchill, President and Chief Executive Officer
1978   Ernest W. Barr, Director of Pacific and CEO Heinz Australia
                    Anthony J. Bardsley, Managing Director
                    Barry S. Gilbert, Managing Director

1974	Fred V. Kellow, Chairman
	Ernest W. Barr, Managing Director and Chief Executive Officer
1964	John A. W. Ross, Chairman
	Fred V. Kellow, Managing Director
1951	Henry G. Dennett, Managing Director (Finance)
	John A. W. Ross, Managing Director (Operations)
1948	Henry G. Dennett, Managing Director
1935	Christopher P. Berry, Managing Director
	William B. Cormack, Senior Management

WATTIE'S LIMITED.
Auckland, New Zealand
Established 1992

1992–present	David A. Irving, President and Chief Executive Officer

HEINZ JAPAN LTD.
Tokyo, Japan
Established 1961

1986–present	Masahira Ogawa, President
1982	Masahira Ogawa, Representative Director
	Jerry G. Scharer, Representative Director
1980	Kazuo Asai, President
1977	Keith A. Hauge, Representative Director
1976	Hisashi Tezuka, Representative Director
1970	Kazuo Asai, President
1969	Ernest W. Barr, President
1965	Albert F. Margus, President
1964	Gilbert H. Morris, President
1961	Eizo Amemiya, President

HEINZ-UFE LTD.
Guangzhou, People's Republic of China
Established 1984

1993–present	James Chen, Sr., President
1993	Ronald R. Steingart, President
1991	Wah-Hui Chu, President
1988	Edward P. W. Tsang, Managing Director
1985	Wah-Hui Chu, Managing Director
1984	Roy King, General Manager

Index